RAF LIBERATOR
OVER THE
EASTERN FRONT

A Bomb Aimer's Second World War and Cold War Story

Jim Auton MBE

ISIS
LARGE PRINT
Oxford

Copyright © Jim Auton, 2008

First published in Great Britain 2008
by
Pen & Sword Aviation
an imprint of Pen & Sword Books Ltd.

Published in Large Print 2009 by ISIS Publishing Ltd.,
7 Centremead, Osney Mead, Oxford OX2 0ES
by arrangement with
Pen & Sword Books Ltd.

British Library Cataloguing in Publication Data
Auton, Jim
    RAF Liberator over the Eastern Front: a bomb
    aimer's Second World War and Cold War story.
    – Large print ed.
    (Isis reminiscence series)
    1. Auton, Jim
    2. Great Britain. Royal Air Force. Squadron, 178
    3. World War, 1939–1945 – Campaigns –
    Eastern Front
    4. World War, 1939–1945 – Aerial operations, British
    5. World War, 1939–1945 – Personal narratives, British
    6. Large type books
    I. Title
    940.5'44'941'092

ISBN 978–0–7531–9520–8 (hb)
ISBN 978–0–7531–9521–5 (pb)

Printed and bound in Great Britain by
T. J. International Ltd., Padstow, Cornwall

Dedication

To the memory of my friend, the late Colonel Wojciech Borzobohaty VM, Regional Commander of the Polish *Armia Krajowa (Okreg Radomsko-Kielecki* 1939–1945).

Contents

Acknowledgements

I am particularly grateful to the following distinguished friends and organizations for their help and encouragement during the preparation of this book:

Colonel Wojciech Borzobohaty VM
(Regional Commander of the Polish *Armia Krajowa*)

Polish Ambassadors Gertych and DeVirion
(Members of the wartime Polish Resistance forces)

Bickham Sweet-Escott
(Wartime brigadier in the Special Operations Executive)

Joan Band
(Widow of Flight Lieutenant Gordon Band, Medical Officer, 178 Squadron)

Count Edward Raczynski
(Polish Ambassador in London throughout the Second World War)

Ken Travenna
(Flight Commander on 178 Squadron)

Wing Commander Cecil Harper
(Wartime Senior Operations Officer of the RAF Balkan Air Force)

Fellow members and other friends of the Air Bridge Association

Fellow members of the *Armia Krajowa* Association in Poland

The Polish Directors of the former concentration camp at Auschwitz

Veterans of the Polish, Czechoslovak and German Air Forces

The Royal Air Force School of Aviation Medicine

Staff of the National Archives, Kew

CHAPTER ONE

Training for War

"Balls up! Balls up! Get your balls up, man!" We stood there in rows, scores of us, in the Long Room at Lord's, our trousers down round our ankles, our shirt tails trapped under our chins, while a man in civilian clothes carried out an inspection of our most private parts.

"Get your balls up," he bellowed at the top of his voice as he paused in front of each of us. We were rather surprised by his vulgarity and we could not understand why he seemed to be so angry. I suppose he thought the whole process was a waste of his time. We certainly thought it was a waste of ours. "Get fell in for an FFI!" the corporal had shouted. "What on earth does that mean?" we asked each other. "They want to see if you've got a dose of the clap." We tried not to stare at each other's works, as we stood there exposed and red-faced.

"Fall out, that man!" we heard the corporal bark, and we craned our necks to see what was happening. Was it the clap? If so, what did it look like? As one of our number was hauled out of the ranks, we saw that one of his testicles was rather larger than an orange. The other one was the usual size. How the hell did that happen?

1

Surely not the clap — but we didn't know the symptoms. The lad with his extraordinary ball was led meekly away, never to be seen or heard of again. Since that time, I have never gone back to Lord's. Years later, when I mentioned to a cricketing friend that we had exposed our willies in the sacred Long Room, he exclaimed in horror, "Good Lord, and you were not even members!"

We had enlisted in the Royal Air Force voluntarily and enthusiastically, to be trained as pilots. Why did it seem to us like such a good idea at the time? Our side didn't appear to stand any chance of winning the war. The United States had not yet shown any signs of joining in as combatants. Our newspapers indicated that Stalin with his millions of troops was allied with Hitler. Our gallant allies, the French, had swiftly capitulated to the Germans, and the British Army had been humiliatingly kicked out of the Continent at Dunkirk. However, despite the apparent invincibility of Hitler's forces, we had been impatient to join up. What drove us to such foolishness? Most of us were still at grammar school when the decision had finally been made in 1939 to "teach little old Hitler a lesson". At our age, nobody would have allowed us to drive a car, borrow a motorbike or vote, but the Royal Air Force offered us the chance to leave home and fly an aeroplane. So we were hooked. The RAF didn't ask for birth certificates. We were whatever age we said we were. All we had to do was to pass the strict medical and educational tests and we were in. The youngest pilot I ever met was a lanky lad of fifteen. Joining the

Air Force made us feel that we were real men. Little did we realize what was in store for us — some of it good, much of it bad.

For the first few days, we would have put up with anything. We were so elated to think that we would soon be up in the sky. However, we had a lot to learn on the ground before we were to see any aeroplanes, and we would generally be treated with contempt both by the people who were directly in charge of us and the remote and unseen people who ran the Air Force. Uniforms were shoved at us by grumpy storekeepers in a garage that the Air Force had commandeered in St John's Wood. Some of the uniforms almost fitted us. Unfortunately, they had no new footwear of my size, so I had to hobble around in a crippling pair of repaired boots — one with rubber soles and heels and the other one leather with steel heel-plates and studs. We spent our first weeks learning how to salute officers, how to march back and forth for hours and how to carry out ridiculous drill movements while wondering how such knowledge should help us to win the war. "What are you supposed to be?" the drill corporals would snarl. "Pilots! You couldn't pile shit!"

In our spare time, we practised such manly pursuits as beer drinking and smoking. Most of us were still virgins, but keen to learn the ropes as soon as the opportunity presented itself. Every night there were plenty of "ladies of easy virtue" loitering in the streets between our billets near Regent's Park and the West End, but they were wary of us because an aircrew cadet had recently murdered several prostitutes in the

3

vicinity. Although the cadet was eventually caught, the girls were still scared of any man with the customary white aircrew flash in his cap. The solution was obvious: take out the white flash. The next hurdle was that the girls seemed rather intimidating. After all, they had been at it quite a while and we were mere beginners. Each night after "lights out" at 10.30, we related our latest experiences of "chatting up the birds". One of the more intrepid lads told how he had spent two pounds, which, we learned, was the current local rate for sexual services. We excitedly encouraged him to disclose all the details. "She was a nice-looking girl. I was a bit surprised when she invited me to go with her. She took me to a flat near St John's Wood station. When we got to her room, she took two quid off me and put it under the clock on the mantelpiece. She told me to undress and lie on the bed, while she went off to the bathroom. Of course, I wanted to get my money's worth, so when she came back into the room I asked her to take off all her clothes. She kept her stockings on though, and I remembered reading that girls had been strangled with stockings, so I guessed why." "What happened then?" we wanted to know. "Did you shag her? You lucky sod." "Well, no. She got me so worked up while she was putting a French letter on me that I came, and she said, 'You're finished.' I said no I wasn't. 'Oh yes you are,' she said. I said, 'But I haven't had it yet!' 'Well, you're finished, anyway,' she said. Then I suddenly thought about my two pounds on the mantelpiece, and so did she. We both jumped off the bed together, but she was a bit quicker than me and

4

she grabbed the money. Then she told me to get dressed and go. I felt such a fool, and that's all my money gone until next pay day." We sympathized with him. As pupil pilots we were paid only two shillings (10p) a day, so two pounds was a lot to lose.

That year the government started a "Holidays at Home" campaign to discourage civilians from travelling. "Is your journey really necessary?" asked the posters on the railway stations. The local council organized dances in Regent's Park in the evenings. Dancing was a painful business for us. We had been inoculated in both sides of the chest, jabbed in both arms and both buttocks and we had been vaccinated too. Wearing a heavy respirator (gas mask) slung across the chest was agony. Why did they have to do so many jabs at the same time? We had queued up — minus our trousers — dozens at a time — up the stairs and along the corridor in a commandeered private house. The same blunt needle was used on all of us. One big hefty lad fainted and as he lay there on the floor in his short vest, the medical orderly bent down and jabbed the dreaded needle into him. We would encounter many more blunt needles before the Air Force was finished with us.

At one time, there were three thousand of us doing ground training at Torquay. Much of this training seemed utterly pointless, and it appeared to do nothing to prepare us for flying duties. We were paraded and inspected several times each day. The bottoms of our boots between the sole and heel had to be polished, and the backs of our cap badges, otherwise we were in trouble. We regularly did route marches in steel helmets and full marching order — that is heavy backpacks, side-packs, water-bottles, overcoats, gas masks, rifles and bayonets.

In wet weather, the route marches were sheer hell. We felt miserable and we looked miserable. The drill corporals had been told that servicemen should help to raise the morale of the civilian population by demonstrating that the troops were in good heart. The nearby towns of Plymouth and Exeter had been badly bombed and civilian morale had been badly shaken. During route marches, the corporals would rush back and forth, exhorting us to "Sing, you bastards, sing!" We didn't really feel like singing anything that might be likely to cheer up the civilians — we were cold, tired and hungry, but sing we certainly did. We sang vulgar words to hymn tunes. A favourite was "We are the Royal Air Force, what fuckin' good are we? The only time we double is breakfast, dinner and tea. And when the Sergeant calls us we shout with all our might, Per Ardua ad Astra, up you Jack, I'm all right."

This mournful dirge bellowed out by several hundred men was always quite an impressive performance. We had a large repertoire of rude songs, some of which had originated in the First World War.

When the weather became warmer, they had another torture in store for us. We had to put on our gas masks, and gas capes and run a couple of miles uphill. What on earth was the point of it? We would be exhausted and bathed in sweat when we arrived at a place where we were to spend many hours learning Morse code that few of us would ever use. We had to clean the dust off our boots at least twice a day — usually by standing on one leg and rubbing the boots up the back of the trouser legs — and we had to get our hair cut a couple of times each week. A favourite remark of the drill corporals as they walked up and down behind us on parade was, "Am I hurting you, lad? No? Well, I should be, I'm standing on your back hair — get it cut!" The remark was usually accompanied by a jab in the back that made the recipient stagger forward. "Stand still!" was the next snarling rebuke. As a mild form of protest, some of the lads got the barber to run the clippers over their heads, leaving a raised portion in the form of individual letters that, when they stood together, would spell a vile word. Each fresh drill instructor would address us with statements such as, "You play ball with me and I'll play ball with you — otherwise I'll have you in the bloody guard room so fast your feet won't touch the deck." Another favourite statement was, "You might have broke your mother's heart, but you won't break mine." We had to carry gas masks at all times and we were forbidden to carry any extraneous objects, such as our knives and forks, in the gas mask cases. To make sure that regulations were being observed, spot checks were carried out on parade. There was great hilarity in the ranks one day when a lad was found to be carrying a pair of his girl-friend's knickers in his gas mask case. Foot drill and marching — a daily torture — was accompanied by much unnecessary swearing by the drill instructors. Occasionally we were made to take

7

over from the instructors and drill a squad ourselves. We always managed very well without any swearing at all. This didn't suit the instructors. I heard one of them shout, "Bollock 'em! For Christ's sake, bollock 'em!" "But they aren't doing anything wrong, Corporal," protested the pupil. "That doesn't matter, bollock 'em, anyway!" was the reply. Constant verbal abuse did nothing to instil discipline, it merely fostered in us a rebelliousness that became general among aircrew personnel.

Some of our spare time was spent in trying to lure girls away from cadets of Dartmouth Naval College. This form of inter-service rivalry gave us much satisfaction. Being always hard up, we found it useful to have several girl-friends on the go at the same time. For example, girls in the chemists to provide gifts of essentials such as soap and razor blades, others working in cafés who would let us off without paying, and one or two working at the cinema, so that we could get in free. Of course, the girls had their price — they expected us to take them out on dates. We did our best to fulfil our obligations, but there were simply too many of them. When we failed to show up for a date, we could sometimes get away with the excuse that we had been unexpectedly put on guard duty. After that lie failed to work any longer, we would be forced to flee into the nearest public toilet at the sight of an irate girl bearing down on us in the street. In time the streets of Torquay became ever more hazardous in that respect, and we had to keep a sharp lookout in public at all times.

Civilian clothes were banned, so we always had to wear uniform, complete with blancoed webbing belts. The blanco would come off onto the clothes of any girl with whom we made contact. When walking out in town, we were supposed to walk in twos and in step. We were not allowed to carry anything, such as a girl-friend's shopping or a bunch of flowers — nor were we allowed to hold hands with a girl. The Air Force considered that we didn't need as much food on Sundays as we had on weekdays, so to make up for the deficit, we visited the Salvation Army hall, where we could be sure of getting a free cup of tea and a sandwich after a short religious service. Following the customary prayers, I once heard the Salvation Army man ask a soldier in our midst where he expected to be in eternity. The soldier's reply was, "Wiv all me mates." A suitable reply, at that time, we all thought. We greatly admired the good social work of the Salvation Army, but we would have been happy to forego the prayers.

One of the most ridiculous ideas thought up by somebody remote from the horrors of air combat was the use of Torquay's Palace Hotel as a sort of convalescent home for officer pilots who had had their faces burnt off. Many of these unfortunate young men were not only hideously disfigured, but also blind, and we would often see them in their smart uniforms being led through the streets, hand in hand, by companions who were fortunate enough to be able to see where they were going. When we looked at these men, who were only a little older than we were, we could see clearly a fate that awaited many of us — a fate of which we did not need to be constantly reminded. The recollection of those poor men and their dreadful disfigurements would constantly haunt us when we came to face the enemy and the possibility of being trapped in burning aircraft ourselves. Our government, which was so concerned about boosting the morale of the civil population, paid scant regard to the state of our morale. One Sunday, a couple of German FW 190 fighter-bombers flew in low from over the sea without encountering any opposition, and dropped their bombs on the Palace Hotel, killing some of the patients. The bombs fell on the gymnasium. Fortunately, it was Sunday. If it had been any other day, the gymnasium would have been crowded and many more people would have died. As the Palace Hotel was occupied solely by severely wounded Royal Air Force men, we wondered if the Germans had deliberately chosen it alone as their target. An unofficial plaque was later placed in the hotel to commemorate the sad occasion.

After more ground training, including marching about at the ridiculous speed of 140 paces per minute, we at last reached Elementary Flying Training School. The aeroplanes were beautiful — de Havilland Tiger Moths — open cockpits — real flying. We were in our element. This made it all worthwhile. We completely forgot about the war. We were too busy to think about the future or the past. Even girls were no longer quite so important now. When we were not actually up in the sky, we spent all our time talking about flying.

"Tell us about your first solo, Bert." We never tired of Bert's account of his first solo flight. It was Friday afternoon when Bert was cleared for take-off alone. We all rushed out of the flight hut to see him go off. After one circuit of the aerodrome, he came in to land. As he touched down everything seemed to go wrong. The plane started to perform cartwheels — nose — wingtip — tail — wingtip — nose — finally coming to rest upside-down with Bert hanging in his safety straps. He carefully removed the retaining pin from his straps and, holding fast to the sides of the open cockpit, he lowered himself gently to the ground. "I weren't a bloody fool." Bert told us later, in his deliberately exaggerated northern accent, "I didn't pull the pin straight out of the safety straps and fall on me 'ead and break me soddin' neck." Having extricated himself from the wreck, Bert wondered what to do next. Nothing in his training so far had prepared him for dealing with this kind of situation. He stood a little way off and looked at the plane. What would they do to punish him? Would they kick him off the flying course? He was near to tears. Should he walk back across the aerodrome to the flight hut and find his instructor? Everything had gone very quiet — no sound of an ambulance or fire engine. Didn't they know he had crashed? Suddenly the sound of a motorcycle. It was the Medical Officer. He circled the plane, and then he circled Bert. "You all right, lad?" he shouted above the noise of the motor bike. "Yes, sir," replied Bert, standing to attention and wondering if he ought to salute. "Right ho, then," shouted the MO, still circling, "I'm just off on a forty-eight [weekend leave

11

pass]. Report to me at the sick bay on Monday morning." One more quick circle and he was gone. Bert trudged back across the aerodrome to face an interrogation by his fellow pupil pilots who still had to face their first solo flights.

Most inconsiderate of Bert to crash on a Friday afternoon! If he had broken his neck, he might have upset the Medical Officer's plans for the weekend.

It was February. The weather became freezing cold. Our unlined metal huts had stoves, but no coal except what we could steal from the coal dump. After dark, we took turns to crawl across open ground and wait for the armed sentry to disappear from view. Then we hastily filled our buckets and silently crawled back to the hut. The Germans were not the only enemy. The coal was not of the best quality and the stove needed much poking to keep it going. One evening the top flap was open and someone was poking about as usual in the stove, when a shout went up, "There's a round in the fire!" We all dived under the beds, and almost immediately a bullet shot out through the side of the stove and through the wall of the hut. Fortunately, nobody was hit, but we were all a little shaken by the experience. Who put the bullet in the stove? Was it one of us? We soon forgot the incident. That is, until someone hit upon the silly idea of shouting, "There's a round in the fire!" just for the hell of it, and then laughing hysterically at the sight of the rest of us diving under the beds. In due course, we would be facing a great many more bullets, and that would not be a laughing matter.

February was not the best time of year for flying in planes with open cockpits. The weather was dreadful and we spent many hours waiting for clear skies. One day, the Air Force sprayed camouflage paint on the aerodrome so that it looked like a series of small fields, and in consequence it became more difficult for us to see it from the air. To add to our difficulties, the large name boards were removed from all the railway stations. We had used those boards as an aid to our navigation. How the devil were we going to find our way back to the aerodrome now? At the end of a practice flight, we would head back in the general direction of base until we came to the local railway line, turn right and fly for five minutes, and if we didn't see the aerodrome we would turn around and fly along the line in the opposite direction for ten minutes. In spite of the cold, we had sweaty palms by the time the aerodrome eventually came into view. Luckily, there was a large factory chimney on the aerodrome. Without that chimney, we would often have needed the proverbial bicycle clips and brown trousers, especially as all the fields of a suitable size for emergency landings had telegraph poles planted in them to stop the Germans invading. I lost the aerodrome the day after it had been camouflaged. I was supposed to be doing "circuits and bumps" — that is, repeatedly flying round the aerodrome, landing and taking off again — reaching a maximum height of a mere 800ft. Nobody would expect to lose an aerodrome at that height, but I did. When I realized what had happened, I was on my downwind leg of the circuit and the aerodrome was

13

neither on my right nor on my left side. After a couple of minutes I knew it must be somewhere behind me and I would have to fly over to the nearest railway line, which I knew to be somewhere straight ahead, to fix my position, and then fly back to the aerodrome. Circuits and bumps was not very exciting, so I decided to climb up to 3,000ft, stick my chewing gum onto the top of the compass, so that I would not choke on it, and do a few spins instead — my favourite exercise. When I eventually returned to the aerodrome, I found that my lack of discipline had been duly noted.

Our training planes were painted bright orange — apparently to show that we were unarmed — but this meant that we were sitting ducks for German raiders, and at advanced flying school, one of my friends was shot down and killed during a training flight in a Fairy Battle. After a while, the Air Force set up what was called the Empire Air Training Scheme in order to send us abroad to what we expected to be safer places.

As flying schools were so overloaded, delays were inevitable before we were able to leave for foreign parts. During our "waste-of-time periods", we spent many weeks in disposal centres with nothing much to occupy ourselves with in the daytime, so in the evenings and at weekends we concentrated on our second most favourite interest — girls.

I was fast asleep in the billet when Pompey returned to the room that we shared in a private house. "Meet the new girl-friend!" he said, sticking his fingers under my nose. I held my breath and shoved his hand away.

We were lucky to be billeted out. Most of the three thousand men at the disposal centre were accommodated in huts in a municipal park that was locked up at night, and they were supposed to be back in the park before midnight, or 23.59, as they called it. There was no restriction on men in private billets, and we could stay out all night if we wished. Pompey and I usually went out together every evening, not returning until long after midnight, but we happened to be between girl-friends at the moment and also out of cash, so I had decided to stay in and have an early night. We had both turned in at about nine o'clock that evening, but about half past nine Pompey suddenly exclaimed, "Sod this for a game of soldiers! I've got nothing to read and no cigarettes. I'm off out."

It was well after midnight when he reappeared. "We'll be all right now," he announced, "I met a lad who owed me half a crown, and I managed to get it back off him. Then we went into a pub for a swift half and a packet of cigarettes, but they hadn't got any cigarettes. The usual story — only for their regular customers. There were a couple of birds sitting there near the bar. They heard me ask for cigarettes and one of them offered me one of hers, so we sat down with them. The one with the cigarettes wasn't bad looking," Pompey continued, "but must have been getting on for thirty. She said that her husband was in the Army. He'd been called up a couple of weeks after they got married and she had hardly seen him since then — they had just a couple of days together before he was sent abroad. She said he spent most of his embarkation leave at his

15

mother's house, miles away. He's been abroad two years and she said she wishes she had never got married. She used to be a hairdresser before being directed into a munitions factory. Munitions work is better paid than hairdressing, and with overtime she isn't badly off. She seemed to have had plenty to drink, and after a while she asked me if I would like to go back to her place for supper. Of course, it was mainly the supper that I was after, but I knew what she had in mind. She kept touching me on the knee and leaning on me while she was talking. On the way back to her place, she bought us fish and chips and we ate it in the street. Her place was a bed-sit with not much furniture except a big double bed, and it wasn't long before we were in it. She had sobered up by then, and what a goer! She nearly wore me out. She got a bit maudlin and cried afterwards and said she wanted to see me again tomorrow, but I said I didn't go out when I had no money. Then she offered to lend me a fiver that she said she was saving for the rent, but I didn't take it. I don't want to get too involved with her because she is the type that would probably become too possessive, and I know what that can be like. I've had some of it. I had a young clippy when I was on the buses who was like that. It's worse than being married."

Pompey had been a bus driver. He was married and he seemed old enough to be my father. I could not understand how the Air Force had believed him to be under the maximum age limit of twenty-five for potential pilots. "I never got on well with my wife," he had informed me when I first met him. "We were always arguing about something — money usually. Anyway, one day I told her I'd had enough and I had a good mind to join up. She said I hadn't got the guts, and that annoyed me, so when we were walking past the Labour Exchange I called in and pretended I wanted to volunteer for the Navy to avoid being called up for the Army. I didn't really want to go in the forces at all, and I was only doing it to frighten the wife. She knew that the service marriage allowance was less than the money that she was already getting from me, and I thought she would stop her nagging if she thought I had been to put my name down."

The people at the Labour Exchange gave Pompey some forms to fill in, and while he was doing that, he noticed a poster on the wall, saying that the Air Force needed recruits for flying duties. He volunteered, thinking they would surely never accept him, a bus driver, for training as a pilot! Then he could go back home to wait for eventual conscription into the forces or civilian war work. He told me, "I was a bit surprised when I was accepted for pilot training. They said I was fit and up to the required standard of education, so I would be sent for in a few days. I had only done it for bravado, but there was no way out." A railway warrant arrived through the post a couple of days later, and a note to say that he had to report for attestation. His wife hadn't believed him when he said he had volunteered — that is, not until the railway warrant arrived — and there was a hell of a row. She said he had joined up simply to spite her, so he needn't think she would still be waiting for him when he got back. She was off to live with her mother. Pompey sighed, "I have written to her at her mother's place a couple of times, but she hasn't replied, so I suppose it's all over between us, but I'm not really sorry. We weren't suited. There is nothing that I can do about it now. Anyway, it's fortunate that we don't have any kids — she didn't want any." That was my friend Pompey's story. I was soon to learn a lot about many interesting things from this mature "man of the world".

All day long, from Monday to Friday and half of Saturday, we were confined in the park. The gates were locked and we usually had nothing to do except wander about aimlessly and wait for mealtimes — the only times when we were able to be under cover. There were no lectures, no sports facilities, just utter boredom. Most of us were too hard up to buy cigarettes, and it was quite common to see three or four men passing one cigarette around. Woe betide anyone who took more than two puffs before passing it on! Dreadful music was continually broadcast over a loudspeaker system. After hearing the same songs hundreds of times, we came to loathe the sound of Vera Lynn, the so-called "Forces Sweetheart". She was certainly no sweetheart of ours.

Occasionally, the authorities broke the monotony by ordering us to form up on parade — all three thousand of us. What a performance! We soon realized that they could not possibly control a body of three thousand men — especially on wet and windy days. An officer stood on a little mound and bleated his orders. "Can't hear you!" we shouted. Even if we could hear, we didn't want to. We were fed up with hanging around for months when we thought that we should have been continuing our flying training. "Left turn! Quick march!" the officer screeched. Some of us turned left and some turned right. Consequently, hundreds of men collided with each other. People were knocked to the ground. Hats fell off and were trampled underfoot. Hundreds of men who were still on their feet marched away into the distance — deaf to the pursuing corporals' frantic cries of "Halt! Halt!" Absolute pandemonium! A welcome change, however, from the usual boredom and hours of nothing to do. It was worth getting a few bruises, which were the inevitable result of three thousand men being totally out of control and walking into each other. Occasionally, we were formed up for compulsory church parades — more pandemonium. Roman Catholics, Church of Englands, Jews and ODs (other denominations) had to be separated from each other. Many of us had claimed to have no religious affiliations when we were asked to state our religion on enlistment. "If you are not RC and not OD, then you are C of E, because you have got to be something," we were told, and our identity discs were stamped accordingly. On church parade, many of us claimed to be members of some obscure religious sect that did not allow us to join in with any of the others. It sometimes worked, but sometimes we were marched off to the cookhouse to peel potatoes while the others were sitting in church, blatantly reading newspapers under the Padre's nose as a silent protest against compulsory church attendance.

Once in a while some of us asked to see the Commanding Officer to protest that we had volunteered to fly and it was disgraceful that we were kept hanging about in idleness while our country was losing the war. The most militant protesters during my time were Belgian volunteers, who continually pointed out that their families were suffering under enemy occupation while they themselves were being denied the opportunity of helping them. Nobody in authority paid us any attention, and so our silent non-cooperation continued at every opportunity.

Things rarely got dangerously out of hand, although on one or two occasions attempts were made to burn down the bandstand in the park. The most dangerous thing that happened was when the service police were slow to open the park gates and let us out one Saturday afternoon. People started to become impatient. About a thousand men surged forward, and those at the front were in danger of being crushed to death. Rather foolishly, instead of opening the gates immediately, the police drew their revolvers and threatened to shoot the men at the front, who were helpless to prevent the hundreds behind them from surging forward. A dreadful disaster was only narrowly avoided when the gates eventually gave way. I made sure that I was never again trapped in the path of any large crowd.

After a couple of months of enforced idleness, some of us were informed that we were to be sent away for an infantry tactics course. This news made us wonder if we were to be transferred into the Army. "I shan't be going," announced Pompey, "I'm reporting sick." "But there's nothing wrong with you," I replied. "I know there isn't," he said, "but I've told the Medical Officer that I need to be circumcised, and I'll be admitted into the sick bay while you lot are buggering about playing at soldiers."

The infantry course was interesting, and we welcomed the change from the boredom of the disposal centre, but it was rather hard on us in our flabby condition. We could have done with some toughening-up first. During the course, we slept on the ground in bell-tents. All daytime activities took place in the open air, regardless of the weather. In addition to "playing at soldiers", we took turns to do what were known as "fatigues", which meant working in the field kitchen and doing such tasks as peeling potatoes for eight hours.

Cookhouse fatigues were not as bad as we had feared. We were able to follow the example of the cooks and help ourselves to such items as tins of Spam, condensed milk, jam and other rare treats. In the middle of the morning, a woman voluntary worker from the Church Army or some such organization would turn up and serve tea and cakes from a small van to those of us who had any money. Some of the lads would drink one cup of tea and then buy a second one to take back to the tent and use as shaving water. At breakfast on one particularly stormy day, I collected my plateful of dry cornflakes at the cookhouse tent. When I turned to walk away the wind blew the cornflakes off the plate. I decided to pour a drop of tea on the corn flakes in future to stick them to the plate.

We had to erect our own lavatories, which consisted of buckets in a trench and a rustic pole on which to perch. One of the least popular fatigue duties was assisting the corporal in charge of the "crap cooker". The lavatory buckets had to be emptied onto a grill over an open fire situated down by the river. One of the lads returned to the tent after "crap cooker fatigues" looking rather perturbed. He described how the grill above the fire had become clogged, and he had broken a stick off a willow tree and tried to clear the blockage. The stick became jammed between the bars of the grill, and when he yanked it out a lump of boiling turd had flicked off the flexible stick and stuck onto the corporal's forehead. No laughing matter for the poor corporal! Our instructors demonstrated how to creep silently up behind people, such as German sentries, and strangle them. (I only heard of one shot-down airman who had to kill a sentry during the war, and he did it with a brick.) Among other things, we experienced the excitement of firing live ammunition and the terror of throwing live grenades.

At the end of the course, we were dumped back at the disposal centre and I resumed contact with Pompey. Some of the lads, who knew the crafty way he had avoided being sent on the infantry course, took great delight in telling him repeatedly, "When they did your operation, they threw the wrong end away."

To compensate for the daytime boredom we made frequent visits to the local dance-halls in the evenings. There was nowhere else to go when we had no money, which was most of the time. Entry into the dance-halls was free to servicemen, and as there were never enough men available, we were very popular. When we had money we would be out drinking with the lads until the pubs closed and then we'd go to a dance-hall for what we called "the last roundup". The girls were pleased to see us roll up. They had had to dance with each other until we arrived. As we were usually in twos, we tried to pick up two girls who were together. It seemed that there were never two pretty ones together, and it was quite common to hear the lads say, "I don't think much of yours" before the girls had even been approached. Actually, it was usually the girls who made the selection, and it was no good if we tried to frustrate their choice. We soon learned to avoid being taken home to meet the parents. Being viewed as potential husbands was too high a price to pay for a free supper.

As the Air Force's food was quite inadequate, much of our spare time was spent in the pursuit of something to eat. All girls who showed interest in us were interrogated to establish their financial status. Any girl who was engaged in munitions work was of interest, because such people were far better paid than we were, and we were just as keen to get a free meal as we were to get whatever else might be on offer. The thought of sexual harassment by landladies had never occurred to us until one morning we heard that one of the billeted-out lads had turned up at the guard room in the park in the middle of the night to complain that his landlady had got into his bed. He got no sympathy from us. We asked him if she was young and if she was good looking. If she was ugly, he was told, he should have put a paper bag over her head, or he could have tackled her from the rear — doggy fashion. We suggested that there must surely be something strange about him, and the poor lad had to tolerate our crude jokes for many days. We never found out if the billeting officer crossed that landlady off his list, neither did we discover her name and address. We would have liked her to know that her airman was not typical. She should have had someone like Pompey, who would certainly have obliged her if she had lent him a fiver.

Pompey and I were billeted in a nice house, and our landlady, who had two little children, told us that her husband was abroad in the Colonial Service. When we returned to the billet late one night an inebriated man in civilian clothes was trying to insert a key into the front door lock. "Come on, old son," said Pompey, as he attempted to propel him out through the front gate, "you don't belong here." As the man had difficulty in remaining on his feet, Pompey was almost forced to carry him out into the street. "Now you get off home, before you get into trouble," Pompey advised him. The man struggled to get free of Pompey's grasp. "But this is my house," he protested. "Look here," replied Pompey, "you are pissed — you don't live here — you are at the wrong house. Now clear off, or I will have to thump you!" "I know where I am and I know this is my house," he insisted. "Ask him to show us his identity card," I suggested. With great difficulty, the man produced a document giving his name and indicating that he was a consular official.

"Blimey, he's her husband!" said Pompey. "I thought he was supposed to be abroad." "Yes, I was, but I've come home on leave," was the slurred explanation. After removing our boots, which we always did when returning to the billet, we silently opened the front door and let him in the house, which was in total darkness. As we entered, he tried to explain that he had been to visit relatives and had inadvertently had a drop too much. "Shush, quiet, we don't want to wake up the landlady and the children!" whispered Pompey. "You can't shush him, it's his house," I reminded my friend. As we crept upstairs to our room we realized how near the apparent intruder had come to being thumped and dumped outside in the gutter in front of his own house. We never saw him again and the incident was never mentioned by the landlady.

Time seemed to drag at the park — hours and hours of utter boredom, relieved only by mealtimes. The food was fairly monotonous. The cooks were busy trying to cope with three thousand men three times a day. The usual punishment for defaulters was work in the kitchen — quite an eye-opener. Sprouts were one of the cooks' favourite vegetables, as they did not require, or rather, they did not get, much preparation. Whereas at home sprouts had to be rinsed, the outside leaves removed and little crosses cut into the bottom of them, our cooks tipped them straight out of the sacks into the cookers. After boiling, the scum was skimmed off the water and the sprouts were ready to be served onto the plates. Each of us had a set of "eating irons" — knife, fork and spoon that we had to keep with us and bring along to every meal. Our eating irons were always getting lost and many men would turn up at mealtimes without any, and the plea would be heard, "After you with the fork, chum!" The requested fork would then be licked clean and passed over. It always paid to sit next to someone who had a complete set of "irons". Although the Air Force would not help, there was one sure way of getting a replacement set of "irons". We waited until we had saved up a shilling (5p) — the price of a meal at one of the government's "British Restaurants" — and pocketed their irons. The British Restaurant's staff soon got wise to us and demanded an Air Force cap, as deposit, in return for the use of the irons. Our solution to the problem was to "borrow" a cap from somebody before a visit to the restaurant, hand it in and leave it behind in return for the (permanent) use of the cutlery. In time, the restaurants had a surfeit of caps. Men from whom the caps had been "borrowed" were made to wear steel helmets instead, as a punishment for their lack of vigilance.

It seemed to us that we were condemned to hanging about in idleness until the end of the war. We were told nothing, and morale was only buoyed up by our nightly forays in search of new "crumpet", which was freely available. The only trouble was that the government had introduced "Double British Summertime". It never seemed to get dark in summer. It was still daylight when the pubs and dance-halls closed, and there was usually nowhere to take the girls for a bit of unseen "hanky-panky". During her husband's leave, our landlady went away for a few days, giving us, we thought, a good opportunity to sneak two of our favourite girl-friends, Joyce and Betty, into the house. Betty was the flirty one of the two and I thought that she would be most likely to accept our proposal with enthusiasm. I was unsure about Joyce, however. I had always felt a bit inhibited by her extraordinary good looks and striking figure. I was happy to keep quiet and leave the arrangements to the smooth-tongued Pompey. He only needed a couple of minutes to explain what we had in mind, and both girls agreed to stay with us all night. We wanted to avoid the risk of being seen by the neighbours, so we went to a pub and waited excitedly for darkness to descend. The girls phoned home to say that each would be spending the night with the other one. It was all set and we were on to a good thing, we thought.

When the pub closed, the blasted sun was still shining. Would it never get dark? We went for a walk to pass the time away. We explained that we were anxious not to lose the privilege of being billeted out in private accommodation, so we didn't want to risk being reported to the authorities if the neighbours should see what we were up to. The girls did not seem to understand our fears. Their intrepid airmen had turned into wimps. We had been wandering about for an hour, waiting for darkness. If we did not pluck up our courage soon, the girls might get fed up and go home. We decided to go in first, make sure the coast was clear and leave the front door unlocked. The girls followed a few minutes later. Once they were in the house, the first thing they had to do, of course, was to go to the toilet, and they made so much noise in there together, talking and giggling, that we were afraid the neighbours might hear them through the wall. When they were ready, we introduced them to our rickety, narrow RAF beds and awful three-piece mattresses. Soon Pompey's bed was rattling like a steam hammer. But Joyce and I were not doing at all well. Despite Joyce's enthusiastic co-operation, it didn't work. There seemed to be no way in. We tried for about an hour. Then I asked accusingly, "Don't you want to do it? Haven't you done it before?" "Yes, I have," replied Joyce. "I'm sure you couldn't have. Who was it with?" I wanted to know. "I did it once with a soldier, and of course I do want to do it," she whispered. We lay quietly for a while, before making another attempt. Penetration was impossible and I felt sure that there had never been a soldier or anyone else. Joyce had closed up completely. She seemed to be as frustrated as I was. We lay in each other's arms until dawn before, at her suggestion, making a final unsuccessful attempt. Meanwhile Pompey's frequent rattling continued to break the silence. About 5 o'clock, we reckoned that the buses would have started running and it was time for the girls to leave. I watched in silence, as Joyce slowly got dressed. Suddenly she turned to me and whispered, "I'm sorry, I really couldn't help it. I suppose you won't want to see me again after this." I could see that she was on the brink of tears. "Don't worry about it, Joyce," I muttered, feeling guilty that I had made her feel the need to apologize. I hoped that the other two would not notice that she looked upset. When they were ready, we let the girls out of the house. "How did it go?" enquired Pompey. "Marvellous," I replied. There was no way that I was going to tell him about our failure. "You get on okay?" "Oh yes," he assured me, unnecessarily, "didn't get more than five minutes' sleep; I think I'll be about knackered by tonight." Within a couple of weeks, Pompey became tired of Betty's company and moved on to a new girl-friend. Joyce and I remained good friends, going to the cinema and to dances together occasionally. There was the usual furtive fumbling in the dark on the back row of the cinema, but we never again tried anything else. In time, our meetings became less frequent. The last time I saw her she was with another aircrew cadet, and she shyly told me that they were engaged to be married. I made no comment.

CHAPTER
TWO

Air School in South Africa

Every few weeks a couple of hundred men disappeared from the park at dead of night, bound for secret destinations abroad. We knew that flying schools had been opened in Canada, the USA, Rhodesia and South Africa. I thought Canada and America might be too similar to England, and as I preferred to go somewhere really foreign I was delighted when we were suddenly issued with tropical kit and told to appear in the dining hall that evening. After we had been fed we were given a pep talk by a young officer who told us in a silly acquired accent (typical of newly commissioned officers) that we were going abroad to a secret destination and that we must always bear in mind that we would be regarded as ambassadors for our country. Therefore, we should be on our best behaviour, so as not to disgrace the United Kingdom. A few of us, who had spent the evening in the pubs celebrating our impending departure for foreign parts, were in no mood for a lecture. As the officer repeated the bit about being ambassadors, a voice rang out from the back of the hall, "Oh, piss off, you daft prat!" The officer immediately tore off his tunic and flung it down on a chair. Red faced, he spluttered, "If that man will have the courage to come here, I will fight him. We can forget about rank, I will fight him." Of course, nobody accepted the challenge, and after a minute or two of laughter from us, he picked up his tunic and left the hall. One of the lads turned to me: "George should have gone forward. He's got a professional licence, and he would have made mincemeat of him."

In thin drizzle, and loaded down with two kitbags, we struggled through the pitch-black streets to the station. We climbed aboard a blacked-out train. We sat crowded together in dim blue lighting and speculated about our secret destination. "We must be going to end up in Africa because we have been issued with tropical kit." "Not necessarily; I've heard that sometimes people who were going to Canada were given tropical kit, just to mislead the Germans." "What does it matter where we go, as long as we get out of this bloody place!" Still in darkness and rain, we were eventually transferred onto a pinnace for a short journey in rough seas to a troopship. As dawn was breaking, another pinnace arrived at the ship and twenty or more sailors in chains were led aboard. As soon as they were aboard, the sailors had their chains removed and we were all shown to our bunks on the troop decks. Our accommodation was very near the engines, and the stink of hot oil was dreadful. We were surprised to discover that the bunks, although closely crowded together, were quite comfortable. The next day we ascertained that we were on a mass-produced, all-welded American "liberty" ship, manned mainly by men from the Philippines and by black Americans. Our destination was still not disclosed to us, and we assumed that the ordinary ship's crewmen did not know anything, as we could not get any information out of them. During the first few days at sea, we challenged the crew to a boxing tournament and our team won. We were pleased by the quality of the food, served on a tray, like an airways meal; it was much better than our usual rations. We were fed at seven in the morning and seven at night. It was always exactly the same meal, and after a few days we realized that it was hardly sufficient to keep us alive. There were always two slices of very light white bread on the tray, and I ate only one slice with the meal. I kept the other slice in my pocket for six hours and then broke small pieces off and sucked them until they disintegrated in my mouth. By this means, I attempted to keep the pangs of hunger at bay during the twelve hours between meals. After three weeks, we dropped anchor off the coast of Freetown in West Africa, and the ship took on more fuel. We were within a mile of land, but we were not taken ashore. The ship was immediately sur- rounded by "bum boats", from which young black boys dived into the sea to collect coins or anything else that we threw overboard. They were remarkably strong underwater swimmers. The seawater looked calm and inviting. The weather was scorching hot, but we were not allowed to swim. We had to remain all day on the hot steel decks.

For the first three weeks of the voyage, the "Officer in Charge of Troops" had incorrectly assumed that we were cadet officers, because we wore white flashes in our caps. Due to this misunderstanding, we had been excused all sentry and fire-picket duties. Somehow, he realized his mistake and he announced, to our dismay, that we were to take over all fatigue duties for the remainder of the trip. While we were lying off Freetown, the weather was so hot and humid that sleep below on the troop decks was impossible. We decided to move onto the open deck at night, but we got very little sleep there, and we were severely bitten by mosquitoes. When I was put on sentry duty for twenty-four hours, I managed to find a collapsible chair to sit on in the shade of a hatchway. By midday, I was sitting there fast asleep when I was abruptly awakened by a dreadful bellow from the warrant officer who accompanied the "Officer in Charge of Troops" on his rounds: "What the hell do you think you are on — sleeping duty?" he screeched. "Yes, sir," I instinctively replied, having been conditioned never to say "no" to anyone in authority. Suddenly both of them were screaming at me, "You're under close arrest in five minutes." As they both disappeared down to the troop decks, I slowly realized in my dazed state that I had been found asleep on sentry duty — in wartime. "You can be shot for that!" I thought.

I was still having difficulty in keeping my eyes open, as I was hauled off and locked in the "brig". I had expected to be incarcerated alone, but I found that there were already eleven men in the brig and nine of them were my fellow aircrew cadets. The brig was below the waterline and pleasantly cool. Sleep at last! We were taken to meals by the ship's police, who kept their caps on and escorted us round once to collect a meal. Then they took off their caps and went round with us again. So, we and the police had four meals instead of two each day. We also received a quite unnecessary warning to "keep your trap shut!". Imprisonment in the brig was far better than "freedom" on the troop decks.

After the other criminals were released, I was joined by a rather fierce sailor who told me that he had been sunk twice in submarines and he could not bear to be shut in anywhere. He would scream and shout and bang on the steel cell door for hours until the policemen opened it. He would then demand that the door be left open, and it would take four of them to fight him off and shut it again each time. He sobbed as he told me that he wanted to get out of the Navy and go home, because his mother needed him. He described his experiences of being sunk in submarines, and he said that he had the urge to kill somebody, "with a chair leg or something like that". I spent many hours trying to humour him. He was one of the men who had been brought aboard in chains. I felt convinced that he was mentally unbalanced — no use to the Navy. Why on earth didn't the authorities recognize that he was as much a casualty of war as if he had been wounded, and why didn't they treat him accordingly?

After a few days, I was released from the brig and I rejoined the others on starvation rations. By now, we were under way again. We were not allowed to stay below during daylight, but the top deck was so crowded that there was standing room only for most people. If anyone found a place to sit down on the steel deck he was lucky, and if he stood up someone else would immediately sit down in the vacant space. Standing up all day was tiring, and a few of us took to perching on the ship's rails until we were warned that we were in shark-infested waters and the ship would not stop to pick up anyone who fell overboard. We regularly had to put on our kapok-filled life-vests when a siren sounded for "submarine alert", and we never knew whether it was just a drill or a real emergency. We had been at sea for about four weeks when we were challenged by the ship's crew to a return boxing match. This time we lost almost every bout.

One day I got into conversation with some of the black members of the crew, and I asked them if they had the same meagre food rations. They told me that they had plenty to eat and said that if I would agree to work in their galley, washing up greasy tin dishes, I could eat with them. So I worked in the galley for a week or so, and was well fed. In fact, I was able to provide food to some of my friends on the troop decks until the heat in the galley eventually became unbearable and I had to leave the job and return to starvation rations with the other lads until the end of the voyage.

After six weeks at sea, we arrived in afternoon sunshine off the coast of South Africa in Table Bay, where we dropped anchor. What a welcome sight! We were about a quarter of a mile from the docks and we could see two dock workers waving to us. We waved back and tried to shout to them. They couldn't hear us, but they began to chalk messages on a large sheet of rusty steel plate. "Welcome to Cape Town — plenty of beer — plenty of food — plenty of women", and other good news. After what seemed like an eternity, the anchor was raised and we entered the harbour and the ship was tied up to the quay. We hastily packed up our kit and tried to smarten ourselves up ready to disembark. Keeping clean during the voyage had not been easy. We had the use of shower baths and washbasins, but only cold seawater with soap that refused to lather. Anyway, that was now all behind us — we were there. South Africa. What joy!

However, our excitement was short-lived. An announcement over the loudspeaker informed us that we would not be allowed to leave the ship until the next day. Our mood changed and it looked as though there might be mutiny. Within an hour there was another announcement: we could go ashore until midnight; we must then return to the ship and we would be officially discharged the next morning. We hurled ourselves down the gangway and rushed through the docks into the town. It was paradise. The shops were filled with things such as tropical fruits that we had not seen for years. I and another lad immediately bought six bananas and ate them. We came across a services restaurant staffed by matronly ladies where we ordered a three-course meal. When we had finished we were asked if we wished to have anything else. We sheepishly enquired, "Could we have it again, please?" "What! The whole lot — soup, main course and pudding?" we were asked. "Yes, please, if it's all right with you," we said.

After dinner, we had a few beers and then rode around in a horse-drawn carriage for a while. I leant out of the window to speak to the black driver just as he was whipping up the horse, and I got a stinging blow around the ear. On the way back to the docks, we had a few more beers and bought a pineapple and a coconut. Somehow, we eventually found the ship. We stood on the quay looking at it. We had never been able to study it from the outside. It was very short from bow to stern and very high. No wonder it rolled so badly in rough seas.

The following day we were off by train and three-ton truck to a transit camp in the woods at the foot of Table Mountain. The truck was driven over dirt roads at breakneck speed by a black man. We soon learnt that all black men drove at the same terrifying speed. We were told by the other inmates that we would be staying in the transit camp for just a few days, and there would be nothing to stop us from spending our time sightseeing in Cape Town, "But don't take a taxi at night, because you will end up in District Six with your throat cut. A boatload of Aussies once ran riot in District Six and when the next boatload arrived the inhabitants killed some of them, so keep away!" We were learning something more about South Africa, to add to the information that had been given to us on the troopship. We had been told that on no account were we to mention the Boer War to South Africans. They were very sensitive about it, so we should not get into any discussions about the subject, especially in bars. How the hell were we likely to talk to anyone about the Boer War? After all, we didn't know anything about it ourselves. As far as we could remember, it had never been mentioned to us at school. We assumed that we won, but we didn't know why it was fought.

Another taboo subject was apartheid, a form of strict racial discrimination enforced by law. We were not to have any contact with black women — the penalty for a white man caught with a black girl, we were informed, was seven years in prison, and incidentally, if a black man was caught with a white girl, he got the death penalty. During my first day at the transit camp, I was chatting with a young pilot officer who had been in South Africa for some time and was waiting to be shipped back to the United Kingdom. "Would you like to see my girl-friend?" he asked with a grin. From his pocket, he pulled out a photograph of himself, sitting, smiling at the camera, in a tin bath, naked, with an equally naked black girl. The photo, taken in the open air, showed native huts in the background. I wondered if the black girl was the reason for him being sent back to England. She was the first of many naked black girls that I would see in Africa, but none of them would be in a tin bath.

Pompey was still with me. One day he told me that we could visit his sister and her husband who lived not far away, in Simonstown. The brother-in-law, a dockyard worker, had recently been transferred to

Simonstown from Portsmouth dockyard. We set off to get a train, but before we could reach the station, a man and woman in a car hailed us. "Where are you gentlemen going? Jump in, we will take you there," they said. As it happened, their destination was on the way to Simonstown, so we stopped off for a drink at their house. "If ever you are in the neighbourhood again, call in and if we are not here, don't worry — just help yourselves to drinks out of the cabinet over there, or anything else you want. The house is never locked up and the girls (black servants) are always here." This was our first experience of typical South African hospitality.

When we reached Simonstown, Pompey's sister and her husband were keen to tell us all about their new life in the sun. Baboons stealing their washing off the clothes line — oranges as big as saucers at giveaway prices in the shops. What heaven after life in dreary wartime England! The South Africans' callous attitude to black people troubled them, however. A few days previously, they had been travelling home in the dark when they had run into a black man. They stopped the car and examined him, decided he was dead and called the police from the nearest public telephone. "We have run over and killed a black man," they said. "What have you done with the body?" they were asked. "We haven't moved him or the car. He is still lying in the road at the place where we hit him. We don't want to touch anything until you come out and see that it wasn't our fault — he ran in front of us — we couldn't see him in the dark," they answered. "We are all closed down and locked up for the night here, so we can't come out now.

Just pull him over to the side of the road and we will come out and collect him in the morning. You can go home, there is nothing else to be done," they were told. They returned to where they had left the car and were discussing the phone call as they prepared to move the body. At the sound of the word "police" the body suddenly came alive and scuttled away into the darkness — not dead after all! Although they had given the police their names and address, they never heard another word about the matter. They had since learnt that the police station was always locked up at night and the police never came out after dark.

In a couple of days, we were off on a long train journey to an air school near the town of East London. It did not take us long to establish contact with the abundant local female talent. Our favourite hunting grounds were Woolworths stores and the Saturday-night dances at the town hall. One evening, Pompey and I had a date with two girls we had selected during a quick look around one of the department stores. Mine wanted to go to the Café Bioscope, where food and drinks were served during the film. Pompey and the other girl went for a walk along the beach and we all met up again later. By the time we parted from the girls, we had missed the last bus back to the air school and we had no money for a taxi, so we set off on foot. Every time we came to a street lamp, Pompey took out his penis and examined it. He complained that he had an awful pain, but there was no visible injury, and he explained what had happened. As soon as it was dark, he had got down on a steep grass bank with the girl.

While they were busy in the "missionary position" she slipped straight down the bank from under him, bending his erect penis the wrong way. "You are lucky," I sniggered, "you could have snapped it right off at the root." The moral: always choose a level playing-field.

One day we were informed that the Royal Air Force now had too many pilots and we were to be trained as navigators instead. This news did not suit most of us, and there was much discontented murmuring in the ranks. We had volunteered to be pilots, nothing else. We were told that the system of aircrew training had been revised. "You will be changed around as necessary to suit current requirements of the Royal Air Force. The important thing is that you all do what is required to win the war. Personal choice does not enter into it," we were told. "You might well have volunteered in, but you cannot volunteer out. You must follow orders and make the best of it."

I reluctantly worked my way through the navigation course, at the end of which I quite unexpectedly met up with my old pal Maurice, the "Halifax Cockney", who had been with me at pilots' flying school. I was moaning to him about the amount of classroom work on the navigation course. "I am not doing the navigators' course, they have remustered me as a pupil air bomber," he told me. "Never heard of it. What on earth is that?" I wanted to know. "It's good — we are to act as second pilots and bomb aimers," he said. "After the introduction of large four-engine aircraft like the Lancaster and Halifax, the category of observer has

41

become obsolete, and the other aircrew categories have been changed, with the introduction of flight engineers and air bombers."

Maurice's enthusiasm for his new job was contagious. Co-pilot of a bomber sounded acceptable as a second choice, if they would not let us train as Spitfire pilots — our ambition since long before we joined the Air Force. I toyed with the idea of asking to be remustered, so that I could join Maurice, but I was discouraged when I learned that other people's similar requests had been turned down. At every stage throughout the navigation course, I had moaned to each of the instructors about being denied the opportunity of completing my pilot training, until one day I was summoned to appear before the Commanding Officer. "Why don't you like being a navigator?" he enquired. I explained that I felt it was unfair that men who volunteered for one job were then compelled to do something different, in which they had no particular interest. I had piloted Airspeed Oxfords and Avro Ansons, and it was not right that such experience was now to be wasted. Instead of the expected threat to "stick you in the bloody Army", he asked me if I would be willing to accept a transfer to an air bombers' course, and I gladly accepted. Air bombers, I was informed, were men who had had some training as pilots, and consequently would be able to take over control from the captain of the aircraft in an emergency.

After a short conversion course, I was informed that people with the best examination results could choose where they would go for further training. Things were looking up! Port Elizabeth was reputed to be the best place, so those of us who were given the choice opted to go there, and surprisingly our request was granted. We had always understood that the Air Force never sent anyone to where he wanted to go. It was Christmas time when I bade farewell to my local girl-friends. One said she was upset that I was not being transferred to another training school nearby. I blamed the Air Force! She had invited me to spend Christmas on the family's banana farm, but I was keen to see more of South Africa, and there would be other girls and banana farms elsewhere.

After a very long, but most interesting, train journey, we arrived at Port Elizabeth's air school on a Sunday afternoon. Our first shock was the news that twenty-five people (five staff pilots and twenty pupils) had been killed on a training flight that day. It was said that the wife of one of the staff pilots was a nurse at a hospital out in the country. The staff pilots decided to "shoot up" the hospital — to pretend to bomb it at low level. Five Ansons crashed. All of us were instructed the next day to blow the whistle on any staff pilots who carried out unauthorized low flying in future. We all liked the excitement of low flying, so we were most unlikely to comply, although the twenty-five deaths did certainly shake our confidence in the competence of our staff pilots.

The next shock was to find that we were to waste time in the "pool squadron" doing nothing for a couple of weeks, instead of immediately continuing our training. Well, not exactly doing nothing — we had to endure a few pep talks. "You will have no problem in finding plenty of cunt in town," we were informed by the Squadron Commander. "The place is seething with it, but don't you come back with a dose of VD and tell me that you caught it from pissing up a cartwheel! You are all to pass through the ET room each time you return to camp." The ET (early treatment) room, we found out, was a room attached to the guard room, and it was impossible to gain re-entry to the camp without being bullied by the RAF police into passing through it. "But we have only been to the cinema — we haven't touched a girl," some of the lads would protest on returning from town. "You get into the ET room, quick sharp, or I'll have you on a charge!" was always the reply. The lads would then enter the ET room and merely stand for a few minutes, reading the notices and the instructions on the use of the various anti-venereal-disease ointments. The authorities apparently assumed that we would not be able to understand the proper words, so the instructions in all ET rooms were in what they thought to be "soldiers' language". "Squirt the contents of the tube right up your pipe", we read. "Rub the ointment well in around the knob end and the balls. To help to prevent catching VD you should always have a piss as soon as you have finished with a woman." Strangely, the use of condoms was not mentioned.

While wasting time in the pool squadron we had to attend morning parades, after which we were free to do anything except what we really wanted to do, namely, fly. We would stand around the perimeter of the parade ground and wait for the command "On parade!" and then we would form up in ranks on the parade ground and wait for inspection. What was the point of it, we wondered. One morning our fat little Squadron Leader arrived in his baggy shorts, parked his bike in its customary position, up against the flagpole, and waited to do his inspection. On receiving the order "On parade!" we moved forward as usual, but we all made a loud moaning noise without moving our lips. What a din! Our fat little officer was red-faced and furious. He grabbed his bike and rode straight across the parade ground swishing his rolled-up newspaper at us and shouting, "Get back, get back!" It was like a cavalry charge. What fun! His reaction was so amusing, we decided to repeat the performance on the following day. Sensibly, he completely ignored our noise the next time, so the fun was over and we gave up our silly game.

When our course started, we were up in the air nearly every day and night. The aircraft were the familiar Oxfords and Ansons, and I was itching to get my hands on the controls again. We found that our doubts about the competence of the staff pilots were, in some cases, well founded. Old Benjie, a South African, repeatedly used a flashlight at night to read the instruments, blinding both of us. It was the task of the air bomber to sit in the second pilot's seat and wind the undercarriage of the Anson up and down with a cranking handle. One day after we had returned from an exercise in daylight over the sea, Benjie commenced his descent and instructed me, "Lower the undercarriage!" I did as I was told, while keeping a watchful eye on him. After a while, I realized that we were not approaching the aerodrome — it was the waterworks! I waited a few seconds, and then shouted above the roar of the engines, "It's not the 'drome, sir!" Benjie's startled reaction was to bellow, "Of course it's not, you bloody fool — wind up the undercarriage!"

A few days later, I was flying with Benjie again, this time in an Airspeed Oxford, with two pupil navigators. The Oxford's undercarriage was raised and lowered automatically, by the pilot. I knew that the pupil navigators were new boys. They had done very little flying, and I noticed that they had been made a little nervous by Benjie's erratic flying. As we came in to land, I braced myself and jokingly shouted to them, "He's forgotten to put the wheels down!" The colour drained from their faces. After we had made a normal landing — one of Benjie's better efforts, as it happened — I tried not to laugh as I said, "Well, you know, I really could have sworn he hadn't got the wheels down."

Night-flying with Benjie was always a little fraught. He would repeatedly taxi from one end of the airfield to the other, trying to figure out which was the correct end for take-off. One night I realized at the last minute that I had left my parachute behind in the flight hut. There was no way I was going to fly with Benjie without a parachute. "Hang on a minute, sir," I shouted, as I wrenched the door open and jumped to the ground. I then ran about half a mile to collect the parachute. I was exhausted by the time I got back to the plane. I never forgot my parachute again. Another of Benjie's quirks was to keep switching his landing-lights on and off during night flights. I never found out why.

One day I was due to carry out a daylight navigation and bombing flight with another pupil air bomber and two pupil navigators, when the staff pilot (not Benjie this time) asked, "Have any of you chaps flown twins?" I told him that I had flown Oxfords and Ansons. He said that he was feeling ill, and if I would take the controls he would go up to the back of the plane and "get his head down" on the dinghy. While he slept, I flew the plane for two and a half hours. I was back in my element! All went well until one of the sprog navigators became hopelessly lost over the sea, so I turned back to the coast, and after recognizing the church spire at Grahamstown I flew low along the seashore, looking at the bathers, until Port Elizabeth came into view. As I turned inland, the sprog navigator was still sweating over his calculations. I passed him a note: "The airfield is on the port bow." His scribbled reply came back, "Not according to my calculations." We then flew right across the aerodrome and headed out over the bundu. After ten minutes of waiting in vain for a course to steer, I decided to turn back to the aerodrome. By this time Archie, my fellow air bomber had become thoroughly miserable about the likelihood of his planned rendezvous in town being ruined by our delayed return, and he hastily aroused the staff pilot, who took over control just as I was joining the landing circuit. Our worried sprog navigator accompanied us to the plotting office, where, to my disgust, he reported that his log was in a mess "because the air bomber was piloting the aircraft and he didn't fly his 'three drift winds' accurately enough". The rest of us thought that "lying bastard" was the appropriate response.

We had approximately equal numbers of South African cadets training with us. They were issued with smooth barathea uniforms, the same as their officers, but while under training they had a light blue band around their peaked caps. At the completion of training they were immediately promoted to commissioned rank, which meant that they merely had to remove the blue hat bands and put up a couple of "pips", whereas most of us Royal Air Force cadets became mere sergeants, although we might well have achieved better examination results than the South Africans.

The Afrikaans language was given complete equality with English, and the words of command on morning parades were given on alternate days in English and Afrikaans. Although no Afrikaans language lessons were given to us, except by some of our girl-friends, we had no difficulty in understanding the words of command, but we secretly objected on principle to being addressed in a foreign language, so we pretended not to understand. As each command was given, we turned to each other and asked in mock bewilderment, "What on earth does that mean?" Despite the resulting delays and confusion, the use of Afrikaans continued on alternate days, and I doubt if the South Africans realized that we were being deliberately obstructive. They must have concluded that we had no talent for understanding foreign languages.

One of the South African cadets, Skaap, was considerably wealthier than the rest. His father, in the diamond business at Kimberley, had provided him with a car, which he had brought with him to the air school as freight on the train. Pompey and I often tried to hitch a lift into town with him, but Skaap was not always willing to turn out with the car, as its use restricted his drinking. The car was called "Sweet Pea", and Skaap usually told us that he would have to consult "Sweet Pea" before making a decision about a trip into town. Skaap often consulted "Joseph", too. "Joseph" was the name of Skaap's penis. When Joseph was not in the mood, Skaap stayed in the air school to study his books and we had to find other means of transport into town. We noticed that Skaap always went into town on Friday nights, but then he never took us with him and he didn't want us to know where he went. Every Friday we pestered him, trying to find out his secret rendezvous. Finally, we wore him down and he agreed to let us accompany him. To our surprise, in view of Skaap's wealthy family, we found that he was attending the Friday-night dance of the local Communist Party branch, where he was very well known. We were warmly welcomed by the men at the dance, who were mostly skilled tradesmen, not the kind of rich South African civilians that we usually met. We were told that black people were not able to become skilled workers, apparently to protect the interests of the whites. We were not able to understand how Communist principles could be reconciled with the apartheid system of discrimination, but thought it safer to concentrate on dancing with the daughters of the Communists, rather than to risk getting involved in more serious, and perhaps dangerous matters.

We were constantly troubled by the callous attitude to the black people of otherwise very nice, kind, generous, white people. The blacks were commonly referred to as Africans, or Kaffirs, and we were often criticized for being considerate to them. Cigarettes were normally sold in packets of fifty, and we used to buy a packet every day. We didn't smoke most of them, and by the end of the day those that were left were extremely dry, so we gave them to the black men of the Cape Corps. Our friend Skaap told me, "You shouldn't spoil those Kaffirs. You are making a problem for us. We have to live with them after you have gone back to England." Another thing that upset our South African friends was that we each paid threepence per week to a member of the Cape Corps for keeping our barrack hut clean and doing our laundry. "They are like dogs and they need to be treated like dogs," we were told.

The black men of the Cape Corps were dressed like soldiers, but they were non-combatants. They were used as drivers, lavatory cleaners and such. They also did duty as sentries, but they had no rifles, only native assegais. They loved to march and do arms drill with their spears. Their natural sense of rhythm and their enthusiasm meant that they were very good at it. When I saw them being drilled by a white sergeant on the parade ground after normal working hours one hot summer evening, I enquired if they were being punished for some misdemeanour. "Not at all," I was told, "they have asked to be drilled as a privilege, and so the sergeant has had to give up an hour of his free time."

In those days, black people were very seldom seen in England, and most of us had never previously had the opportunity of speaking to one. They were quite a novelty to us, and we were curious about them, particularly as we understood that men of the Cape Corps were recruited straight from the tribes. We gained the confidence of our hut cleaner/laundry boy, and he explained that he had joined the Cape Corps in order to save up enough money to buy a wife. He already had a woman in mind, back in the tribe. He would have to buy her from her father and pay, not in money, but in cows. The prices of wives varied, we were told, according to their childbearing potential, and that was assessed according to the size of the breasts. The marriage was not finalized until the first child was born. His woman had good big breasts, so he would have to work for at least two years to save the required money. Being partial to big breasts ourselves, we certainly did not begrudge him our contribution of threepence per week, and we learned more from him about South Africa than we did from the whites.

The Air Force authorities occasionally arranged lectures on hot afternoons about South Africa's social and economic problems, and we had great difficulty in keeping awake. One day, the topic was "soil erosion",

51

and when the South African captain giving the lecture was finished, he asked for questions. None of us could think of anything that we wanted to know about soil erosion, but some bright spark asked him if he was willing to answer a more general question. "Yes, provided that it concerns South Africa," he answered. "Well," said the questioner, "we have all been wondering why the South African girls are so much more sexy than our English girls." Suddenly, everybody in the lecture room was alert and waiting for the captain's reaction. The subject of soil erosion was forgotten. "You chaps have the better of me, because I have never been out of the Union (South Africa) and I can't make the comparison," the captain smilingly replied, "but I do understand from what many of my English colleagues have told me that they have discovered our girls to be very sexy indeed. Perhaps it has something to do with the sunshine and hot weather, or maybe it's due to the amount of fruit in the diet." There followed a general discussion on South African women and their sexual prowess. The final comment was, "Whatever the reason — it's good, isn't it!"

One of our number did not agree, however. The randy Pompey had finally met his Waterloo, as far as girls were concerned. He now spent nearly every evening poring over his navigation books, preparing for the final exams and afraid to go into town. Woman trouble! When he first met his tall, blonde, athletic Sheila, he was enraptured, but his enthusiasm soon faded. Pompey was at first the envy of all as we ogled at Sheila on the beach in her tiny bikini. She seemed to be the perfect female specimen — beautiful face, gorgeous figure. It was customary for all new liaisons to be the subject of close interrogation by the rest of us. "What's she like? Did you get anything? You want to get in there, you jammy bastard! Get in, knob, I'm right behind you!" The questions and crude comments would come thick and fast, but the answers would not always be believed. To goad the victim into revealing all the intimate details, the interrogators would often feign disbelief: "Oh, cut out the crap! I bet she didn't let you have anything, you bullshitter! Anyway, you wouldn't know what to do with it!"

In Pompey's case, no interrogation was necessary, and his reluctance to continue seeing Sheila was plain for all to see. He told us, "She got married eighteen months ago, and during the honeymoon her husband volunteered to join the Army. Immediately he was in, he volunteered to serve in North Africa, and within a few weeks he was with the troops in the desert campaign up north." "Why did he do that?" we wanted to know. "She said that she used to wake him up several times every night, and it was too much for him," Pompey explained. "But don't tell us that she was too much for you, you randy bastard," someone commented, "you always said your ideal woman would be a nymphomaniac whose father owned a brewery." Before long we all realized that Pompey was not kidding — he was certainly frightened of any further contact with Sheila. Each time he had stayed at her flat, she had kept him awake the whole night. Once he had two consecutive nights without sleep, and when he returned to the air school he was so exhausted that he was unfit for flying and had to report sick. He did not disclose the true reason for his exhaustion to the Medical Officer, otherwise he might have been charged with the punishable offence of "self-inflicted injury".

I liked Pompey's company, and when I managed to persuade him to come into town with me one evening, he made me promise that we would go straight off the bus into the Café Bioscope — no women! When the bus stopped at the town depot, we scrambled off and ran down the street and into the cinema. We had no sooner settled down in our seats, than our two girl-friends came down the aisle, searching for us. They must have been waiting at the depot to see if we got off the bus. Pompey wriggled down in his cinema seat, but to no avail. In order that food and drinks could be served in the Café Bioscope, the lighting was not as dim as in ordinary cinemas, and after scouring the rows of seats for a couple of minutes Sheila spotted him. The girls sat down next to us and there was much intense whispering between Sheila and Pompey. During the interval, Pompey gave me the secret word "Dinghy!" (part of the Royal Air Force's patter for preparing to land an aircraft on water: "Dinghy, dinghy, prepare for ditching!"). We had adopted the word "dinghy" as part of our secret language, for use in the following circumstances. If we were with a couple of new girls, in a pub, for example, we would rapidly assess our chances. If we thought that we were wasting our time with them, one of us would say the word "dinghy". We would both excuse ourselves, go to the toilet and then escape out and away through a door from another room. We used to joke that there were dozens of girls sitting in English pubs, waiting for us to come back from the toilet. I followed Pompey into the toilet of the Café Bioscope. Surely, we were not going to leave in the middle of the programme, long before the bus was due to leave for the air school! No, Pompey merely wanted to explain his plan, so that I would back him up. He had told Sheila that the reason he had not been able to meet her lately was because he had been confined to camp, and tonight we had to return to the air school immediately after the film programme and report for night-flying duty. After that episode, Pompey never dared to go into town again, and within a couple of weeks he completed his navigator's course and was posted away. I don't know if he survived the war.

I continued as a pupil air bomber. Life consisted mainly of lectures and bombing and gunnery practice. A couple of times a week, in my free time, I hired a horse and went riding across the veldt for a couple of hours. I persuaded a couple of the lads to share my interest in riding, after promising them that I would teach them to ride. As I thought that men who could fly aeroplanes should have no difficulty in riding horses, they did not actually get much tuition from me, but surprisingly nobody met with disaster. As the veldt was full of dangerous holes, we preferred to use the cinder track of the railway for fast galloping. Clouds of black cinders and dust would fly up from the horses' hooves, so it was best to be on the one in front. For a bit of excitement, we often galloped through the native locations. The inhabitants always ran out of their shacks, made out of cardboard, corrugated iron and old bedsteads, to wave and cheer as we galloped past, pursued by scores of dogs. Although we would have liked to learn more about life in the shanty towns, we never paused there, because the stink and the flies were so dreadful.

We were allowed to have one complete day and night free each week, and the usual programme was horse riding in the morning, swimming in the afternoon and boozing in the evening. Sub-tropical paradise! The open-air swimming-pool, surrounded by palm trees in a beautiful public park, was an ideal place for picking up girls. During the very hot weather, we had to get out of the water to cool off from time to time, and that was when we selected our female companions for the evening from among the multitude of beauties beside the pool. What a life! As far as we were concerned, it could have gone on for ever. The authorities arranged (quite unnecessarily, we thought) to transport us once a week during working hours to the swimming-pool in a three-ton truck. We were accompanied by a gorgeous young South African Air Force corporal who was to teach us to swim. Most of us did not need lessons, but the crafty ones among us pretended to be non-swimmers, and floundered about with her in the shallow end, grabbing her by the waist in mock panic. "Just watch the movement of my legs," she would say, as she demonstrated the way to swim. We did not need any encouragement to ogle at her legs and her other interesting bits. Even when fully dressed she was highly attractive in her tight tropical-weight uniform shirt and skirt. On the way to and from the air school, in the truck, which had standing-room only, we deliberately pressed up against her as though there was not enough room. She never objected. We were fortunate in having the glamorous corporal as our swimming instructor. Her colleague was a rather more mature woman, a jolly plump sergeant. "Ting-a-ling," the lads would shout and wave to her whenever she appeared, and she always smiled and waved back to them. "Why do you call her Ting-a-ling?" I asked. "She's the air school bike — everybody rides her," I was informed. The gorgeous corporal, on the other hand, had no such reputation.

One of the "facts" that we were taught was that the black mamba, a deadly snake, can move as quickly as a galloping horse. This bit of information always came to mind when we were lying in the grass with girl-friends, who would often teasingly announce, "There are snakes in the grass here." On such occasions, a quick decision had to be made, either to show cowardice (or common sense) and leave the scene, or bravely trust that the girl was merely testing our courage and remain with her in the grass. Strong sexual urges usually dictated that we remained. We never heard of anyone being bitten by a snake, but I have no doubt that if anyone had been bitten, frolicking in the grass would have quickly become a thing of the past.

Some of the lads concentrated much of their free time on making contacts with daughters of rich parents. Many eligible young South African men were away in the Army "up north". (It was said that South Africa had the world's largest volunteer army.) When the daughters reached marriageable age, the parents often turned their attentions to us. Some of us, crafty single lads, pretended to be already married when the girls started looking into furniture stores or staring at engagement rings in jewellers' shop windows. If the girls still associated with us "married men", we were usually onto a good thing. One evening I saw two lads sitting on their beds in the barrack hut, and I noticed that one was listening intently as his friend gave him instructions on how to pass himself off as a Jew. I understood that one of them really was Jewish. It appeared that he had met a wealthy Jewish family with two unattached daughters. The family had asked him to bring along a friend and accompany them to the synagogue.

We very soon learned to avoid married women. One night, Lofty was lying in bed with his woman in a fourth-floor apartment when all hell broke loose. Her soldier husband had arrived with an Army mate. Fortunately, the door of the flat was securely bolted on the inside. Lofty sprang out of bed. "You told me your husband was in North Africa!" he said as he hastily pulled on his trousers and shoes, throwing the rest of his clothes down off the balcony. "I know I did, but he was only at the barracks in Pretoria," she replied. At breakneck speed, Lofty scrambled over four balconies and down onto the ground. Before he had covered a hundred yards, the irate husband and his friend were in pursuit, and they chased him all the way back to the air school. Lofty described himself as "totally knackered" as he staggered into our hut. Needless to say, he did not dare to go into town for some weeks.

Although South Africa was a land of plenty, with the most wonderful food on sale in restaurants, the rubbish offered to us in the pupils' mess at the air school was hardly fit to eat. Meat that could have been part of an old elephant, and vegetables boiled into a tasteless mass, were the usual midday fare. After a few weeks, most of us only visited the dining hall for breakfast, when the best thing available was a kind of maize pudding called "mealies", which the South African cadets scorned as "Kaffir scoff". Bread and jam was appreciated by us, as jam was available ad lib, unlike in England, where we had been strictly rationed to one slice of dry bread with jam and one slice of bread and margarine with our meals. Every mealtime an officer accompanied by a sergeant entered the dining room and the following ritual was performed. The sergeant shouted, "Orderly Officer — any complaints?" We had to stop eating and "sit to attention" while the officer looked around the room. If any of us wished to complain about the food, he had to stand up. The officer and sergeant would then act as though they had not seen him and casually go to look at the food on the serving-counter. If the man was still standing up after about five minutes of being totally ignored, the sergeant pretended to have just noticed him. "What's the trouble, lad?" he growled. "The peas are hard and I can't eat them, sergeant," was a typical complaint.

"Then come with me, lad, and bring your dinner with you." And the lad followed the sergeant to the food counter. "Corporal! Give this man another dinner," the cook would be instructed, "without peas!" It was not long before we realized that to complain was futile, and we simply left the worst portions uneaten.

One day a new boy — just arrived at the air school — stood up to complain. We were alarmed to hear him tell the sergeant, "There's a worm in my soup!" as he dangled the huge, wiggly creature on his fork. The cook was summoned to the table. He took the worm between his fingers and examined it closely, before exclaiming loudly, "That's not a worm, you silly sod, it is bacon rind. We always cook rind in the soup to give it a bit of flavour, but we usually chop it up small." Too late! We had heard so many horrifying tales about what went on in the kitchens. Our appetites had vanished and we were quite prepared to believe that it really was a cooked worm. One story put about by a lad who allegedly witnessed an incident while undergoing cookhouse (punishment) fatigues, was that the cooks had accidentally spilled the entire contents of a cauldron of stew onto the tiled kitchen floor. "No time to cook another lot," exclaimed the corporal in charge of the cookhouse, "shovel it up and heat it up again! It will have to do."

Not surprisingly, much of our meagre wages went on decent food during our trips into town. Little did we know it, but after our time in South Africa was finished things would get even worse, so far as food was concerned, and we would yearn to be back again in the land of plenty. Meanwhile, strong bonds of comrade-ship were being formed between the lads on the air bombers' course. As former pupil pilots, we had all flown various types of training aircraft in the past. Johnnie had been training on Miles Masters until he had the most horrific crash at night, from which he was very lucky to escape with his life. In fact, the crash was so alarming that a photograph of it was displayed, as a warning to others, in the pupils' dining hall. Following an interview with the Chief Flying Instructor, Johnnie was sent before an aircrew assessment board at Pretoria. To ensure impartiality, the members of the board were not allowed to know anything of his past flying history. After examinations by psychoanalysts, the report on Johnnie contained the comment, "This man is the typical fighter pilot type." Within a short time of resuming pilot training, Johnnie was returning from a night-flying exercise when he crashed again and a second aircraft was written off. By now, he had decided that he did not want to continue training as a pilot. Once more, he appeared before the board in Pretoria, and this time the psychiatrists' report contained the astonishing comment, "This man will make a good fighter pilot." After reading the report, the Chief Flying Instructor declared, "I don't care what they say; I don't want you back here!" Johnnie appeared before the assessment board again, but this time he was accompanied by a note advising them that he should be assessed as suitable for something other than a pilot. In view of the psychoanalysts' previous decisions, they didn't know what to do with him, so they asked him for his own views, and he told them that he would be prepared to accept reassessment for training as an air bomber.

Confidential information of this nature was contained in personal records, which were handed to us in sealed envelopes at the completion of our training. Naturally, we carefully unstuck the envelopes and read everyone's documents. Some of the entries in the documents were laughable, and our general opinion was that the field of psychoanalysis, as applied to aircrews, was a load of nonsense. We would meet many psychoanalysts before we were finished, and we would not change our opinion that they were all "bloody crazy". Post-war perusal of official (School of Aviation Medicine) records proved that they thought the same about us.

Bomb-aiming practice was good fun, although it was quite difficult at first to get the front sight and the back sight of the primitive Mk 9 bombsight lined up with the target when directing the pilot through a sort of rubber hosepipe called a Gosport tube. If we did not achieve a sufficient number of "groups" of all individually dropped bombs within a certain radius, we were grounded for more practice in the AMBT — a tower in which a moving picture of the ground travelled beneath us. While one of us aimed imaginary bombs, the other pupil operated the controls of the "aeroplane" in accordance with the pupil bomb aimer's instructions. As we were not in a real aeroplane, it was the projection of the ground that moved to the left and right, and when the imaginary bomb was dropped the moving picture stopped and indicated whether the bomb would have hit or missed the target. All good fun, but nobody wanted the indignity of being grounded and condemned to return to the AMBT instead of being up in the sky, so there was great rivalry to achieve accurate "groups".

When the old Mk 9 bombsight was used, bombing accuracy depended not only on the bomb aimer's skill, but also on the pilot's good co-operation and accurate flying. We soon discovered that not every staff pilot was up to the desired standard. Some of them had been flying for years, but were unable to make accurate corrections to the right, and although none of us wanted to fly with such "ropy" pilots, we had no choice. One of my favourites was a pilot called Fletch. He was upset if pupils flying with him got bad bombing results, and his tantrums in the air were alarming for new boys who did not expect them. In the Airspeed Oxford, the pupil bomb aimer would lie down on the floor of the aircraft with his legs beside the pilot. If an inexperienced pupil kept over-correcting and causing the pilot to zigzag on the bombing run, Fletch stamped on the offending lad's legs and shouted, "Left — right — left — right — left — right — you're driving me fuckin' mad up here!"

As two bomb aimers flew in each aircraft, I often witnessed such a scene. One day, we were running up towards the target when Fletch suddenly became so enraged that he took his feet off the rudder pedals, turned sideways in his seat and stamped with both feet on the unlucky pupil. He then caused the aircraft to behave like a bucking bronco. I could not understand what could have caused such rage, so after another couple of stampings and more of Fletch's violent manoeuvres of the aircraft, I got down on the floor and crawled forward into the nose to find out what the pupil was doing. We were now approaching the target again and the pupil was giving corrections that Fletch could not hear because the speaking tube had become disconnected. The pupil was distressed and tearful because Fletch was apparently ignoring his instructions and Fletch was enraged because he was not getting any instructions. When we landed and got out of the plane, I was expecting ructions, particularly as the pupil was a fairly hefty lad, but Fletch immediately defused the situation by taking out his cigarettes and offering them round as though nothing untoward had occurred. I was glad that I never got stamped on myself.

Although we were grounded once due to high winds, the weather was perfect most of the time. Only on one occasion did we have unexpected cloud, and then several things went wrong. One of the pupils bombed the waterworks, which looked deceptively like the inland practice-bombing target in the dark. He was taken by car to apologize to the people at the waterworks the following day. I was supposed to be bombing the other target, which was in the sea, and although it was lit up with a triangle of lights, I could not find it, and it seemed as though the exercise would have to be aborted, until the dense clouds suddenly parted and I saw a triangle of lights. I dropped one bomb and shortly afterwards the lights went out. I had bombed the bombing-range signal, the triangular tip of an arrow on land that pointed to the target, situated about a mile away. The bombing-range staff switched out the lights and jumped into a slit trench that had been provided for such an occasion. A message from the bombing range was ready for me when we landed, and I was ready with my explanation that through a small gap in the clouds the tip of the signals was identical to the target. Fortunately, nobody was killed on that occasion. But a few days later one of the pupil navigators walked into an aircraft's propeller, and that was the end of him. He was the twenty-sixth casualty in a couple of months, and we had not seen the enemy yet!

Most of us were very wary of propellers. They were invisible when they were rotating, and I always gave them a wide berth. At pilots' training school, every pupil was occasionally required to start the Tiger Moth's engine by swinging the propeller. In the bad weather I was always afraid of losing my footing, sliding forward in the mud and getting my head chopped off. Prop swinging was certainly one of the most frightening things that I encountered during my flying training.

As the time for our final exams approached, our social lives were suspended. Every evening we sat around in groups in the barrack hut, asking each other questions that we thought likely to crop up at the exams. We carried our notebooks with us at all times and revised whenever we could — even sitting on the lavatory or when waiting for aircraft to take off. When the exams started, we all wore khaki shorts instead of long trousers, so that we could copy our cribs onto our thighs and take a quick glance when the invigilator was not looking. Out of the twenty-five of us, only "Benny the Dip" failed the exams, and we concluded that he must have been too honest to use a crib. Most of us had no compunction about cheating, as we regarded much of the theory that we were supposed to learn as totally unnecessary. For example, we could not see that it mattered to us what the explosive in the bombs was called, so long as we were competent to drop them in the right place. Nor did we think it was important to know by heart the names of all the ships in the Japanese Navy.

On a scorching hot day, we were lined up on the parade ground in thick blue uniforms, and for some inexplicable reason we had to carry rifles. While we waited in the sizzling heat for the South African "Fortress Commander" who was to conduct the passing-out parade, several lads fainted and their rifles went clattering to the ground. Eventually the Fortress Commander arrived and slowly passed along the ranks, attaching our flying badges to our thick tunics with the aid of a tin of pins. The process took about an hour and was accompanied by the clatter of more falling rifles. "Congratulations," said the elderly Fortress Commander to each of us in turn, "I suppose you will be glad to be getting into combat at last." "Yes, sir," we replied, "thank you, sir." Our thoughts were on the lines of, "For God's sake get on with it, you old duffer, we can't stand here much longer in these thick uniforms!" That afternoon we spent our time in the bars in town, celebrating. One of the lads was called Govett, and we named a cocktail of our own invention after him. We then marched into bars and asked the barmen for a round of Govett cocktails, knowing full well that they would not know what we meant. Invariably, the barmen disappeared to consult their colleagues before shamefacedly asking, "Excuse me, gentlemen, would you care to refresh my memory regarding the ingredients of the Govett cocktail — brandy based, is it?" Soon all the barmen in town had been taught the secret of mixing Govett cocktails, and most of us had suffered the dire effects of drinking too many of them.

It was now time to take leave of our local girl-friends and for some of us to embark on a four-day train journey via a transit camp in Durban to an aerodrome between Pretoria and Johannesburg. The remainder were told that they would be returning to England, but some who did not wish to go back to England sold their postings for five pounds to others who were desperate to return home. As we clambered aboard a truck and left the air school, there was much jeering at us by the lads who expected to be soon on "the boat going home". "Never mind, lads, when we get back to Blighty we'll write to the Prime Minister and make sure that you get wide legs on the trousers of your demob' suits," they laughed. There were those among us who did not believe in interfering with fate by buying a posting. "If you get your leg shot off you will spend the rest of your life looking at the stump and knowing you bought that for five pounds," we said. Although we had all volunteered to fly in the Air Force, very few of us would ever volunteer for anything again, because that would be tempting fate, and fate should be allowed to take its own course. We would soon find that we, like sailors and other people who depended on uncontrollable elements such as the weather, would develop a multitude of superstitions as we got nearer to real danger.

Our stay in Clairwood Transit Camp, Durban, was fortunately only for a few days. The camp itself would not have been too unpleasant if the beds had not been infested with fleas that seemed to have developed immunity to flea powder. Within a couple of days our chums who had expected to be on the boat back to "Blighty" arrived and joined us. The return to England was cancelled. They all looked very crestfallen, and it was our turn to jeer: "What about the wide legs on our trousers?" They had no sooner arrived than they were instructed to go to the sick bay for injections. "Hang on," protested "young Blondie" (so called because he was fair haired and only eighteen), "we've had nothing to eat for twenty-four hours. They disconnected the train's restaurant-car yesterday. Can't we get something to eat first?" "No. This is an emergency," he was told, "you must be inoculated immediately." We continued to snigger at the discomfort of the new arrivals as they reluctantly slouched off into the sick bay for injections against yellow fever and black-water fever and other nasty things. Fortunately, we who had not expected to return to England had already had our jabs before leaving the air school, so it was a case of "Fuck you, Jack, I'm all right" — the customary remark to those less fortunate. The name black-water fever intrigued us. Was the injection to protect us from the effects of drinking black water or was it to stop us from passing black water? We never found out. The only remarkable things at this transit camp, apart from the fleas, were the lavatories. Rows of about six men sat in line over porcelain troughs of running water, and a common trick was for a ball of newspaper to be lighted and dropped in the water so that it singed each man's bottom as it sailed beneath him.

After Clairwood Camp, our next stop was at an airfield on the main road between Johannesburg and Pretoria, from where we expected to fly off to Egypt. We were told that we should remain permanently on twenty-four hours "standby", and we were at liberty to go sightseeing in Johannesburg if we wished, as there was nothing else for us to do. Pretoria was nearer, but we were advised by the military police to stay away from there, unless we went in a large group, because airmen had recently been beaten up with bicycle-chain whips by gangs of anti-British (white) Afrikaaners.

We found that the only way to get to Johannesburg was to wait by the side of the road opposite the gates of the aerodrome for a lift. It was never more than ten minutes before a car came into view and stopped to pick us up. Never did a driver ignore us, but one day as I waited alone for a lift, a huge American-made car drove about a hundred yards past me before stopping. As I trotted up to the car, women in Indian dress moved from the front to the back seat. As I opened the front door, I said to the driver that I had thought that he was not going to stop. He then told me that he did not want to stop near me, because he was afraid that I might refuse to travel with him when I saw that he was an Indian. "But I'm English," I said. "Exactly," he replied. "We know that no white South African would accept a lift from us, but it would have been very hurtful if an Englishman refused to ride in our car." He told me that he was a businessman and graduate of Calcutta University. Like many other wealthy Indians, he had been encouraged to immigrate to South Africa, only to find on arrival that he was subjected to the strict colour bar and that the only form of commerce open to him was the soft-fruit trade. He explained, "We face the same discrimination as the black Africans. We are all treated the same. We are only allowed in one cinema in Johannesburg, but we don't go there. I couldn't have my wife sitting next to a primitive black man." From what he told me during the journey, I felt that an even greater gulf existed between the Indians and the black Africans than between the whites and the non-whites. I was grateful for the ride in his car, but I was left with the uneasy feeling that the country was heading for a bloody civil war in which the two-and-a-quarter million whites would be slaughtered by the ten million people that they were oppressing. I decided that I would definitely not accept the many invitations that I had received to go back and settle there after the war.

Although we were supposed to return to the aerodrome each evening to check if our departure was scheduled for the next day, the girls of Johannesburg proved too enticing, and we often risked staying the night with them. On our return to the aerodrome, we compared experiences. "Wow! I saw what you had with you yesterday. She looked a bit of all right. Did you get anything?" were typical remarks. "Rotten sod if he did — silly bugger if he didn't." "Well, I was doing fine until I noticed the Sacred Heart of Jesus embroidered on her vest. That put me right off." Bragging, exaggerating, and lying. What did it matter? Just live for the moment! How many of us would still be alive at this time next year? Don't give it a thought!

My own Jo'burg connections were in the gold-mining business. The white family had several black servant-girls, and when I turned up at the house all sweaty I always went out to the back of the property and shouted for one of them who would wash, dry and iron my shirt during the time that it took me to have a shower. One scorching hot day the girls did not respond to my shout, so I went to the corrugated-iron shed that was their accommodation. I pushed open the door and saw an old iron double bed standing on an earth floor and two of the black girls asleep on it. There was no other furniture in the hut. Their primitive accommodation was probably worse than the mud huts in which they had lived back home in the tribe. After our dinner one evening, I saw them squatting on the ground eating theirs, which obviously included the scraps that we had left on our plates. I recognized a piece of gristly meat that I had chewed a while and then rejected. Although I was shocked at the time, this was not, by any means, the most unappetizing food that I would see being eaten a few months later.

CHAPTER
THREE

Egypt and the Middle East

After three or four weeks of enjoying the delights of Johannesburg, we left South Africa in a DC3 Dakota. While waiting for the order to embark, I saw my old friend Maurice, the "Halifax Cockney", who had been so satisfied to have been selected to train as an air bomber last time we met, but now he was sporting a pilot's brevet. "How did you get that?" I wanted to know, as I pointed to his brand-new wings. "Well, you know how they fart around. Before I got started on my air bombers' course, they said that they had run short of pupil pilots and they stuck me back on a pilots' course. I have just finished training on Harvards, so I guess I will be going on to Spits or Mustangs," he replied. "But what are you doing as an air bomber?" he asked. "I thought you were on the navigation course." "Maurice, old son, it's all your fault," I told him. "Come on, let's get aboard and see if we can get seats together, and I'll tell you all about it."

I was glad to meet up with Maurice again. We had been good pals at pilots' flying school. We used to travel

into Coventry together on one bicycle to attend the
GEC dances. Maurice would do the pedalling and I
would sit behind him on the carrier. As there were no
footrests, my legs would be nearly dropping off by
the time we reached our destination. "Where did
you get the bike, Maurice?" I asked him. "I borrowed
it from the police sergeant," he answered. "Does he
know?" I asked. "What a daft question, of course
he doesn't bloody know," was Maurice's reply. Our first
few excursions into Coventry during the wartime
blackout on unlit roads were difficult due to the lack of
a lamp on the bike. There was hardly any traffic, but we
could scarcely see the edge of the road. The problem
was solved when somebody left a lamp on his bike
outside a country pub.

Our flight from South Africa to Cairo took three
days. We flew only during daylight — landing each day
for lunch and then again at teatime. As the entire flight
was below the clouds, we could watch herds of animals
stampeding and admire the interesting African
landscape all the way. We landed on isolated dirt strips
that were still being constructed by black men and
women, whose only equipment was shovels and wicker
baskets. We explored the neighbourhood at each place
where we stopped overnight. Near Kisumu on Lake
Victoria, we wandered into a hotel bar and smilingly
greeted the middle-aged colonial whites. They fiercely
scowled back at us in complete silence. From their
hostile looks, it was clear that we, "Ambassadors for the
United Kingdom", were certainly not wanted there. As
we got nothing more than a couple of ignorant grunts

out of the white barman, we soon gave up our attempts to converse with him and left. We now knew how black people must have felt in the face of similar hostility, but they were accustomed to it — we were not.

In Cairo, we were accommodated in the magnificent Heliopolis Palace Hotel. Unfortunately, it was completely unfurnished, and we had to sleep on the cold marble floors. We might have been more comfortable outside in the grounds on the bare earth. Our only bedding was two small blankets, so we slept on top of the few clothes that we had worn on the plane. All our kitbags had been left in South Africa to follow on by ship. I wrapped my shoes in a towel for use as a pillow. We knew that to complain would be quite futile. The response would have been the usual snarling rebuke, "Don't you realize there's a bloody war on?" Was our discomfort simply another unavoidable sacrifice on the difficult path to victory, or the result of some silly bastard's incompetence? We would have welcomed the chance to express our opinions to the locally based, but remote, chair-bound warriors at General Headquarters.

Cairo was a most fascinating place during wartime. We were the only tourists. When we arrived, the jacaranda trees were in blossom. The streets were filled with camel and donkey transport — scarcely any cars. The dozens of ragged shoeshine boys would start work on our shoes every time we stopped walking. If we refused another unnecessary shine, they spat on our shoes before running away. The cinemas were luxurious, but full of fleas. At the end of every programme, the Egyptian National Anthem was played and our troops sang their own words: "Up your pipe King Farouk, hang your bollocks on a hook . . ." The Egyptians smiled and nodded benignly at us, apparently not realizing that we were not singing a correct translation of their anthem.

Cairo nightlife was hectic and dangerous. The streets were full of touts for Egyptian-style cabarets with their floorshows or "exhibitions". On all sides the cry would be heard, "Exhibish, exhibish! See a lady fuck a donkey!" When accosted our response was, "Don't believe it! — Don't want to see it! — Too expensive!" We very soon learned enough "Soldiers' Arabic" to be able to say, "You are crazy!" — "Go away!" — "I have no money" — "Show us your fanny", and dozens of other useful phrases. Nearly every morning we set out for the pyramids, but were diverted by more modern attractions and usually ended up in the Waterloo Club, where long trousers were essential for any man who wished to prevent the dancing girls from feeling up the legs of his shorts.

One evening, some of the lads wandered into what they thought was a fairly cheap and cheerful cabaret show. The usual striptease and belly-dancing acts were nothing remarkable, and most members of the entirely male audience were more intent on guzzling the watery Egyptian beer, but then a fairly nude dancer appeared, smoking a cigar. After a few puffs she placed the cigar in her vagina, and as she vigorously gyrated around the dance-floor it seemed as though puffs of smoke were still appearing and that the cigar was being smoked in this unusual fashion. The word quickly went round,

"There's a woman smoking a cigar with her quim!" The men all craned their necks, left their beer on the tables and surged forward around the dance-floor to watch this unusual phenomenon. The dancer beckoned one of the young Air Force lads to join her. Not wanting to show his shyness in front of the others, he went and stood in the centre while she circled around him. Suddenly, to his consternation, and to the delight of the others, she unexpectedly whipped the cigar out of her vagina and thrust it towards his mouth. With a look of absolute horror on his young face, he turned and scampered back to his companions to the sound of loud whistling, laughter and applause from the delighted onlookers. Although the cigar had not actually touched him, he seemed compelled to rub his mouth repeatedly with the back of his hand.

As the alleyways of Cairo harboured a multitude of perils, such as pickpockets and muggers, we tried to keep to well-lit streets after dark and walk in the middle of the road in the hope that we would avoid being jumped on by people lurking in the shadows. As an added precaution, Johnnie and I pooled our financial resources and bought a leather-bound truncheon from a street trader. We never had occasion to defend ourselves with the "cosh", but it added to our confidence during our nightly adventures. The only way to carry the thing was in a trousers pocket, which made sitting down rather uncomfortable. Before setting out each evening, there was always an argument over whose turn it was to carry the cosh. Neither of us wanted it, so we sometimes invited our pal Ginger to join us, on condition that he carried it. Ginger, a fiery fellow of Irish extraction, maintained that the cosh was designed for coshing people, so we should take every opportunity to use it for that purpose, otherwise we had wasted our money on it. I was more inclined to make a run for it when trouble looked likely — which was quite often the case in the bars at closing time. The barkeepers would try to call the troops to order by getting the band to play our national anthem — "God save the King". As the last notes died away, someone was certain to shout, "Fuck him!", which was the signal for all hell to break loose. I would then get down on all fours and crawl to the exit, keeping close to the wall and hoping that nobody would fall on me.

Day and night, the streets were full of youths offering "filthy pictures", which were often merely well-handled postcard views of nude statues. As the vendors clamoured around us, we would tell them, "Not filthy enough!" Their vigorous tugging at our sleeves and prodding at us was often a method of disguising the crafty way that they were trying to rifle through our pockets. When we caught them at it and took a kick at them, they would cry, "Sorry, sir", as they took to their heels. We had been issued with revolvers, but I never heard of anyone taking one with him on a night out in Egypt.

One morning we were told to assemble at the railway station, where we discovered that our destination was the British mandated territory of Palestine. We travelled uncomfortably on slatted wooden seats in carriages crowded with people in Arab dress, tethered goats and crates of chickens. The journey took about twenty hours. We were not provided with any food or drinks, so we bought hard-boiled eggs and bread rolls from Arab pedlars on the stations. The bread stank strangely and we conjectured that it had been made with water out of the River Nile. During the night the ancient steam train made numerous stops in the desert for no apparent reason, and we all got off and wandered about for a while each time. We were happy to be on our way to somewhere new, and we assumed that when we left the train we might proceed to an operational training unit (OTU) for the final stage before joining an operational squadron and commencing combat-flying. Nobody complained about the discomfort, and there was a general air of excitement among us.

After crossing the frontier into Palestine, we all bought bags of cheap oranges — far more than we could eat. As we crossed the desert at a speed of around ten miles per hour, we saw another train slowly approaching from the opposite direction, and when it drew level we noticed that every carriage was filled with Australian soldiers. Both trains were completely open at the sides, and as we crawled past within about six feet of the other train, we quickly assembled all our spare oranges and pelted the Australians with them. With great glee, we saw their bush hats being knocked off and the looks of consternation on their faces. Due to the surprise of the attack, none of them had time to throw the oranges back at us. Luckily for us, as we were outnumbered, the trains kept moving. The Australian airmen among us enjoyed this typical example of inter-service warfare just as much as the rest of us. We would have played the same trick on any "brown jobs", as soldiers were called. They did not necessarily need to be Australians.

Upon arrival at our destination, Jerusalem, we learned to our dismay that we would not be doing any flying for quite a while, as we were to be held at a disposal centre once again. Why, we wondered, were we being shunted around? We might just as well have remained in the disposal centre in Cairo! We soon learned that Jerusalem was in the middle of a three-sided armed conflict between the British Palestine Police, Arab terrorists and Jewish terrorists, so we assumed that we were to act as a military force. We were billeted in hotels in the centre of the town. In answer to my question to men already in occupation — "What's it like here, lads?" — I was informed that an aircrew man had been shot dead by one of the Arab cleaners the previous day. The terrorists were regularly blowing up buildings, such as hotels and the radio station. "What are our duties?" I enquired. "There aren't any. There is sweet FA to do here all day." I was told, "If you are interested, you can go and look at the 'holy places'. They say there are two lots: one lot is run by the Arabs and the other lot by the Jews, so you can take your pick." At this moment, a lad entered the room. "We have just been telling him about the holy places. You've been, haven't you?" He proudly produced a matchstick-sized piece of wood from his pocket: "Yes, I was there yesterday and look what I bought — a piece of the original Cross." "The original

Cross, my arse! If you believe that you would believe anything," his companion scoffed. "They have been selling bits of wood like that for years. They must have got through a complete forest by now." "Isn't there anything else to do?" I wanted to know. "There are plenty of bars and cinemas, but as far as women are concerned, it's a dead loss. Worse than bloody Cairo! There's no social life here at all. And no decent bints [girls] will have anything to do with us. The Arabs and Jews are going at it hammer and tongs every day — blowing things up and shooting at the police, but they don't bother much with us. Oh, and incidentally, we aren't allowed to keep our revolvers. There's a notice on the board — new arrivals have to hand them in at the armoury, down in the cellar." I wandered down to the armoury and handed over my Smith & Wesson thirty-eight inscribed with the words "US Army Pattern 1918". I had never used it. We had fired pistols once during our infantry course and I had not succeeded in hitting a four-inch-wide target at fairly close range. In the armoury, I watched policemen mounting twin 0.303 Browning machine-guns onto a tripod, fixed to the back of a fifteen-hundredweight truck.

After dinner, I wandered through the town. The streets seemed quiet compared with Cairo. I wondered how to distinguish Jews from Arabs. I found out later that the bearded men in black frock-coats and black hats were Orthodox Jews. I had never heard of "Orthodox" Jews before. Nobody looked like a terrorist, and I wondered why they were fighting. Our authorities had not told us anything at all, and here we were, unexpectedly dumped in the middle of a bloody civil war, unarmed and in uniform. As I wandered along a quiet tree-lined avenue, I suddenly became aware that I was in the direct line of fire of a group of policemen who had their rifles aimed at a house that I was passing. "I bet you nearly shit a brick!" was the response of my friends when I told them of the incident. I felt angry. I was prepared to risk being shot by the enemy in combat, but not by the British Palestine Police. But we would all be involved in many other conflicts that we did not understand in due course.

We usually paid scant regard to the numerous instructions that appeared on the official notice-board in our billet, one of which stated that we were to wear khaki drill tropical kit instead of our thick blue uniforms. The clown who wrote this instruction was obviously straight out from chilly England. Although the days were fine, the temperature was much lower than the heat to which we had become accustomed during our time in Africa. We protested, but to no avail, so to withstand the cool climate we wore singlets and long-sleeved sweaters under our tropical shirts, and thick woollen shorts under our thin khaki slacks. Most of the day we spent lying on our beds, waiting for mealtimes. We spent our evenings in bars or cinemas. Where servicemen were stationed, the lavatories, or "bogs", as they were called, always had graffiti such as, "It's no use to stand upon the seat, the crabs in here can jump six feet!" (a reference to pubic lice). In

Jerusalem, every closet bore the scribbled inscription, "JC was here!"

Time passed dreadfully slowly, and after about six weeks we were glad to leave Jerusalem for a place called Lydda, that we understood to be somewhere near Tel Aviv. These places were totally unknown to us, and as usual we had no idea what to expect at our destination. To our delight, we found that Lydda was an aerodrome — a heavy conversion unit — so we would be up in the air again at last. Two things troubled us, however. The other aircrew personnel at Lydda were already formed into crews of five. They had previously been flying together in Vickers Wellingtons at an operational training unit. We were concerned that, as we had skipped OTU, a presumably important stage of our own advanced training had been missed. Also, as we were converting to American B24 Liberator aircraft, we feared that we might be destined for the remote Far East conflict to fight against the Japanese, who had dragged the USA into the war after we had enlisted. We thought that we ought to be countering the threat of a German occupation of Britain, and the war against Japan seemed to us like a purely American affair. As usual, we were told nothing. It transpired that a sixth man, a flight engineer, had recently joined the crews of five, and now they were to get us, air bombers. To our surprise, we were not allocated to a crew; we just had to wait to be invited to join one. A few days after our arrival, I was chatting to a young sergeant navigator in the dining room. After a short but thorough interrogation, he asked if I had already joined a crew, and told me, "We are all sergeants in our crew. We have a very good pilot. A really steady type. He does not smoke or drink. If you like, I will introduce you." I was attracted to the thought of a non-drinking pilot, and I willingly made the acquaintance of the 21-year-old Glaswegian called Andy, who would become a life-long friend. Andy welcomed me into his crew. Until that moment, he had been the youngest member. The oldest was twenty-two.

Life on the heavy conversion unit was hectic. Sometimes we were up in the air for seven or eight hours out of twenty-four. We did simulation bombing, which meant that a photograph was taken of a chosen target when I pressed the bomb-release "tit". We also did night-fighter affiliation over Cyprus, where Bristol Beaufighters made mock attacks, taking photographs of us instead of shooting at us. Searchlight co-operation with an anti-aircraft training unit at Haifa convinced me that we would not last long once we went into combat. Every time the searchlights picked us up, we found it was impossible to shake them off. Inexplicably, nobody told us that operational squadrons were able to use "window", foil strips, as an effective method of evading radar-controlled searchlights and anti-aircraft fire. We carried out navigation exercises over Egypt, Palestine and Syria. Sometimes the inexperienced (sprog) navigators would miss the blacked-out island of Cyprus in the dark and find themselves over the illuminated coastal towns of Turkey. They would fly up and down the coast trying to "get a pinpoint" (find out exactly where they were). Turkey was a neutral country, and the Turks would immediately switch off the towns' lights and then send protests through the British Embassy. We were told that in the event of an emergency landing in Turkey, we were to declare that we were "distressed mariners", and we would then be eligible for repatriation as non-combatants instead of being interned until the end of the war. "Our Ambassador says don't just turn up at the British Embassy unannounced. Phone first for an appointment!" we were told. We were also instructed to memorize the telephone number of the Embassy, and not to write it down. Nobody told us how we were to obtain the necessary Turkish coins for the telephone. We assumed that the Ambassador had a comfortable nine-to-five job and would be unlikely to be on duty when we needed him. Without money, we would not be able to enjoy a bit of "Turkish Delight" while we waited for the Embassy to open. We thought that the address of the Ambassador's personal residence might have been of more use to us in an emergency.

Nobody landed in Turkey during my time at Lydda, but one night an air gunner mysteriously disappeared from a plane over the sea about thirty miles off the coast of Cyprus. A few days after I joined Andy's crew, he crashed and wrote off a Liberator. I joked that we might have been better advised to join one of the "pissy-arsed" pilots who drank. Fortunately, nobody was hurt, but everybody was rather shaken. Andy was doing night-time circuits and bumps. He was using the throttles to turn on to the runway for his first take-off,

85

and before he had straightened up the flight engineer placed his hand behind Andy's and caused all four throttles to be opened together. It was customary for the flight engineer to follow up to make sure that none of the four throttle levers was missed on take-off, but this time he was too hasty, and because the plane was not straight on the runway one of the main wheels ran off the edge. Andy continued with the take-off, but the trouble was that one leg of the undercarriage was being sawn off by the edge of the concrete runway, which was a couple of feet higher than the surrounding land. He selected "undercarriage up", and only one wheel retracted. He then selected "down", and as the rest of the crew shone torches out of the windows to see what was happening, the retracted wheel came down again, but on the other side the whole leg of the undercarriage dropped off. He flew round the circuit and landed, trying to keep the aircraft tilted over onto the "good leg" as he touched down. The loss of the damaged leg and wheel meant that all hydraulic power was also lost, and of course there were no brakes. The plane raced past the control tower before the wing on the damaged side touched the runway, then it slewed around ninety degrees and travelled a couple of hundred yards across open ground before embedding its nose in the sand dunes.

The following morning the engines and instruments were salvaged and the fuselage remained stuck in the sand, where we could see it on each subsequent take-off and landing. Andy appeared less perturbed by the incident than the rest of us. Then a nasty endorsement was entered in his flying-logbook by the Commanding Officer, who considered that he had acted carelessly, whereas the rest of us thought that he had performed brilliantly, in view of his lack of experience of four-engined aircraft. We had not noticed the flight engineer's involvement in the mishap, and Andy did not mention it to the Commanding Officer or anyone else at the time.

Once a week, if we were not scheduled to fly, we travelled in an Air Force bus to Tel Aviv, where we strolled along the seafront, had something to eat and then perched on the railings of the promenade while we waited for the bus back to Lydda. We could not risk missing the bus because we knew that we would be on the rota to fly on the following day. The bus was invariably late in reaching the pickup point, and we always got there early, so we often had to wait about three-quarters of an hour. There were always half a dozen young women loitering on the promenade, ready to begin soliciting as soon as we turned up. Instead of telling them that we had to return to Lydda, we spent the time until the bus arrived in teasing them and pretending to haggle over the price. The girls were quite pretty and very persistent. We were surprised how flexible they were over the price, but of course, we could not go with them, and we were only amusing ourselves in what we later realized was a rather cruel manner. Although we did not know it at the time, many of the girls were illegal immigrants who had to support their parents and a host of other unemployed family members out of their immoral earnings. Some of us felt rather ashamed when we realized that our light-hearted banter must have unwittingly added to the humiliation caused by their unfortunate circumstances.

It was in Tel Aviv that Johnnie and I met our first Germans. Two men stopped us in the street and asked if we would soon be bombing Germany. When we said that we thought so, they said, "Give it to the Nazi bastards! We are refugees from Germany and we lost everything because of Hitler. Palestine is the only country that we could get into. We hate the Nazi swine." They had been in Palestine since before the war, and they told us that they owned a restaurant. We accepted their invitation to a free meal, and as we listened to their account of the way their relatives and other innocent (non-Jewish as well as Jewish) German people were suffering at the hands of the Nazis we gained a better understanding of the misery that was being caused by the war. Although we had read newspaper reports about the German concentration camps, we had previously assumed that such stories were mostly British government propaganda — exaggerated accounts intended to foster hatred of the Germans. We regarded all newspaper reports with scepticism, because so many of them were quite obviously untrue. Now we were hearing horrifying details of the Nazi death-camps from men who had been quite ordinary German citizens until Hitler and his villainous gang of Nazis came to power.

Most of us had never seen Germans before, and we knew very little about the political circumstances that had led up to the British involvement in the war. From tales in books about the "Great War" of 1914–18 that we had read during childhood, we had gained the impression that all Germans were evil people, so we blindly assumed that Britain's entry into the war must have been necessary and justified. A common wartime saying was, "The only good German is a dead one." We now learned from our hosts that not all the people in Germany were Nazis — supporters of the National Socialist German Workers' Party. Many Germans were indeed anti-Nazi Communists. Our principal incentive for joining the Air Force had been our obsession with flying, not a desire to kill anyone, but now we were becoming aware of the gravity of the task that lay before us. We would soon be killing people, and, contrary to the vague impression that we had previously carried around in our heads, they would not all be wicked Nazis.

Andy had tried to form an all-Scottish crew, but his navigator and air gunners had dropped out during operational training, and although he had managed to get a Glaswegian replacement as rear gunner, the new mid-upper gunner was an English lad, and so was the navigator. Then the flight engineer arrived. He was from the Shetlands and spoke with a strange accent. Some people asked if he was from Scandinavia.

Most of our training flights from Lydda were carried out at high altitude, and we were occasionally able to scrounge something from the mess waiters to take with us to eat during the trip. The waiters were very tall black Sudanese men, dressed in what looked like long white nightshirts, with red sashes round the waist. They never responded unless they were spoken to in Arabic. We quickly learned to communicate with them. On my first flight with the crew I had managed to get a piece of prune pie, and when I came to eat it I found that the prunes had frozen solid and the juice had turned into scrunchy granules of ice. On future trips, I kept my pie warm underneath the electrically heated muff of the automatic camera. When the cold caused the camera to stop working, a hefty kick got it going again.

On my first trip with them, I was alarmed to find that the broad accents of the Scottish members of the crew were unintelligible to me on the aircraft's "intercom" communication system. We Englishmen soon learned to decipher the guttural sounds of our Scotsmen, knowing that our survival would depend on understanding each other in an emergency. Half an hour after take-off, Andy set the aircraft to fly on "George", as the autopilot was called, and he wandered around chatting to the crew. I was enjoying the view from the beam hatches when he stopped for a word and took the opportunity of using the "pee tube", a funnel with a pipe leading out of the plane. As he looked over his shoulder and talked to me, neither of us noticed that the funnel was blocked up with cigarette ends and that my lunch, a sandwich in a paper bag, was being soaked with urine. I found a safer place, away from the "pee tube", to store my sandwiches after that. Instead of the dreadful old Mk 9 CSBS, I now had the splendid new Mk 14 Sperry gyroscopic bombsight, which I found perfectly simple to use after only a few minutes' practice. We did only twenty-eight hours' flying at Lydda, and our conversion course onto heavy bombers was over. We now expected that we would soon be attacking enemy targets with high-explosive bombs, but we did not know where.

Quite unexpectedly, we were transported back to Egypt by train. Once again, we were given no food for the journey across the desert to Cairo. The carriages of the steam train were as uncomfortable as before. At dusk, I climbed onto the slatted wooden luggage rack and fastened myself with my belt, so that I would not roll off during the night. We reached the Egyptian frontier at midnight. There seemed to be nothing except cigarettes on sale, and we had not eaten for twelve hours. I asked the Arab moneychangers if they had any food, and I thought I was lucky when they sold me a tin of peaches. I spent an hour opening it with a pocket-knife. With a pound of peaches slopping around inside my otherwise empty stomach, I wished I had been able to find something more solid. After dawn we stopped at a small station where we heard the welcome shouts of "Eks-a-bret, eks-a-bret" of the eggs-and-bread pedlars, as they offered their tiny hard-boiled eggs and smelly bread rolls to us through the windows of the train. We shared the crowded carriages with men and women in Arab dress. Presumably, no Egyptian able to afford a western-style suit would travel like us in third-class carriages. We got off the train to stretch our legs at every station. We watched manacled Arab prisoners in a chain gang shuffling bare-footed along the platform, deftly picking up every cigarette-end in sight with their toes. Their faces lit up with gratitude when we deliberately threw a few cigarettes onto the ground for them. It would not be the last time that we would feel a definite affinity with prisoners.

The train crawled across the desert, and as the sun rose we leaned out of the windows to get away from the stink of goats and chickens in the carriages. We gazed at the dry landscape. Arab life seemed very strange to us — full-grown men riding on the haunches of little donkeys while their women walked behind — blindfolded camels and donkeys condemned to a lifetime of trudging in circles at the end of long poles as a means of pumping water, each one urged on by a little child with a stick.

When the train reached Cairo, we were given railway warrants and leave passes. A few of us decided to spend nine days in Alexandria. One of our companions, Bob, had been there before. He had been an engine fitter on a Hawker Hurricane squadron at a time when the Air Force ran short of pupil pilots and put up notices asking for volunteers. Thinking that as a pilot he would have a chance of being posted back to England, Bob volunteered. Very soon, after he had remustered for pilot training, he was transferred onto an air gunners' course. Now he was giving us the "gen" about Alexandria. "What's it like and what is there to do there?" we asked. We learned that there were good beaches, good restaurants and plenty of nightlife — bars and cabarets — but the only women available to us would be those in the British government's brothels.

Official brothels! Surely not! He knew that none of us had been in contact with women since we left South Africa. Was he joking? Some of us appeared to be disgusted by the idea of anyone wanting to frequent a brothel, but we were all keen to hear what he had to say. "There are separate brothels for the Navy and for the Military and for different ranks," we heard. "They have a large number painted on the blast wall outside, so you know which is which. The girls are from all over the place — Syria — Lebanon — Cyprus. They are regularly inspected to make sure they are clean and you can't catch anything off them." "Have you been there yourself? What does it cost? What are the women like? Horrible old bags, I bet!" We crowded round him. "No, they are certainly not old bags. They are all young and some are quite nice. Some of the lads had their favourites and asked for the same one every time. They always got upset if the one they wanted was busy. It is best to get there early in the morning, before they get tired. Don't pick the best-looking ones, because they get the most use. Actually, it's best to choose a black one — they are more enthusiastic than the white ones." Most of us did not believe him. "Black girls provided by the British government! What a load of old bollocks! He's just taking the piss, because he knows we've been deprived since we left Jo'burg, the rotten sod." "Well, we will soon find out when we get to Alexandria, but if it is true, how many of us will have the nerve to go to a brothel?"

Bob had started a topic that would occupy our thoughts for the rest of the journey. "You know what

Bob's like — always shooting the line about his time in the desert. I wouldn't believe everything that he tells you." "Well, even if it's true, I wouldn't fancy it. I think it's pretty disgusting, shagging a woman after someone else has just had her." Mike had also served in the Middle East before. We asked him if he knew anything about the government brothels. "Yes, they had them in the Sudan when I was there," he told us. "I was with the lads near Khartoum. One night we were riding in the back of a three-ton truck and we came to a building with a red light on it. The driver stopped and the others all went into the place. You know how cold it gets in the Sudan at night. I was only wearing khaki drill and I didn't want to stay outside in the cold on my own, so I went in with them." About twenty of us crowded around Mike as he told his story. "What was it like there, Mike?" "What were the girls like?" "The only ones I saw were black ones," Mike continued. "The British military police ran the place. They took the money and entered the clients' details in a register. There was no privacy. The girls operated behind a sort of screen of army blankets. Each time when the girls were finished they came out and squatted down to sluice out their flues with the spout of a sort of little watering-can. I had never had anything to do with a woman. I really didn't know anything about it and I was bloody terrified." A voice chimed in, "Surely you had a go, didn't you?" "Well, I felt a bit daft," Mike replied, "because I had already paid, but I just couldn't face it. One of the girls kept on telling me she liked me and urging me to go with her. I said I was just waiting for my pal to come out and I didn't want to go with her. She pulled up her frock and stretched open her quim with her fingers. She giggled and said, 'Look, it's the same as a white girl inside!' It was the first time I had seen anything like that. I couldn't get out of the place quickly enough. Of course, the other lads took the piss when they found out about it, but I will never go near a place like that again."

Mike told us that before he had left home to join the Air Force, his mother had urged his father to explain the "facts of life" to him. They sat down at the kitchen table and chatted while father drank a cup of tea. Mike waited expectantly. Father picked up a biscuit. "Now, son," he announced gravely, "you must be very careful where you dunk your biscuit while you are away. Otherwise you might get it burned." That had been the full extent of Mike's sex education when he left home at the age of seventeen. Nor had many of us been any wiser than Mike when we joined the Air Force.

It was early evening when we pulled into Alexandria's railway station. We would rather have been posted straight to a squadron, but now we would see what Alexandria had to offer, and we had no idea what plans the Air Force had for us after that. We went to the Red Shield Hostel and paired off in twin-bedded rooms. I was glad Tob was sharing with me. He was a delightful companion, always giggling and joking. There was never a dull moment in Tob's company. It would be a pleasant nine days. We spent each morning on the beach, and in the afternoons we drank ourselves silly in Athenio's café. Tom Collins was our favourite drink, and each day it was a different colour. It did not seem to be very strong, but it certainly was lethal in the quantities that we consumed.

We met up with the other lads at Athenio's in groups of half a dozen — the drinkers congregating at tables together, and Andy and the other abstainers, including Deaky the navigator and Reg the mid-upper gunner, sitting separately and eating ice cream. When any of us wanted to go to the lavatory the question was heard, "Anyone for a slash?" It was necessary to go to the lavatory in twos, to avoid being mugged. In Athenio's one afternoon, we got into conversation with some soldiers who were stationed locally. We pumped them for information about places of interest and things to do. They told us that they had worked out a system for seeing all the floorshows in thirteen cabarets in one night, and they invited Tob and me to accompany them. Their system was to have one compulsory drink in each place, leave as the last act was finishing, then run to the place where the next show was just starting. I soon noticed that the same performers were appearing in several different shows. For instance, a belly-dancer in one place was a Mexican singer in another place. Before we reached the thirteenth place, the compulsory drinks had gone to my legs and I needed help to remain upright. Our Army friends, being older and more accomplished drinkers than we were, made sure that we found our way safely back to the Red Shield Hostel at the end of the night.

The next morning we decided not to go to the beach, but to go straight to Athenio's café and meet our

Army friends. As always, we sat near to the large first-floor windows, where we could watch the fascinating street scene, and this morning we noticed a continual procession of horse-drawn open gharries full of eager-looking sailors. "They are from one of the ships in the harbour and on their way to the Navy brothel for the day," we were told by our Army friends. "Probably been at sea for months — the poor buggers. They won't go back on board until this evening — pale-faced and totally shagged out. It's always the same when a ship comes in." So it was true about official brothels, and Bob had not been joking. We were keen to learn more. "There used to be places open for soldiers and airmen, but they were closed down as soon as Monty [General Montgomery] arrived. He seems to be a bit of a Bible puncher, and he didn't agree with it, but he had no jurisdiction over the Navy, and they have kept their places open." Suddenly, even those among us who would have been too shy or too prudish to visit a brothel themselves were indignant that the "Senior Service" should have retained facilities that were denied to the rest of us. The discussion and light-hearted banter continued: "Well, good on yer, Monty, I say. Your Mums wouldn't want you young lads going to nasty places like that!" — "I'm not at all sure that they were wise to close the places down. Presumably, the girls are still on the game, but without proper supervision and medical inspections they surely must now be all poxed up." — "I have heard that people at home think that most of the men in the Eighth Army have got the clap and ought to be put in quarantine when they get back." — "Didn't some woman write to the newspapers that men returning from the Middle East should be made to wear yellow armbands as a warning to English women, because her two daughters had caught the clap?"

After our nine days' leave we returned on the train to Cairo. We had now had enough of the Middle East, and were hoping to be sent to an operational squadron. To our dismay, we were sent instead to yet another disposal centre. This one was on the edge of the Western Desert, where we were given a couple of blankets and a tent. We slept on the sand. There were no beds, but the sand was soft and preferable to the cold marble floors of Cairo's Heliopolis Palace Hotel. The trouble was that the sand penetrated everything — our eyes, our teeth, our hair. We quickly got into the habit of tipping the sand (and the odd scorpion) out of our boots each morning. Asphalt paths had been recently laid between the tents, but in the heat they had retained the consistency of sticky black toffee, and we still had to walk on the sand. Fortunately, the disposal centre was not too far from the tram terminus, and, having nothing else to do, we could travel into Cairo and wander around, or visit the open-air swimming-baths in Heliopolis, which had the most aggressive biting flies I have ever come across.

We learned from a notice at the gate of the disposal centre that the Egyptians had complained about our shorts being too short. It was fashionable for those of us who had been abroad for some time to have turned-up cuffs on the legs of our shorts to make them as short as possible, and in some cases the shorts really had no legs at all. One day on the tram into Cairo, I realized why the Egyptians had complained. I noticed that the airman sitting on the low seat opposite to me was inadvertently displaying his entire works, putting me in mind of a handful of pork sausages. I thought to myself that it was probably only the Egyptian men who had complained about us, not their poor downtrodden-looking women in their long black costumes and veils.

CHAPTER
FOUR

A First Experience of Italy

After a month of idleness, the members of our crew were suddenly ordered to pack up and report at Payne Field, an American airfield on the outskirts of Cairo. There, we and our kitbags of flying kit were weighed, and we were informed that we were to be transported by air to Italy. We boarded what we were told was an American Skymaster, and we took off with a load of Americans. Unexpectedly, lunch was served during the flight, and after nine hours we landed. We wandered into the airport building and looked around. Was this Italy? Apparently not. We noticed that the French flag was flying from a flagpole and everybody was speaking French. Surely, we were not in France, but where the devil were we? Deaky tried out his schoolboy French on a couple of people. "This is Maison Blanche," we were told.

Nobody took any interest in us, so we sat outside in the shade and looked around for someone to talk to. Fortunately, we found a French airman who spoke a variation of the English language, and from him we gathered that we were in Algeria. Had we got onto the wrong plane? What did we do now? "There is a transit hostel for aircrews and officers nearby. You can stay there and you will have to make your own way into Algiers tomorrow and report to the transport officer. If you show him your documents he will know what to do with you." We looked around for our kitbags. There was no sign of them. They must have been left behind in Cairo. What a cock-up! "Never mind," said Deaky, "we will probably be on our way to Italy tomorrow." I sincerely hoped so. I had only one shirt, shaving kit, flying helmet and the clothes I was wearing, and we had no money.

We found the Maison Blanche Hotel and booked in. We were allocated accommodation in one of the huts in the grounds, and to our delight we found that the two-tier bunks had sheets. What luxury after irritating blankets on the sand! Our next surprise came when we entered the dining room. The tables, with clean white cloths, each had a plate of dates in the centre. After finishing off the dates while waiting for dinner to be served, we moved to a different table and started on another lot. The next day we reported to a corporal who seemed to be in sole charge of the RTO's office in town. We explained that we thought we should be in Italy and we didn't know what we were doing in Algeria. We handed over the sealed documents that had been given to us on departure from Cairo. They did not get more than a quick glance, and he offhandedly informed us that bomber crews were priority three, so we were likely to be in Algeria for ages. "But I thought

101

we were priority one," said Deaky. "No, certainly not, only fighter pilots are priority one," said the corporal, and the superior expression on his face said, "Don't you bloody lot try to teach me my job!"

As soon as we were back outside in the street, Deaky said, "I know we are priority one, not priority three, because I opened the documents and read them." "Well, you keep your mouth shut! It's good here," one of the gunners retorted. "Don't tempt fate; the war might be over in a couple of weeks." We managed to locate an accounts office and obtain what was called a "casual payment" in local currency. The next three weeks were mainly spent in sightseeing, mooching about in the Casbah, visiting the cinema and doing our best to support the local wine industry. In preparation for Italy, I bought a phrase book, but unfortunately it was for French-speaking people, and as I had opted for German at school I was constantly pestering Deaky to translate the French texts.

We were fascinated by the groups of pretty girls in Arab dress, wandering around the department stores. They wore a token veil that looked like a tiny handkerchief folded into a triangle. We could see clearly that they were all wearing make-up, and although we had been warned by some Frenchmen that we should not stare at them, we found it hard to resist the temptation. I was having a surreptitious sideways look at a particularly pretty one in a group walking around Woolworths, when she suddenly turned to me and asked, "Have you got any chewing gum?" I was quite startled, and having already seen that each group of girls was accompanied by a fierce man with a broad-bladed sword, I scampered away without replying to her. We understood that the groups of girls, some of them Arabs and some French, were the harems of wealthy Arabs. We often saw them squatting on the grass beside the road, waiting for their motor vehicle to take them back to wherever they belonged. Some of them stood up as we passed and teasingly extended their arms wide to open and readjust the loose sheets that seemed to be their only garments. In the presence of the man with the sword, we tried not to look. They giggled, chattered to each other and stared at us. We would have liked to know what they were saying about us.

After three weeks, we could not restrain Deaky any longer. During one of our daily visits to the RTO's office, and as the corporal was assuring us once again that because of our unimportant status we would be staying in Algiers for a very long time, Deaky quietly suggested that he really ought to have a closer look at our travel documents. Condescendingly, the corporal slowly opened the envelope and tipped the contents out onto the desk. He then turned away and kept us waiting while he chatted on the phone for a few minutes. When he eventually deigned to read our documents, he looked as though he would have a fit. "It says here that you are top priority. Get ready to leave this afternoon," he blurted out. "We have been ready for the past three weeks," we told him. Within a couple of hours, we were sitting on the floor of a freight-carrying DC3 Dakota, on our way to Italy. The aircraft was almost completely full of large boxes and a heavy aeroplane tyre that was not properly secured, and we had to take care that it did not run over us during the bumpy flight. The pilot was a Belgian. We did not get any information out of him, except that he would be landing at an aerodrome near Naples.

We were ready for a new adventure. After three weeks, life in Algiers had become rather dull. There was no social life, such as we had been used to in England and in South Africa. The French people either totally ignored us or were openly hostile. "No wonder they aren't too keen on us. I heard that our people sank the French fleet in North Africa," said one of our gunners. "It seems that we had to stop them from joining forces with the Germans." The French nation did not rate very highly in our estimation. We had heard tales of French soldiers being evacuated from Dunkirk with our troops and then going back home to France when they heard that their government had surrendered to the Germans. We felt that they should have stayed with our forces in England, like the Poles and Czechoslovaks. We had also heard that the French Air Force in North Africa had bombed our base in Gibraltar at the time of the Battle of Britain. We received very little official information about the progress of the war — just the odd newsreel in the cinema that invariably gave the impression that we were winning. Most of what we knew was gleaned from casual meetings with Army people who had been in action, and their accounts rarely corresponded with the newsreel reports.

We heard that some of the Italians had changed sides. Our preconceptions regarding the Italians were based on accounts that we had read about their invasions of Abyssinia, Greece and Yugoslavia, their pathetic attempts to use biplanes against the Royal Air Force during the Battle of Britain and on Winston Churchill's frequent disparaging remarks about them. We were expecting to encounter a decidedly hostile attitude in Italy, but in fact we were to be pleasantly surprised.

When we landed and entered the airport building, the scene was chaotic. There was no obvious place where we should announce our arrival. In common with all overseas airports that we used, this one was purely for military personnel, and there were no customs or immigration formalities. We had no baggage — our kitbags were presumably still in Cairo, although they had been checked in and weighed before we took off three weeks previously, so we had expected that they would have flown with us. After landing, we did what every serviceman does in such circumstances; we looked around for a "shai and a wad" (tea and a bun), which we soon found in a canteen staffed by jolly Italian girls. As we selected something to eat and figured out how to pay for it, the girls chattered away in Italian and laughed at our attempts to make ourselves understood. It seemed that none of them understood a single word of English, but they repeatedly asked what sounded like "Cabbage? Cabbage?" I told them, "No cabbage — only tea and cake." As I found out much later, they were saying "Capisc?", the Neapolitan way of asking, "Do you understand?" Judging by the way the Italian girls looked at us we would not lack incentive to learn Italian. We flashed our travel documents at the sort of people in the airport whom we thought likely to be interested in them, and eventually we ended up in the suburb of Naples called Portici. By this stage in our Air Force careers, we were not surprised to find that we were in yet another disposal centre, where we had nothing much to do all day except explore our new surroundings. We were billeted in large villas that had been commandeered for our exclusive use on the steep slopes of Vesuvius. The use of multi-tiered bunks meant that every room was crowded, but at least we were under cover. We knew that when we eventually moved on, there was nowhere else to go except to an operational squadron.

We were interested to find that, in addition to "new boys" like us, the disposal centre contained people who had already survived an operational tour and were expecting to be sent back to the Middle East for a "rest period". Our curiosity about operational flying naturally prompted us to seek information from these experienced crews. What we discovered was rather disconcerting. It was clear that the strain of operational flying had taken its toll. In contrast to us, they were rather morose, almost lifeless, creatures. They had no eagerness. They seldom smiled. We had to drag every word out of them. They appeared to have no patience with us and our naive questions. They looked pityingly, almost contemptuously, at us. We were in awe of these experienced men, but to them we were mere "sprogs", hardly worth wasting their time on. At Portici we saw the first cases of what we were later to know as "the operational twitch" and "flak-happy" behaviour — manifestations of psychological disorders in aircrew men that would become very familiar to us when we reached an operational squadron. We also heard the term LMF (lack of moral fibre), with which any man was branded if he cracked under the stress of combat. LMF was commonly regarded as weakness and cowardice. In our ignorance, we felt no sympathy for such cases. We still had a lot to learn! In retrospect, I think that the presence of "tour-expired" crews with us in Portici was likely to have been as demoralizing to some of us as the appearance of the burned pilots in Torquay.

On my first morning at Portici, I wandered down to the seashore and looked at girls lying on the black volcanic sand and on the roofs of bathing huts. As I leaned on the wooden railings in front of the huts I noticed a little fat soldier, fully clad in battledress, lying beside a scantily clad young woman. "You look to be doing all right," I greeted him. He stood up and came over to me. "Yes, she's a bit of hot stuff. Her husband is a prisoner of war in England. I'm looking after her," he grinned. "Are you based here in the Naples area?" I enquired. "Yes," he replied, "RASC driver. Been here since the invasion. You've just arrived, I suppose. Anything here you fancy? That one over there on the roof is OK — she's called Gina — tightest little hole in Portici." I looked where he was indicating. He waved and the long-legged, bikini-clad girl reciprocated as she climbed down from the roof. "Yes, she looks nice," I agreed. "Hey, Tony," he called to the youth who was in charge of the beach huts, "Gina come down — you open hut for my friend!" "You will be OK there, but don't spoil it for the boys! Give her a hundred lire — not more," he told me.

As Gina approached, I saw that she was holding a pretty little girl by the hand. The door of one of the huts was now unlocked and she indicated to me to enter. Thinking that the little girl was to remain outside, and not wanting to feel foolish in front of the soldier who had winked and given me the "thumbs up" as he returned to his girl on the beach, I entered the hut. Gina followed, still accompanied by the child. She locked the door, and after turning the child to stand facing the corner, she removed the top of her bikini, which to my surprise was padded out with tissue paper. She rolled the paper into little balls and carefully blocked up all the knotholes in the sides of the hut. "Boy no possible look!" she said. She took off the bottom half of her bikini. I was still fully dressed. She stood naked in front of me looking puzzled. "What, you no like?" she asked. I looked at the silent child. I assumed that she was her daughter. About three years old, I guessed. Perhaps she did not understand now, but surely she would remember. The presence of the little girl was making me feel ashamed and embarrassed. "Why you no like?" asked Gina, pointing to herself. She looked puzzled and I noticed that she had not smiled at me once. "Yes, I like, I like, OK" I assured her. I hastily fumbled for a L100 note and thrust it at her. She looked bewildered. "OK, I go now, it is OK!" I muttered. I felt foolish as I unlocked the door of the hut and left. I did not look back. The soldier on the beach called out to me, "OK?" I gave him the thumbs-up sign as I scuttled away. I hoped Gina would not tell him that I had given her the money for nothing. I decided that I would not go near the beach again and I certainly would not mention the episode to any of the lads.

As I climbed the steeply winding street back to the billet, I was passed by an ornate funeral hearse and a procession of about a hundred black-clad mourners. I had never seen people sobbing and wailing in public before. As I stood waiting for them to pass, I noticed that the hearse was steered by a man in a top hat and pushed up the steep hill by the mourners. Obviously, there was no petrol for the vehicle. The next day I went to look at the bomb damage in Naples. The harbour was full of sunken ships, their funnels and masts sticking up out of the water. Most of the harbour buildings were in ruins. As I gazed at the dreadful devastation, an old woman dressed in black clothes spoke to me in English. "You did this!" she said, with a sweep of her hand towards the bombed buildings. "No, I did not. I did not do it," I foolishly replied, not understanding that she meant "you people", and not me personally. However, I knew that I would soon be doing the same sort of thing, and not merely ships and buildings would be destroyed.

One day a notice appeared in the billet asking all men who were able to drive to report for an important assignment. Surprisingly, in view of our normal reluctance to volunteer for anything, several men responded. They were away for a couple of days, and they returned looking totally exhausted. They told us only that they had been driving trucks, delivering mustard-gas bombs. As they seemed reluctant to talk about it, we assumed that they had been warned to say nothing. I knew about the dreadful effects of mustard-gas from my father, who had encountered it in the First World War. I felt uneasy about the prospect of being ordered to drop gas bombs, but I consoled myself with the thought that such weapons would surely be used only as a reprisal. I wondered if such bombs were already in use and I wondered why they were being moved.

Our meals were served in a nearby villa, and after each meal we had to scrape our plates into large oil-drums that constantly stood over an open fire in the courtyard. The swill simmering in the drums consisted of bits of orange peel, gristle and anything else that we had discarded. The unappetizing mess was given the consistency of soup by the dregs of tea with which we rinsed the debris off our plates. By five in the morning, the streets near the villa were filled with old people and children — each one with a small container of some sort. Around nine, the cooks opened the gates into the courtyard, and as the old people and children silently shuffled past the drums they received a scoop of hot swill, which they immediately ate while crouching down on the ground against the courtyard railings. It was clear to me that the people were near to starvation. They were all unnaturally quiet. The legs of the bare-footed children were covered in malnutrition sores. As I walked to breakfast each morning I passed a pretty little girl, four or five years old, who looked at me with sorrowful dark eyes and always said the same words to me, "*Poco pane, poco pane.*" In response, I always put a slice of bread in my pocket and handed it to her on my way back to the billet. I began to look forward to seeing this sad little figure waiting alone for me at the side of the street each day.

Situated diagonally opposite the villa, where we could not fail to notice it, was a military detention centre with a compound that extended to the edge of the road. The compound was surrounded by a fence, about twenty feet high. We often saw the prisoners undergoing punishment drill at the double in the compound. Occasionally we saw them in full marching order, in the heat of the day, running back up the hill to the detention centre. We understood that some of the prisoners were aircrew men, but most of them were Army deserters from the front line. As the place was situated so prominently near the villa, we assumed that its presence was intended as a warning to us. Each morning as we passed the compound, we made sure that nobody was around before hurling packets of cigarettes over the high fence. In due course, a notice appeared on the fence to inform us that anyone caught committing the "serious offence" of throwing anything into the compound would find himself inside with the other prisoners. The notice made us more cautious, but did not entirely stop us from delivering cigarettes.

Some of the enterprising owners of large houses had turned them into temporary cafés, where home-produced eggs and potatoes were cooked and served by the members of the family. It seemed that most of the owners of such places were formerly wealthy people who had fallen on hard times due to the war. There was one such place near our billet, and I had taken to visiting it occasionally for supper. The proprietor was an amiable, portly little old fellow. His two attractive daughters, who served the suppers, added to the appeal of the place, but disappointingly (or wisely) they were never allowed out of his sight. One evening, I rather foolishly told Spud, a crazy lad with an Irish surname, where I was going for supper, and he invited himself to accompany me. I persuaded our cooks to give me some soya link sausages and a couple of slices of bread to take with me, and away we went for what should have been a pleasant evening of eating and drinking. The proprietor's wife cooked the soya links and bread with eggs and chips, and the daughters brought us the suppers with two bottles of wine. Italians could not afford to patronize such places, so we and a crowd of other airmen were the only clients, and the room was packed. Time passed pleasantly enough. Spud, a product of a first-class public school, was an interesting companion, but he was dreadfully unpredictable and likely to start a fight at the least provocation. I had known him since we were on the navigation course together in South Africa, and although I knew that he liked to be with me, I generally tried to avoid him.

112

At the end of the evening, the proprietor presented the bill, and just as I was counting out my contribution, Spud loudly announced, "We are not paying!" I knew it was useless to remonstrate with him, as he was quite likely to turn on me if I said anything. The little Italian, who was not much taller standing up than Spud was when sitting down, explained that the bill did not include any charge for cooking our soya sausages and fried bread. Spud was not listening. "We are not paying!" he repeated. The little man went away looking worried and Spud sat silently scowling as he drained the last dregs out of the wine bottles. I said nothing, but I left my share of the money on the table as a mild form of protest at his behaviour.

Suddenly, we were aware of two aircrew warrant officers as they leaned across from the next table. "There's nothing wrong with the food here and it is really quite cheap," one of them said. Spud noticed the "Canada" label on their shoulders and snarled, "Mind your own bloody business — I don't hold with you fucking colonials!" I knew that if a fight started now, everybody would join in and the place would be wrecked. Luckily, the Canadians turned away without another word. The little Italian reappeared at our table, smiled nervously at Spud and gabbled what sounded like, "Looka me! Soldat italiano — no like-a Tedeschi, like-a Tommies — Inglese buono, molto simpatico." He spread a handful of faded photographs on the table. They showed him, very much younger and thinner, but clearly recognizable, in a comical uniform, surrounded by other young Italian soldiers with plumes of feathers in their hats. He pointed to the dates on the backs of the pictures. They had been taken during the 1914–18 war when Italy was allied with us. He pointed to the group of soldiers in one of the photographs and indicated which ones had been killed: "*Morto, morto.*" Spud examined the photographs and passed them over to me. As I handed them back, Spud put his hand on the little man's shoulder, patted him on the back and then counted out the money required for the bill. I did not visit the place again. The last time I saw Spud, several months later, his hand was bound up and in a sling. "I hit an American," was his explanation. I did not bother to ask him the reason.

While I was still in Portici, I heard that two young sergeant pilots had been visiting "eggs-a-chips" places and robbing the proprietors. As Allied servicemen were the Italians' main source of soap, cigarettes and chewing gum, the two scoundrels had indicated that they had some such goods to offer and suggested that they discuss the matter privately in another room. Once they were alone with their victims, they produced a pistol and demanded money. The pistol was never loaded, but the victims did not know that, and money was hastily handed over on each occasion. I never discovered exactly what happened in the end, but the two villains were said to have been caught by the Italian paramilitary police, who handed them over to the RAF police, but instead of being charged they were quickly posted to a Spitfire squadron. We heard that one of them had never flown a Spitfire before — I think he had been trained on Mustangs — so he was given a short explanation by the Flight Commander, and in twenty minutes, he was a Spitfire pilot.

One day when I was wandering around the streets of Portici, I saw on the other side of the street a notice in English with the large heading, "A PRESENT FROM PORTICI". I crossed the street to read it. I was curious, because I had not seen any souvenirs worth buying since I arrived in Italy. On closer scrutiny, I read, "SOMETHING TO TAKE HOME FOR THE WIFE AND FAMILY", and then it continued with a warning in smaller print about an especially dangerous form of venereal disease that was resistant to the commonly used drugs, and if we caught it, we could not be cured. In the next street, I saw a banner proclaiming "LICE CAUSE TYPHUS". I was already aware that, due to bomb damage, effluent from the sewers had contaminated the town's drinking-water, so we should not drink anything or eat ice cream. We assumed that wine was safe and we did not avoid that, but we were distrustful of Italian "whisky" since some Indian soldiers were said to have died after drinking something that, upon investigation, turned out to be a concoction based on wood alcohol and urine. Italy seemed to be full of hidden perils, but we had not yet experienced the worst of them.

We heard that the long-awaited "Second Front" had recently been opened with the invasion of France, and that the war was progressing well, so we began to wonder if it would all be over soon and we might not be needed. The official news bulletins did not quite tally with the information that we gleaned from casual meetings with soldiers "out of the line", who gave horrifying accounts of conditions on the Italian front. Many of the soldiers were Eighth Army men who had served in the North Africa campaign, and some of them were very critical of the Royal Air Force. "Where was the bloody RAF?" they would ask, as they described how they were attacked repeatedly by German Stuka dive-bombers, while there was no sign of the Royal Air Force. We could have told them where we were — in some blasted disposal centre! We heard about parachute troops being dropped in the sea and drowned during the invasion of Sicily. That seemed to be another thing for which we, as representatives of the Royal Air Force, were blamed. We soon learnt to steer clear of Army people.

CHAPTER
FIVE

The Grim Destination of Foggia

Eventually our time in Portici was over. Our crew of seven men assembled on Naples railway station to take the night train across Italy from coast to coast. Destination — Foggia. We had heard about Foggia. It was said to be a town surrounded by dozens of British and American Air Force bases. We did not know exactly what awaited us. We did not talk about it. We concerned ourselves only with what was happening at the moment. What were our feelings? A mixture of excitement and apprehensiveness, such as we had experienced not so very long ago as new boys on the first day at a fresh school.

As we boarded the train, the RTO informed me that I was to take charge of half a dozen ground staff airmen and their tea chest of rations. It was the first time that food had been provided for a train journey. I looked in the box and was surprised to discover that the rations included several packets of tea. There were no facilities for heating water on the train, so I wondered if they were supposed to eat the dry tea-leaves. This was the first time that I had been put in charge of men, and I felt uneasy when I noticed that one of them, a corporal, was wearing the General Service and Victory medals from the 1914–18 war. I had just attained my twentieth birthday, and I realized that the corporal must have been about the same age as my father. A few minutes before the train steamed out of the station, the corporal reported that the box of rations had disappeared. I wondered if the airmen had sold it to the Italians. I did not really care. Twelve hours without food and drink would not be unusual. I had other things to think about. I stood looking out of the window at the bomb damage as the train left the station. The sight was horrifying and fascinating. Huge locomotives lay on their sides where they had been blown off the tracks. We speculated about the size of the bombs that had been powerful enough to cause such devastation. Our sole experience during training had been with smoke bombs and flash bombs weighing a mere eleven and a half pounds, but we had heard about high-explosive bombs weighing up to ten tons.

It was soon dark and I spent most of the night talking to the other six members of the crew and waiting impatiently for daylight. At times like these, when we had nothing else to do, we were able to get to know each other a little better. We did not talk about ourselves much or about our family backgrounds. Andy, the pilot, was twenty-one, a year older than me. He had been trained at flying schools in Rhodesia. He was a quiet, cheerful, confident, modest lad of medium height with fair hair and fresh complexion. When he sat at the controls of the Liberator, he looked far too young to be flying such a huge aeroplane. Like the rest of us, he was intolerant of unnecessary "bullshit" and senior officers, but unlike most of us, he did not swear, drink or smoke. The other members of the crew were between twenty-one and twenty-two. Deaky, the navigator, had been trained in South Africa. He was a quietly cheerful lad, fair haired, tall and slim, decent and reliable and a dog lover. He had adopted a sort of terrier in Palestine and he used to take it up in the plane with him. I am not sure that the dog was a happy aviator. He was sometimes airsick, and eventually he deserted and joined the packs of semi-wild Arab dogs. Deaky carried a photo of that dog for the next fifty years. Smudger was the flight engineer, a big, strong, fearless Shetlander, the type of man who could be pictured exploring the remotest areas of the world. He had never been out of the Shetlands until the day he arrived in Newcastle to join the RAF. He approached a typical Geordie and asked for directions. To his consternation, it appeared that English as spoken on the mainland was unintelligible. Jock, the wireless operator/air gunner, was a humorous, boisterous, quick-tempered Scot with an accent that became even more guttural at times of stress. Mac, the rear gunner, another Scot, cheerful and always fooling around, was like Jock and me — not afraid of the "demon drink". Reg, the mid-upper gunner, was a quiet lad with a fresh complexion, and I doubt if he had started to shave yet. He had a rather vague manner and he kept his eyes screwed up as though he was constantly peering at enemy planes. To sum up, I suppose we were four steady types and three hooligans who fitted together perfectly as a team. In common with most RAF bomber crews of the period, we had been mere schoolboys when the war started.

We arrived at Foggia about five o'clock in the morning. There was no railway station. It had been destroyed by bombing and the rubble had been cleared away. We climbed down from the train and stood waiting beside the track. It was a glorious summer day. Within a few minutes, the cloudless sky became crowded with heavy bombers circling in perfect formations: American B17 Fortresses and B24 Liberators. We heard the familiar roar of Pratt & Whitney engines — a blood-curdling noise that was to remain for ever in our heads. We estimated that there must have been about five hundred aircraft wheeling overhead at the same time. It was the most awesome display of air power that we had ever seen.

Soon a dilapidated three-ton truck with Royal Air Force roundels painted on the bonnet arrived to convey us to our destination, which we expected to be an aerodrome. After a journey of several miles, the truck pulled off the road into a large field and stopped near lines of sad-looking bivouac-style tents. "What's this place?" we asked the driver. He told us it was the domestic site. "Well, where's the aerodrome?" we wanted to know. He grinned at us. "Aerodrome? It's just a strip of perforated steel planking about seven miles away." We stared around us. Dusty flat land and scorched grass as far as the eye could see. No sign of life — not even a dog. We groaned, "Not bloody tents again!" In the middle of the field was an ancient farmhouse. "That's where you report," the driver told us. We wandered in and announced our arrival to a corporal, who sat behind an antiquated typewriter mounted on a bare wooden trestle table. I glanced over his shoulder as he paused from his two-fingered task and began to deal with us. He had been writing out the report on last night's operational sorties. The target had been the railway yards at Munich. I read how many aircraft had been seen going down in flames, and the statement, "No parachutes observed". I realized that we were replacements for men who had died in the night while we were on the train. The list of their names made little immediate impact on me. I had not known them. They were just names on paper. We had more urgent concerns, like the necessity of finding something to eat and drink. It had been many hours since our last meal.

After the Orderly Room Corporal had finished with us, I wandered along the rows of silent tents. The tent sides were rolled up, the end flaps were tied back and I could see men asleep. Obviously, they were the lucky survivors of last night's bombing sorties. In the distance, I could see a lone figure sitting on an upturned metal bowl. With his elbows resting on his knees and his head in both hands, he looked a figure of utter dejection. I approached nearer, and to my surprise I recognized him. It was Brock, an old friend from my time at Bombing and Gunnery School in South Africa.

I was shocked by his appearance. He looked ill. His face was haggard and he appeared to have aged dreadfully. He did not greet me. He just stared at me with tired bloodshot eyes sticking out of their sockets. "Don't stay here, go back, it's suicide! You can't survive a tour. Go back. Go back!" he gabbled excitedly. I realized that he must be a very sick man. I tried to calm him and I wanted to know where he had been since we left South Africa. He told me that he had been sent straight from air school to the squadron. He had not been to the operational training unit or heavy conversion unit. A vital part of his training had been omitted, and obviously he was neither psychologically nor technically prepared for duty on an operational squadron. "You don't know anything about the Mark 14 bombsight and bombing equipment, if you didn't do HCU," I observed. "Of course I don't; I told them I hadn't a clue, and they've made me fly as a gunner. I have already done half a dozen trips. It's terrible. You can't get through forty trips. It's suicide, go back, don't stay here!" he said. I thought it best not to say anything to the rest of the crew about my talk with Brock, and I tried to disregard what he had said. His condition worried me, but I decided that there was nothing that I could do about it. I would soon discover that he was not the only one in such a state. Many years later, I was to read in the Public Record Office (now the National Archives) at Kew that our authorities in Italy had bitterly complained about the low morale of the inadequately trained aircrew men who were being sent to operational squadrons. Pilots who had never even seen aeroplanes of the type that they were expected to fly were being sent to the squadrons in our group. The squadrons had no proper facilities for retraining these pilots, so some of them were given a short flying test by one of the squadrons' more experienced pilots before they were allowed to commence operational flying. How surprising that a so-called "history" of the Royal Air Force, published after the war, stated that the high standard of aircrew training was never relaxed! Obviously, the author knew nothing of the disgraceful situation in our part of the world.

After Brock's worrying outburst I continued to wander around the so-called domestic site, in the hope of meeting someone who might be able to answer the question always asked by newly arrived personnel: "What's it like here, chum?" Tired-eyed men started to appear from the tents with their aluminium plates, tin mugs and eating irons. I followed them to a place where we were to be fed. It was merely a roof supported on poles, next to the primitive, open-air cooking arrangements. Cooking was done in billycans on fires fuelled by a hissing drip-feed of diesel oil and water. I noticed the corporal cook's white hands and black arms. The cooking equipment appeared to be made from old oil-drums. The rest of the crew had now joined me. We collected food on our aluminium plates, sat down on wooden forms at bare trestle tables and attempted to pump everyone for information. We did not learn much that day. We later realized that experienced crews kept pretty much to themselves and seemed loath to associate with strangers, particularly

123

the "new boys", who were thought unlikely to survive more than half a dozen operational trips.

Our first meal on the squadron consisted mainly of one tomato, a raw onion, a slice of canned meat, some reconstituted dehydrated potato, and a mug of tea. After our meal, we wandered around and familiarized ourselves with the site. We found that the old farmhouse incorporated a room used by the Medical Officer, an orderly room and a room that served as an office for the Commanding Officer. There seemed to be other rooms, but they were not for our use. The farmhouse was the only permanent building. The lads had constructed a shack with an earth floor, which was called the sergeants' mess. It had a bar counter, but little else. The officers' mess was an old cowshed. There was no bathhouse on the site. The lavatories were buckets situated in the open about a hundred yards from the tent lines. The site had no electric power. Paraffin lanterns were the only means of lighting. There was no water main. Water was brought to the site in a bowser, and each man was issued with a jerry can. The water stank of chlorine and we were reluctant to drink it. We called at the stores tent to collect a galvanized bowl that was to be used for washing ourselves, a mosquito net, two well-used blankets and a punctured blow-up mattress. We had arrived with only the clothes we were wearing and our "small kit" — a small webbing bag containing a spare shirt, a pair of socks, soap, towel and shaving kit. Apart from those items and my flying helmet, I had nothing.

"Give him some of that dead bloke's shirts," the store man told his assistant. I collected a few other items of used clothing, a set of flying-kit and a parachute. The flying-kit included a pair of well-used and repaired old brown leather flying-boots that presumably had also belonged to "that dead bloke". It seemed that the only clothing available was that which had belonged to men who had been killed. The flying-boots were much better than my ridiculous suede leather ones that I had last seen in South Africa. The more commonly issued type of suede boots were most impractical — very loose — and they invariably dropped off if the wearer had to bale out. No beds were provided for us, and after a couple of nights on the hard ground on the punctured "blow-up" I managed to find a sheet of thick cardboard on a wooden frame — part of a packing case — that had to serve as my bed for the next six months.

Deaky, the navigator, and Reg, the mid-upper gunner, shared a tent with me. Reg's bed was a sheet of corrugated iron! The tent was rather crowded, as it had to accommodate not only us three, but also our parachutes and flying-kit, so in fine weather we spent most of our time outside. In wet weather, the rain ran through the tent like a river. We dug a channel through it with our eating irons and played Pooh sticks to pass the time. The main trouble with the tent was that it had been sprayed with camouflage paint and was no longer waterproof. Every time it rained, our bedding and everything else got damp — no great problem in the hot weather, but the summer would certainly not last for ever. Like servicemen the world over, we often grumbled to each other about our disgusting living conditions, but we had been in the Air Force long enough to know that we would simply have to tolerate them. The usual jocular response to anyone who moaned too much was, "Silly bugger — you shouldn't have joined!" and that remark was often followed by shouts in mock despair, "Dear mother — sell the pig and buy me out!" and "Dear mother, it's a bastard! Dear son, so are you!"

A couple of days after our arrival we made our first visit to the airstrip. It was situated miles away from any sign of habitation, but it had a nice-sounding name — Amendola. There were no buildings, and all aircraft maintenance was being carried out in the open. Our aircraft were American B24 Liberators — mostly old machines, in questionable condition, from maintenance units. As I crawled under the flight deck of one of them I noticed a list of names, addresses, telephone numbers and cheery comments painted on the inside of the fuselage by the American girls at Willow Row who had built it. I said to one of the lads, "Read that! It is the nearest thing you will get to a sex life for a while!" We shared the airstrip with a squadron of B17 Flying Fortresses of the United States 15th Air Force, but we had no official contact with the Americans, although we learned later that the Royal Air Force in Italy was part of the Mediterranean Allied Air Force under United States supreme command.

During our first few days on the domestic site, we found that we were to join "B" Flight, which was commanded by an Australian navigator, and we heard that the squadron's commander was a red-haired officer known as "Red" Smythe. As new boys, we expected to be interviewed by these officers, whom we tended to look upon as a sort of equivalent of our form master and head teacher respectively. They both ignored our presence, and as our training had not prepared us for the routine of an operational squadron, we were left to adapt to our new circumstances the best way we could.

One morning we got instructions to go up for a flight to familiarize ourselves with the surrounding area. We were transported the seven miles to the airstrip in a three-ton truck, and we found a Liberator bomber that had been loaded up with a dozen little (20 lb) smoke bombs that I was to drop on a stone quarry for practice. We flew around for a few minutes and then I directed Andy to the stone quarry and started to drop the bombs one at a time. When I still had four bombs left, Deaky, the navigator, asked me to let him drop them. I agreed, and we lay side by side on the deck as I showed him how to operate the bombsight. We watched three bombs all the way down to the ground, but after he pressed the "tit" to release the last one we did not see it go, and a few seconds later the plane became filled with thick smoke. My immediate thought was of fire, and I quickly scrambled back under the flight deck to see what had happened. I found Smudger and Jock hastily sticking chewing gum onto leaking hydraulic pipes. The last bomb had dropped onto the release gear below it and exploded in the plane. I realized that the practice bomb had been too small to be correctly supported by the "crutches", and it had wobbled after it was released. "Such an accident couldn't have occurred if we had been carrying high-explosive bombs," I assured the other lads. A few minutes later, with the bomb doors and beam hatches open, the smoke cleared away and Andy was able to see well enough to find his way back to the airstrip and land safely.

After landing, we looked at Americans loading bombs onto the B17 Flying Fortresses that shared the airstrip with us. We were told that the Americans flew only during the day, whereas our squadron flew only at night. The airstrip, made of linked perforated steel planking laid on the bare ground, was about 3,000 yards long and far from level compared with the concrete runway at Lydda. Alongside the airstrip was what the Americans called the "dirt strip", a long stretch of bare earth that was available for damaged aircraft to crash-land on instead of blocking the airstrip. When we had returned to our domestic site, I heard that the Americans' domestic site was in a field about a mile away, so I decided to walk there and take a look at it. On the roadside by our domestic site was a small painted board with the simple inscription "178 SQUADRON RAF". When I got to the Americans' site, I found a board that grandly announced "NUMBER 2 HEAVY BOMBARDMENT HIGH ALTITUDE DESTRUCTION UNIT. USAAF".

One evening several of us accepted an invitation to visit the Americans' cinema on their site. This gave us an opportunity to compare their facilities with ours. We found that their tents, unlike ours, had proper beds, lockers, stoves, wooden walls and floors. To our surprise, we discovered that they had an ice-cream-making plant on the site. Their flying-crews had flak jackets and their uniforms and flying clothing were better than ours. If our "American cousins" had known of our primitive living conditions they would certainly have regarded us as their "poor relations", and I wondered why many of us had considered ourselves to be superior to Americans (and all other foreigners). Perhaps our annual Empire Day ceremonies before the war, and the fact that all the millions of people in the vast territories of our Empire, marked pink in our school atlases, were said by our teachers to be fortunate subjects of our King, had convinced us that the British were the most important people on earth. Our visit to the Americans' site left me with feelings of envy and resentment, and I did not go there again.

Each day we scanned the battle order on our notice-board to check if we were scheduled to fly that night. We were anxious to get started. We learned from experienced crews that nobody was allowed to leave the site until the battle order was posted at midday. Crews not on the battle order were free for the rest of the day. The men who were due to fly would have until briefing time, about 4 o'clock, to guess what the night's target was likely to be, using the stated bomb load and fuel load as a guide. On 19 July, the great day arrived, and at last our names were listed on the battle order. At briefing in a marquee, we sat on wooden forms in front of a huge map on which a red tape indicated the route from base to the target. "Red" Smythe began his briefing with the words, "Gentlemen! The target for tonight — another chance to get a crack at the Hun — Fiume oil refinery." As far as I can remember, Smythe never said a word to any of the sergeants individually, but at briefings, he always addressed us as "gentlemen". I recalled with some amusement that when we were doing our stupid foot drill and marching on the promenade at Initial Training Wing, the drill instructors could not rave and swear at us in their customary manner with civilians standing around watching the proceedings, so they would often growl under their breath, "You lot of pregnant bloody earwigs!" Now we were "gentlemen", but I felt that I fitted neither Smythe's description nor the drill instructors'.

After Smythe had said his piece, we were briefed by other officers about various aspects of the operation, such as the enemy opposition that we could expect to encounter. Finally, it was the turn of the Met Officer, who assured us that the weather over the target would be ideal. That was the only occasion on which he was right, as far as I can remember. Many aircraft were to be lost during the next six months when the weather forecasts were hopelessly wrong. We were very lucky to commence our operational tour with the relatively easy trip to Fiume.

After the briefing I prepared my flying-clothing, oxygen mask, throat microphone, parachute, topographical maps, escape kit, emergency food pack and camera magazine. As we departed for the airstrip, together with another crew in a three-ton truck, I felt rather uneasy in case I had forgotten something. There was an air of excited anticipation such as when I, as a seventeen-year-old, had prepared for my first take-off at the controls of a twin-engined plane. There was no thought of danger — just a dread of not doing the job properly. When we reached the airstrip and left the other crew, they each shouted, "Good trip!" and we realized that it was the customary thing to say on parting. The actual flight took only four and a half hours, but the travelling time on the ground and the interrogation after we returned meant that we were busy the whole night.

The high point of the trip was the actual attack on the oil refinery. Flames reached a height of about eight hundred feet. A fantastic sight! The anti-aircraft fire seemed unreal, just like a spectacular fireworks display. It did not worry us unduly. For the moment, we felt elated, but that feeling was not to last. During the next few days we heard from the more experienced crews that Fiume had been "an easy trip" compared with the dreaded Bucharest and Ploesti oil refineries. It became clear that the squadron had a hierarchy based not on rank, but on the number of times that a crew had flown to these targets. With our second trip, we joined the élite band of Bucharest and Ploesti veterans. At briefing, "Red" informed us that we would be bombing the "number one priority target in Europe", the Bucharest/Ploesti complex. As I prepared to guide Andy on the bombing run, the streams of tracer flak looked so close together that I thought we could not possibly pass over the target without being hit. I had heard that the Bucharest and Ploesti defences usually caught three aircraft at a time in the cones of searchlights, and shot them down before dealing with further threes throughout the duration of the attack. As we reached the target, I was relieved to see that three Wellington bombers were already in the searchlights and the flak seemed to be passing straight through them. "Good! We are going to get through OK" was my immediate thought, but after I had released our bombs and we had set course for base I realized that "good" was not an appropriate word to use when other people were being shot to pieces, and I felt rather ashamed. During the next three weeks, I made a total of four attacks on the Bucharest/Ploesti oil refineries, and we had become one of the most senior crews on the squadron by the time of our fourteenth trip.

We were flying "two on and one off", which meant that we flew two consecutive nights and had the third night off. The weather was so hot during the daytime that sleep became impossible after midday, so we waited in the flight tent until that night's battle order appeared. We were keen to get through our forty trips as quickly as possible, and get away from the squadron's dreadful conditions.

I noticed that there were boards around the domestic site bearing the words "CAUTION MALARIOUS AREA". Malaria was not the only hazard. The Medical Officer listed twenty-three cases of enteritis as well as numerous cases of infective hepatitis, scabies and pubic lice during our first few weeks on the squadron. I doubt if any prisoners of war in Europe had to endure such disgusting conditions as ours.

★　★　★

During the mornings, if we had not flown the previous night, we often had to carry out air tests to check the serviceability of aircraft. Air tests gave us an opportunity to do some very low flying over the sea. We sometimes skimmed over Italian fishing boats, and as we climbed away, our slipstream blew the boats over and the fishermen had to lean over the side to try to keep them upright. When we returned to the flight tent after one of our low-flying escapades, we were told that some Army people had noted our aircraft's number and phoned to complain about us. We protested that we had not been particularly low, but the Flight Commander said that we had been observed to fly under a cable that the Royal Engineers had erected between the shore and a rock in the sea. The height of the cable was fifty feet above the water and we had not seen it. The youngest pilot on the squadron, John Rush, aged nineteen, was also in trouble for low flying during an air test. The evidence was a length of a fir tree embedded in the underside of his aircraft. To make matters worse, Red Smythe, the Squadron Commander, had witnessed the incident as he drove his Jeep in the hills and was surprised to see John's Liberator flying in the valley below him. The other members of the crew were waving to people standing on the balconies of houses on the hillsides. Smythe raged at him, "I would have you court-martialled if we were not so damned short of pilots!" Within a very short time, he would be pleased that he had people like Andy and John — intrepid enough to fly at extremely low level — for supply-dropping operations over Warsaw and for mining the Danube.

There were no houses anywhere near our domestic site, and if we had not gone into Foggia we would rarely have seen any civilians. No official transportation was provided for us, but about once a week we waited on the main road until we were able to hitch a lift into town on the back of one of the open American trucks that regularly hauled loads of limestone from the local quarries. The black drivers usually greeted us cheerfully with, "Where ya wanna go — downtown Fowja? Okay, git aboard!" We climbed up on top of the load of dusty limestone and held fast to the sides of the truck to make sure that we did not get bounced off during the journey. Our main aim was to visit the military shower baths in Foggia. Apart from the little galvanized bowls (such as were used as feed pans for the Army's horses during the previous war) and a daily gallon of cold water, we were not provided with any washing facilities on the squadron. Some of our aircrews, who were shot down and captured, must have been the scruffiest airmen the Germans had ever encountered. I will refer again to the matter of our disgraceful appearance later.

The distance into Foggia was perhaps about eighteen miles, and we usually arrived covered in white dust from the limestone. The showers were always crowded with black Americans, white Americans and our own Air Force men. The open-fronted shower cubicles had space for two or three people together, but each one was continually occupied by at least half a dozen men, struggling and shoving each other in an attempt to get wet. There were always at least another dozen of us, stripped off, clutching our soap and waiting for someone to come out of a cubicle so that we could force our way in and try to get under the meagre trickle of warm water. Very many years later, at a reunion of airmen, I met one of the American pilots who had been stationed in the Foggia area. When I asked him if he had visited the showers, he laughed: "Yes, I sure did and I must have seen you there, but I didn't recognize you now with your clothes on."

Foggia had been bombed by the British, the Americans and the Germans, so that it was now scarcely more than a collection of ruins. The town's inhabitants were mainly elderly people, who had apparently evacuated all their young women to somewhere safely out of reach of the thousands of locally based British and American airmen. The town had two cinemas, and they were both for the exclusive use of Allied troops. One cinema was run by the British and one by the Americans. The American troops were allowed to queue up with us at the British cinema, but at the American cinema, we had to queue behind the Americans and drop back each time additional Americans arrived. Consequently, we sometimes failed to get in after waiting a couple of hours in the street outside the cinema. We were quietly resentful because we felt that the same rules should have applied at both cinemas, but I did not see any signs of trouble between our lads and theirs. Actually, we only rarely attempted to get into the cinemas, because so many of the films were made for the entertainment of American civilians who were far away from the horrors of war. War films, starring famous Hollywood actors, were often shown to the accompaniment of jeers and derisive laughter from the audience.

After the shower baths, we usually visited the NAAFI (a sort of military cafe), which had previously been a school, where we sat on hard chairs and consumed tea and cakes for hours at a time. The NAAFI was a great meeting place. In fact, it was the only meeting place, and each time I went there I was certain to meet crews from other squadrons in the locality. Most of the lads who had trained with me in South Africa turned up at the NAAFI sooner or later. The navigators were on the Vickers Wellington squadrons in the same group. We all attacked the same targets, so we were able to compare operational experiences and casualty rates when we met in the NAAFI. It was fleetingly of interest to hear that a mutual acquaintance had been killed, but on such occasions we reported that he had either "gone for a Burton", "got the chop" or simply "had it". The words "killed", "dead" and "death" were never used by us. When aircraft returned to base with dead men on board and when people were killed in crashes, we were invited by our authorities to attend the burials at Foggia cemetery. We usually declined. It was as though death was contagious. We did not want to have any contact with the dead. We continued to talk of them as though they were still alive. Our seemingly casual attitude to the likelihood of our own deaths was totally misunderstood by certain earthbound senior officers, who concluded, "The aircrews are too foolish to realize the dangers. They each think it will not happen to them." We were unaware of this insult at the time, but the official records show that it was typical of the way we were regarded by such people.

As we had practically no opportunity to associate with Italian families in Foggia, the NAAFI became the centre of our social life, if merely sitting around eating rancid-tasting cakes and drinking NAAFI tea can be described as a social life. A surprising amount of information was exchanged in the NAAFI. It was there that I found out that some of the men who had trained with me in South Africa were on attachment to two Liberator squadrons under South African Air Force command. I was interested to know if the living conditions on the other squadrons were as disgusting as ours. It seemed that we were all in the same situation as far as accommodation was concerned. Life on the squadrons under South African command seemed to be made more tolerable by the generous "gifts and comforts" provided by the South African civilians for their servicemen. By contrast, our people back home in wartime Britain, where most foodstuffs and even clothing were strictly rationed by the government, had virtually nothing to send to us. We rarely saw any newspapers, except an occasional *Union Jack* or *Stars and Stripes* produced by the military authorities.

Most of us had very little news from home, so when anyone received a letter from a girl-friend, we crowded around him, urging him to disclose a snippet of news. "What does she say, Reg?" we urged our mid-upper gunner. "You needn't tell us everything. Leave out the lovey-dovey bits, what else does she say?" Reg read

the letter softly, "Mumble — mumble — mumble."
Apparently, every letter was about nothing but love.
"Surely she must have said something apart from how
much she loves you. Isn't there any news from home?"
we kept asking. Reg's girl was serving in the Royal
Navy, so her letters were censored, and Reg was not
allowed to disclose to her where he was or what he was
doing. Like us, the people at home were throttled by
wartime regulations — even the weather was secret,
so what was there left to write about? One day we
discovered that Reg had a photograph of his girl in her
Navy uniform. She looked very attractive, and those of
us who had no photographs of our own girl-friends
would frequently persuade Reg to let us drool over his.
From time to time, men would receive what we called
"Mespots", or "Dear John", letters from wives or
girl-friends with the demoralizing news that it was all
over between them. It was customary for such a letter
to be pinned up on the noticeboard and for everyone to
write an impolite comment on it about the woman. The
letter was then returned to her. My own attitude was
rather different from that of most of us. I felt that
unmarried girls should not be placed under an
obligation to live like nuns while they waited for a man
who might never return from the war. The girls should
be free to try to enjoy themselves as much as possible in
the dreary circumstances of wartime Britain. Reg, the
mid-upper gunner, and Deaky, the navigator, were
seriously intent on getting married to their girls, and
they spent much of their spare time on letter writing.
As each member of the crew depended on the

efficiency of the others, I dreaded the possibility of them being distracted by a "Dear John" letter; we had enough troubles without that. Staying alive was the main concern. I was happy to be unattached and free to take advantage of any local opportunities that might eventually present themselves. Unfortunately, Foggia was what we termed a "crumpet-free zone", but we heard that we might be lucky enough to get nine days' leave if we survived the first twenty operational sorties.

Survival seemed unlikely as trips to bomb the Ploesti oil refineries became more frequent and we were flying "two on and one off" — two consecutive nights in the air and then one night on the ground. Staying awake and vigilant on the second night was a terrible strain, so we began to take "wakey-wakey tablets" that were available ad lib. We soon realized that these Benzedrine pills were not effective unless we could move around, which most of us could not do. I found that they did not stop me from falling asleep in the air, but they kept me awake for hours after I had returned to base and wanted to sleep. During long hours of sitting in darkness, the deafening roar of the four engines became soporific, and each time I dozed off I awakened with a violent lurch into reality. I always asked myself how it was possible to fall asleep when we were in danger of being shot out of the sky at any moment and we were flying thousands of feet up in the air with hundreds of gallons of fuel and tons of high explosives. The impossibility of conversing with the other crew members added to the strain of trying to remain alert. I was sure that our efficiency seriously declined, due to lack of sleep, on the second of the two consecutive nights in the air. I knew when Mac, the rear gunner, had been asleep with his fingers on the triggers, because he always fired off a quick burst as he awoke.

After two particularly difficult long trips, I wearily returned to the tent and lay down on my makeshift bed. I knew that sleep would be impossible after about 10 o'clock, when the sun would have made the air in the tent unbearable, and anyway I was due for a night off after two consecutive nights in the air, so I decided to stay awake all day. I knew that if I slept now, I would not be able to sleep at night. I had an overwhelming need to get away on my own for a while. Deaky and Reg were still discussing the previous night's horrors when I quietly slipped away and hitched a ride into Foggia for a hot shower. Afterwards I felt too tired to call in at the NAAFI, so I stood at the side of the Manfredonia road waiting for a lift back to the domestic site. An American Air Force fifteen-hundredweight truck pulled up and I climbed into the back and flopped down onto the floor.

"Hi! I'm Lootenant Jansen," a voice greeted me enthusiastically. "I really don't care who the hell you are," I thought. I just wanted to be left alone. I was not in the mood for a lively conversation with the young American lieutenant. "I'm a bambadeer," he announced cheerfully in his irritating accent. "You a bambadeer, lootenant?" he asked. I replied that I was a bombardier, but that we were called air bombers in our Air Force and I was not a lootenant, I was a sergeant. "You mean your bambadeers are not officers?" he exclaimed.

"Some of them are, if they live long enough," I said. "You fly those canvas bombers?" he asked. "I saw them being loaded up — they carry more bombs than our B17s." As he chattered away, I realized that he was talking about the Vickers Wellington bombers, and he had mistakenly thought that the bombs being loaded were thousand-pounders, not five-hundred-pounders. He was obviously as green as grass, but seemed full of boyish enthusiasm. "Say, you been to Ploesti?" was his next question. I told him that I had bombed Ploesti twice and the nearby Bucharest oil refineries, at night. "At night!" he exclaimed. "How do you see?" Knowing that the Americans had no night-flying experience, I could not resist the temptation to pull his leg. "The searchlights," I said. He continued to prattle on excitedly about Ploesti, and his naive questions indicated to me that he was a new boy on his squadron and had not yet started "combat-flying". Obviously, the more experienced men had impressed him with horrifying tales of their attacks on the dreaded Ploesti refineries. I knew of the very high casualty rate sustained by the American Air Force during their low-level attacks on Ploesti in daylight, and I sensed that this young man's non-stop tirade was merely an attempt to disguise his trepidation. I could offer him no comfort, but I later regretted my flippant replies to his earnest questions. I often wonder if Lootenant Jansen (or was it Johnson?) was lucky enough to survive the war.

"The target for tonight, gentlemen," announced Smythe in the briefing tent as he waggled a long pointer at the map on the wall, "a torpedo-bomber aerodrome at Valence la Tresorerie in France. You will make two bombing runs to increase the duration of the attack and you must bomb accurately in the centre of the aerodrome. While the attack is in progress and the Germans are in their bunkers, French partisans will be placing explosives in the aircraft that are scattered in the outlying bomb-proof dispersals. By this means it should be possible for every one of the enemy aircraft to be destroyed." We trudged off to get something to eat in our makeshift dining area. It was going to be another long night. "Sorry, lads, there's nothing to eat," we were told by the corporal cook, "the rations didn't come today." "But surely you must have something left over from yesterday. We are going to be flying all night," we protested. The corporal explained that food rations were delivered to the squadron daily, and only in sufficient quantities for one day. There was never anything left over. The cook was a very serious 21-year-old, commonly called Glad by the aircrew sergeants. "Oh come on, Glad, get your finger out and find us something, we are bloody starving," we urged. Although the rubbish that Glad did his best to transform into palatable food was not too good at the best of times, the prospect of flying all night with empty stomachs was even worse. We had once seen a quantity of something that looked like compressed straw delivered to the field kitchen. It turned out to be dehydrated cabbage — quite unsuitable for flying personnel. Our stomachs swelled up enormously at high altitude, and the cabbage caused us to fart furiously throughout the trip. Now, in the absence of anything else, we would have been willing to settle for dried cabbage or any other rubbish. "Come on, Glad, for Christ's sake, see what you can find," we persisted, "there surely must be something left over." After much searching, Glad produced some onions, and we ate them raw — one each. There was no bread. Nothing else. Just a mug each of weak tea and the five boiled sweets that we received at briefing for trips of more than five hours' duration.

That night, after crossing the Alps, we experienced two attacks from aircraft firing rockets. The rockets glowed like the tips of cigarettes in the dark. When we saw them approaching, it was impossible to judge whether they would pass over the top or underneath us. I soon realized that the enemy pilots had fired while out of range, as the rockets dropped in an arc harmlessly below us. "They probably think the war will soon be over and there is no sense in getting killed at this late stage," I concluded. I began to realize that enemy fighters always broke off the attack and turned away if we saw them in time and fired at them with our 0.5in guns. Every fifth one of our bullets was a tracer and looked like a red-hot cannon shell in the dark. Each time I saw one of our bombers shot down by fighters, I noticed that it had not opened fire on the enemy aircraft, which must have approached unseen out of the pitch-blackness below. Nobody had told us that the German fighter planes had been fitted with guns that fired obliquely upwards (although our authorities must surely have known about it), and our gunners spent their time searching the sky, which was usually lighter than the more dangerous area below. We were always at our most vulnerable on the last few miles of the run up to the target, when, due to the danger of collision with other bombers, we all had to fly on the same heading, and we could not take evasive action in the event of attack by fighters. We were warned not to become distracted by the sight of bombers being shot down and not to look at them. I found that it was impossible not to look when a bomber burst into flames a few hundred yards away and continued to fly on beside us for what seemed like ages before slowly dropping down in an increasingly steep curve and exploding as it hit the ground. I hoped to see parachutes appearing, and as the seconds ticked by I always muttered, "Get out, get out, for Christ's sake!" I never saw any parachutes and I always hoped that the men hurtling to their deaths were not people that I knew personally. For obvious reasons, I made no new friends on the squadron. It did not seem to matter that they were killed, if I didn't really know them.

CHAPTER
SIX

Balkan Operations and Squalid Living

We started to drop mines in the River Danube on full-moon nights. We were told that the loads of six mines per plane were so secret that they were never to be dropped where the enemy could get at them. They were dropped, with parachutes attached, from a maximum height of around 200 feet into the main stream of the river. The banks of the Danube were around 200 feet high in places, and the Germans were said to have stretched cables across the river from bank to bank, so we needed to fly lower than the banks. The Liberator was fitted with an excellent radio altimeter, but on our first mining trip it failed to function correctly. Unable to judge his height accurately, Andy seemed to be skimming the water as I directed him on to the main stream. "Bloody hell, we are much too low. Any second we are going down in the drink. Pull up!" I urged him. "It's OK, Jimmy, we are at 100 feet," came Andy's calm response. From our daredevil low flying on air tests over the calm waters of the Adriatic sea, I knew that the ripples on the water of the river were much bigger than they should be. Luckily, we didn't touch the surface of the river, but when the altimeter was checked later, by the ground crew, we discovered that we had flown at only 30 feet. "Shit!" seemed to be the appropriate exclamation in the circumstances. We realized that we had nearly "bought it" (another of our silly euphemisms for being killed). Instead of telling us at briefing that we were being sent on minelaying operations, the Commanding Officer always announced that we would be "gardening", and the mines were referred to as "cucumbers", which were to be "planted" in specified "beds". The use of these codewords, which we had never heard during training, struck me as unnecessary and rather childish, but I never knew if the others shared my view.

During the next few full-moon nights, we succeeded in closing the entire 1,500 miles of the Danube's navigable waterway, by the use of the secret mines that were said to be virtually unsweepable. The mines did not become active until three weeks after they were laid, and they did not explode until the second time that a vessel passed over them. We heard that the Germans tried, without success, to explode the mines by letting empty barges float downstream. The crews of the tugs were said to have deserted, even when an armed sentry was posted on each vessel. The Germans needed the Danube to convey oil from the Rumanian oilfields. Oil was vital to the continuation of the war. It seems likely that the closing of the important Danube waterway was one of the Royal Air Force's greatest achievements, but I think it has scarcely received any publicity. In addition to the obvious hazard of flying over enemy territory in full moonlight and the danger from cables stretched across the river, flak barges were anchored in the main stream, and we knew that at low level we might be brought down by the invisible cables of the barrage balloons attached to them. All in all, mining the Danube caused me and the others greater stress than bombing trips, and we did not see any of the results of our dangerous efforts. There was no immediate "pay off", so we usually tried to relieve the stress by remaining at low level for a while and firing off almost all our ammunition at ships, warehouses and jetties. On these occasions, as soon as I had dropped the mines, I scrambled back from the nose of the aircraft to use the beam guns (known as "waist guns" by the Americans) situated on each side of the aircraft. Using these guns made me aware of the unsuitability of the Liberator for use at night. The reflector sights of the guns, being intended for daytime use, were so bright that nothing could be seen through them, so they had to be switched off, and I aimed the guns by watching the path of the tracer bullets, rather like using a garden hose. The gunners' turrets were fitted with tinted Perspex panels that were intended to stop glare in daylight, but at night it was as though the gunners were peering into the darkness through sunglasses. In time, the tinted panels were permanently removed from the rear gun turrets, and consequently the cold was so intense that the gunners' eyelids froze shut. Another disadvantage of the Liberator was that the exhaust outlets under each engine glowed red-hot in the dark like huge gas-cooker rings — visible for miles. I have no doubt that the Americans found the Liberator perfectly suitable for use in daylight, but as a night-bomber I thought it was a disaster, and I wondered why we had not been given the British Halifax and Lancaster bombers. In due course, I was to discover the likely reason, from men who had previously flown with heavy-bomber squadrons based in the United Kingdom.

We were all rather surprised that we were never told anything about 178 Squadron's history and past achievements. I felt sure that if we had been in the Army we would have been taught something about the regiment's traditions and battle honours. Deaky shared my disappointment. "I wonder why they [the Commanding Officer and his Flight Commanders] never bother to talk to us, except at target briefings," he wrote in his secret diary. The keeping of a diary was strictly forbidden, but as all flights had to be recorded in our flying-logbooks, I always wrote a very detailed account of all operational flights in mine, and for many years after the war I was able to check up on what I had experienced on any particular date.

One afternoon when I had nothing better to do, I looked through some boxes of documents in the flight tent where briefings were conducted. I read that the squadron had been listed as a "semi-mobile" heavy-bomber squadron, and that it had moved to Italy from North Africa the previous year. I was idly flicking through some papers when I came across some booklets of "gooley chits". It appeared that such booklets had been carried by airmen when flying over territory inhabited by Arabs. They were a sort of safe-conduct pass and an inducement to the Arabs to return airmen "intact" (complete with testicles) to the Allies. The vouchers, or "chits", were printed in various languages with English translations. The English wording did not vary much except in so far as the kind of inducement or reward was concerned. In some cases, the reward was a number of goats or sheep. The most interesting explanatory note accompanying the "chits" stated that in a certain territory (I forget where) the airman, on being captured by Arabs, should select the most important man present and shout out a particular Arabic word to him. In doing this, the airman would have placed the selected Arab under an obligation to defend him, according to local custom. The note went on to explain: "If the man you select is not sufficiently important, the Arabs will simply kill both of you, so make sure you pick the right man!"

While rummaging through the documents, I also came across a report about an American Air Force crew that had been shot down by Swiss fighter planes. The Swiss authorities interrogated the crew and asked why they had attacked their town of Schaffhausen, which, although bearing a German-sounding name, lay within neutral Swiss territory. The gunners said that nobody ever bothered to tell them what the target was, or which country it was in. The pilot, navigator and bombardier said, "We always bomb this place if we can't find the primary target!" I knew that European geography was not the Americans' strongest subject, and I learned later that people in the Swiss border towns always switched all their lights on whenever they heard planes overhead, in the hope of reminding Allied airmen that Switzerland was a neutral country. The trouble was that the navigators' charts did not show international frontiers.

When we started to bomb enemy airfields, we were told that we were to drop a mixture of normal high-explosive bombs and delayed-action bombs that would be fitted with three-, six-, nine- and twelve-hour delay devices. This meant that the airfields would be out of action long enough for the American daylight bombers to attack them during the following day, without meeting fighter opposition. Each delayed-action bomb contained an acid bottle and Perspex washers. When the bomb hit the ground, the acid bottle broke and the acid ate through the washers that held back the firing-pin. The more washers, the longer the delay. The German bomb-disposal squads would dig down to the unexploded bombs, thinking they were duds, and attempt to unscrew the fuses to make them safe. However, when a fuse was unscrewed a mere quarter of a turn, the bomb immediately exploded.

We never flew directly to the target, but made several alterations of course en route, so that the enemy fighters would not know our intended target and might be deceived into waiting to intercept us at the wrong place. In order not to betray the location of airfields, the enemy guns usually remained silent until the first bombs dropped. As soon as bombing commenced, attempts would be made by the German pilots to get all their aircraft safely up into the air. With experience, I was able to observe my own bombs all the way to the ground, even when in the middle of a stream of dozens of bombers. On one occasion, our pathfinder force had dropped flares and the enemy airfield was illuminated as brightly as daylight. I watched as a large three-engined Ju 52 transport plane was going along the runway. Bombs were exploding all around it and I saw my own stick of bombs with a pre-set interval of 200ft catching up with it. As I watched the German plane, I thought it had travelled far enough along the runway to be off the ground, and I was silently willing it to get safely into the air. As my bombs caught up with the plane, it slowly turned over and crashed onto its back. I had just seen the certain deaths of airmen whom I felt that I really did not want to kill. I tried to suppress my feelings and I did not mention the matter to anyone else, but the incident remained for ever in my mind. I later realized that by bombing airfields I must have destroyed more enemy planes than any of our fighter pilots in the Battle of Britain.

Since the first worrying encounter with my old friend Brock I continued to avoid him for fear that he might upset me and demoralize the others by his talk about the impossibility of surviving forty trips. One scorching hot afternoon I was resting in the tent alone and wondering what that night's target would be. The fuel and oil load listed on the battle order indicated that it would be another long trip. Unexpectedly, Brock appeared in the tent. He was dressed in khaki drill shirt and slacks, and unusually he was wearing a cap. As he started to talk, I noticed that he was making a great effort to remain calm. He told me, "I'm going to walk out of here now and I'm never coming back. Don't stay here. Come with me." I tried to joke with him and made a flippant remark about his unusually smart appearance. I noticed that he was carrying his side pack of small kit and I realized that he seriously meant to desert. "Come with me. Please come with me. Get ready and let's go together," he pleaded. I asked him where, exactly, he intended to go. "Just away from here!" he told me.

It appeared that he had no particular plan of action — he was simply running away. He was a good-looking, dark-haired lad, a couple of years older than me. I realized that his bronzed appearance would enable him to merge easily into the southern Italian background if he obtained some civilian clothes. I, being fair, would have been certain to attract the attention of the Allied military police, who were constantly on the look-out for deserters from the front line. I attempted to reason with him. "Don't be silly," I told him, "they will catch you and you will get a court martial and then it will be the 'glasshouse' [military prison]." "Well, that would be better than this lot," was his reply. Common sense told me that he was probably right. When I had eventually convinced him that I had no intention of going with him, he quietly left the tent. I well remember his look of utter dejection. I never saw him again. Before long, I was to hear of other men who found that they could not continue to fly, but as I did not know them well their disappearance was of no particular interest to me.

On the way to attack another airfield in Hungary, the Liberator's autopilot stopped working, and Andy faced the choice of turning back or spending the next six hours flying the heavy aircraft manually. I knew that Andy was unlikely to turn back. His motto was, "Press on regardless". I lifted up the flap of his helmet and shouted into his ear, "Would you like me to take over for a while?" Andy grinned at me and nodded. He quickly left his seat and handed over control to me. I had never flown a Liberator, and in fact I had hardly flown anything at all during the last twelve months. I suppose I expected Andy to hover over me for a while and supervise my actions, but when I turned my head he was gone. It was a very dark night, with no visible horizon, and I soon realized that my limited blind-flying experience, mainly in the Link Trainer, was woefully inadequate. After a few minutes Deaky, the navigator, gave me a new course to steer. I attempted to turn onto the requested compass bearing, but overshot by a long way and had to bring the aircraft back onto the correct heading. I decided to do a few gentle right and left turns to get used to the controls. The Liberator seemed to be as stable as an ocean liner. It was completely different from anything I had flown before. I discovered that turns could be accomplished by merely using the ailerons and raising the nose slightly. The rudder controls seemed to be totally unnecessary. After twenty minutes of struggling with the beast, I was glad to hand it back to Andy.

After another attempt later, when the weather had deteriorated and we had encountered some turbulence,

I struggled to maintain the correct course for about half an hour. Suddenly a hand clapped me on the shoulder. I looked round and saw Mac, the rear gunner, who had left his turret and come up to the flight deck to complain. "I thought it was you. The bloody tail's going up and down like this," he bawled in my ear as he waved his arm. "Turbulence!" I shouted. "Get back in your bloody turret!" I decided that the most I would be able to do in an emergency, such as if Andy were to be killed or wounded, would be to keep the beast in the air long enough for the others to bale out. Landing it in the dark would certainly be completely out of the question. I often stood behind Andy as he came in on his characteristically long low landing approach after a tiring trip. Smudger, the flight engineer, read out the airspeed as the sweat kept dropping off Andy's jawbone. At the last moment before touchdown, I flopped down onto the floor of the flight deck with my back pressed up against the bulkhead.

Joining the circuit and landing in the dark was sometimes the most nerve-wracking part of a trip, especially if it was raining. Aircraft from adjacent airstrips sometimes strayed into our circuit and increased the risk of collision. Sometimes when we were on approach, and damaged aircraft with no lights appeared alarmingly in the darkness in front of us, we would have to go around the circuit again. After two or three abortive attempts to land, our nerves were in tatters. I thought it was fortunate that we had men, not girls, in the control tower, as the language used by Jock the wireless operator became ever more colourful each time a red signal from the ground stopped us from landing. The edge of the runway was dimly marked by "goose-neck" flares, which were like little galvanized metal watering-cans full of paraffin, with a lighted wick hanging out of the spouts. Goose-neck flares also marked the taxing tracks to the dispersal areas. The runway was not a safe place to linger in the dark, so Andy always turned off and sped back to the dispersal area as quickly as possible after touchdown. In the poor visibility, he usually ran over a flare or two on the way. One night one of the other pilots had the misfortune to get his sleeve caught in the throttle levers, and in consequence his Liberator swung round and the propellers chewed into another aircraft. One of our more experienced pilots, commonly known as "Trev" to the rest of us, failed to see a B17 Flying Fortress that the Americans had parked near the taxing track, and he sliced a large chunk out of its tailfin with his wingtip. There was a hell of a row about it on our squadron, and the next morning poor Trev had to go with our Commanding Officer and apologize to the American commander. Trev tendered his regrets as instructed, but to his surprise the American officer did not seem to understand what all the fuss was about, and he said, "It's no big deal, son. I'll get a replacement tail unit flown in right away." Trev remarked ruefully, "A bit of a different attitude from that of our Air Force."

One evening, a rather bewildered-looking new boy turned up at our tent. He had just arrived on the squadron and been told that there were no spare tents, so he was looking for somewhere to spend the night. "The Orderly Room Corporal told me that there might be an empty tent tomorrow, so I wonder if I can squeeze in with you lads for tonight," he said. "Yes, if you can find enough room to get your head down, come on in," I told him. We shoved our parachutes out of the way under our makeshift beds to make room for him, and watched him vainly attempting to inflate his punctured blow-up mattress. I was dreading that he would ask us the usual question, "What's it like here?" He was one of the replacements for men who were expected to be lost that night.

I was rather surprised by this new boy's pallor. The rest of us were very bronzed from the sun in Africa and Italy, and by comparison with us he looked quite sickly. He told us that he had just arrived from England, where he had been flying with a squadron of Halifaxes. We had never met anyone before who could tell us what conditions were like on the squadrons back home. As we plied him with questions, we realized that he was in for a shock. Instead of thirty operational sorties from England, he would now have to do forty with our squadron. We agreed with him that this was unfair, as we were bombing some of the same targets as the UK squadrons, such as Munich, Vienna and Milan, and although we did not mention it to him, our casualty rate was much higher. We told him he would no longer get sheets on his bed. In fact, he would not have a bed unless he managed to find some suitable material and make one himself. He would no longer get eggs and bacon for breakfast when he returned from a trip. "And another thing," I told him, "there are no pubs here and no women."

"Don't talk to me about women," he said. "Just before I left England, I got a letter from my parents to say they had taken a girl into their home because she claimed that I had made her pregnant. I wrote back to them that I am not the father of her child — she is a liar and they should have nothing to do with her. My father wrote back that I should behave like a gentleman and face up to my responsibilities. They had provided a cot, pram and baby clothes and furnished their spare room for her. They said she is such a sweet girl, they had become very fond of her and they were looking forward to the birth of their grandchild. I should not worry about anything or feel ashamed — just look after myself, get home safely and then do the decent thing — marry the girl. But, as I told my father on the phone just before I left England, I could never marry her. I know who she is, but I never had anything to do with her. I had plenty of girls, but not her. The girl wrote to me that she loved me and looks forward to me coming home. I wrote and told her that she knows full well that I am not responsible for her pregnancy, so she should leave my parents alone. Then my father phoned and said that he and my mother were very disappointed in me. The trouble is that my parents really want to believe that I am the father of the child, and I will never be able to convince them that I am not." "So it seems you have got all this aggravation without even having the pleasure of shagging her," I said. "Was she worth

157

shagging, by the way?" "Oh, yes, she is not bad looking, but I never even took her out on a date," he replied. "The biggest problem is that I got engaged to another girl just before I left England. She lives in the same town as my parents, and I am dreading her finding out about that little bitch who is living with them."

As I walked to the cookhouse with Deaky to see if we could get some supper, I prophesied, "The poor bugger will have something far worse than woman trouble in a few days." New crews were "getting the chop" after an average of only seven trips, so I felt that he stood little chance of surviving a tour of forty. The next morning our new boy and his fellow crew members inherited a tent from men who had not returned from the night's operations. They also inherited a few chattels such as a paraffin lamp and three washing bowls that the tent's previous occupants had assembled during their short time on the squadron. Most items of value had disappeared during the night. It was customary for us to tell our friends in other crews, "If I don't come back, you can have my Primus stove," or whatever other desirable article we possessed. When an aircraft was so long overdue that it was obviously not going to return to base, the survivors would hastily sort through the equipment in the missing crew's tent and collect their inheritance and anything else they fancied. When the Soviet troops on the Eastern Front advanced into Rumania, the American Air Force flew out there and collected the British and American prisoners of war from a camp near Bucharest, and we heard that one of our boys was being returned to the squadron. "The trouble is," I heard a lad saying to a fellow crew member, "I can't remember where I got this pullover, and I don't want to be wearing it when he gets back here, in case it's his."

We were warned not to take any private letters or photographs with us on operational sorties. "Even an apparently insignificant item such as an old bus ticket might be of value to the enemy if you get shot down," we were told. Of course, there were no buses in our area, but I always obediently emptied my pockets of personal possessions before boarding our aircraft, and I often found that I had inadvertently brought my small leather wallet and some Italian money with me to the airstrip. On such occasions, I sought out Sergeant Jake Hattle, a member of our ground crew, and told him, "You can keep this if I don't come back." When we returned from the trip, he invariably rushed to shove the wallet back into my hands, and I realized that he was squeamish about the thought of inheriting a dead man's property. Another ground crew man told me that whenever any aircraft that he had worked on failed to return from a trip, he was worried by the thought that he might have been responsible for some technical failure. He wondered if he had failed to do something, or if he had done something incorrectly. "I try not to get too friendly with the aircrews," he told me. "If I keep reproaching myself for crashes and casualties, I will go off my bloody head." I had already noticed the apparent reluctance of some ground crew men to associate too closely with us, but I had not realized why.

★ ★ ★

During the last half hour of each operational flight, we always packed up all our equipment so that we would be ready to jump out of the plane as soon as it was back in the dispersal area. As soon as the engines were switched off, the duty ground crew always started shouting, "Any snags? Any snags?" There had usually been some sort of technical trouble, and we would often snarl angrily, "The bloody rear guns wouldn't fire and the portable oxygen bottles were empty," or "The last bomb hung up!" The ground crew dutifully entered our complaints in the "snags book". Although Andy managed to appear unperturbed at all times, the strain of the trip often caused Jock, the wireless operator, and me to fly into fits of rage at the least provocation. A typical aggravation was the occasional delay in getting back to the domestic site. Three-ton trucks waited in the darkness of the dispersals until they had a full load of crews, and if we were the first to board an empty truck we had to wait for the next crew. If the next crew took more than a few minutes to leave their plane and board the truck, Jock flew into a dreadful rage and subjected them to a torrent of swearing, without regard to the fact that they might be of superior rank. When we arrived back at the domestic site, we waited impatiently for our turn to be debriefed in the "flight tent" marquee. While we waited, we helped ourselves to lukewarm tea out of a large billycan. We all used the same half-dozen chipped mugs. There was no water for rinsing them. When the interrogation was reaching its end, a small voice piped up as usual from the shadows behind us, "The met report?" It was the young Meteorology Officer. We loathed him. On one occasion he had told us at briefing, "We had a Spitfire over the target at four o'clock this afternoon, and the signs are that it will be a fine night." Our instructions were to bomb from 13,000 feet or below the cloud base. It was raining so hard in the target area that the powerful wipers on the clear-vision panel could not cope, and the unmarked target was almost invisible, although we had descended low enough to be in danger of blast damage from the 4,000 lb "cookies" being dropped by Wellington bombers. Some of the automatic camera photographs taken that night would show three or four railway trucks filling the whole of the photo frame. On that occasion the target was a railway marshalling yard, about five miles long and over a mile wide, and there was no doubt that my bombs hit some part of it, but bombing in bad visibility when we had been told to expect good weather always infuriated me. It was my task to make notes about the weather throughout the trip, including the altitude of the cloud base. I was never sure how anyone could accurately estimate the height of the base of clouds when flying above them in darkness. "Can I have the weather report?" came the Met Officer's pleading tones, but before I could start reading my report Jock turned on him with clenched fists and snarled, "You hadn't got a fookin' clue!" I prayed that Jock would not hit him, and by the look on the Met man's face, he was praying similarly. I often wondered why the Air Force considered it necessary for the squadrons' Met men to be commissioned officers.

161

Our man was not in command of anyone, and it would have been cheaper if he had been an ordinary airman, although if he had not outranked us he would certainly have been in greater danger of being hit when he got things wrong.

As we had already reported technical trouble to our ground crew and they had entered it in their "snags book", we did not think it necessary to cause them trouble by mentioning the subject again at debriefing. We fully realized that our survival depended, to a great extent, on the competence and diligence of our ground crew. In retrospect, I am surprised that the ground crews were able to keep so many of our clapped-out aircraft in flying condition when maintenance was carried out in the open and they sometimes had to work throughout the night in improvised lighting. Some of our second-hand Liberators had certainly seen better days before we received them. They had passed through maintenance units in North Africa after serving their time on American squadrons. A few had serious defects, such as twisted airframes, caused by high-speed stalls. Whenever we were fortunate enough to be allocated a plane in relatively decent condition, we became even more superstitious than before, and after a few trips in the same "lucky" plane we preferred to fly in the same one every time.

At the start of our operational tour, the squadron was short of aircrews, and we kept the same plane for several trips, but later our preferred aircraft was sometimes flown by new crews and shot down. The loss of what we considered to be "our aeroplane" always upset me, not least because I had made modifications to the bombing equipment, such as tying a strip of white rag onto the bomb-release switch so that I could find it in the dark if it fell among the jumble of wires under the bombsight. I also fitted a loop of white rag on the intercom switch, to allow it to dangle on my wrist so that my hand was free to scribble notes on the margin of my target map while I was bombing. The Royal Air Force did not provide us with handkerchiefs, and bits of white rag were as rare as gold dust. Another of my modifications was the use of a box to divert the fierce hot-air blower away from my face. I strongly resented the use of "our aeroplane" by other crews, especially if they were the more vulnerable new boys.

As we gained experience, our superstitions and neurotic behaviour increased enormously. A common problem was that men who flew together often had conflicting superstitions. Some men were convinced that it was bad luck to fly with dirty boots, while others in the same crew thought that flying boots should never be cleaned at all. Some men had to make sure that they had left some task unfinished, such as a book half read or a letter half written. Some men always made their improvised beds before a trip to convince themselves that they would be coming back to use them. Deaky had to wear his "lucky" shirt on every trip. I tried not to scoff at other men's superstitions, and I thought that I had none of my own. It was quite common for men to wear their pyjamas under their shirts on operational flights. I had not seen my own pyjamas since I left England. When all my kitbags caught up with me at the end of the war, the pyjamas were still in their original Marks & Spencer wrappers, just as they were when my mother bought them for me. "I can't have you going off to the war without decent pyjamas," she had told me when I left home.

I was returning from breakfast when I saw my old pal, Tob, who had shared a room with me on leave in Alexandria. When I tried to engage him in conversation, I found that he was not the giggling extrovert that I had known. Even his appearance was different. The huge black moustache, that had been the envy of the younger lads, was gone. He looked sick. His face was grey with the same sort of hangdog expression that I had seen on my friend Brock. I greeted Tob cheerfully, but he merely grunted and walked away. I began to doubt if it was really him, so I located the rest of his crew and told them. "I thought I had just spoken to my old pal, Tob, but it couldn't have been him, because he didn't seem to recognize me. Anyway, Tob had a big black moustache, so I suppose it was not him." "Oh yes, that's old Tob right enough," they informed me. "He's a very morose individual never talks to anyone." This was one of the very many drastic changes of personality due to stress that I witnessed during my time on the squadron. Sadly, Tob and his crew did not survive more than a couple of weeks after I discovered that he was on the squadron.

During every bombing run (the final run up to the target), my actions were almost automatic and my concentration was so intense that I was always able to perform my task easily, no matter how tired I had felt and regardless of distractions such as anti-aircraft fire and the sight of aircraft being shot down around us. However, after we had set course for base, my limbs became leaden and I felt exhausted. After I had given the order "Close bomb doors", I got up on my knees and looked at Deaky, who had now switched on his lamp. In the dim light, I could see tears running down his cheeks. One day he asked me, "Why do you always laugh so much as soon as you have dropped the bombs? You always turn and look at me, and then you open your mouth wide and laugh like a drain."

His question surprised me. I did not know that I laughed. After all, dropping bombs and being shot at are no laughing matter. "Do I always laugh? I suppose it must be bloody hysteria," I replied. I wondered if he realized that while I was laughing he was in tears, but I did not want to mention that. Sitting alone in darkness during long trips, I had plenty of time to consider such questions as how and why I had got myself into such a situation. I reviewed my nineteen years of past life, only about sixteen years of which I could recall clearly, and I considered the likelihood of my early and violent death. I felt sad that I would be denied such things as ordinary flying for pleasure, riding horses, learning to drive and meeting girls. I actually felt no fear of death itself, and I comforted myself with the thought that being dead would surely be no worse than never having been born. Before I was born I had not existed for millions of years, and what did it matter whether I died now or after living what was considered to be the allotted span of three score years and ten? Gone is gone — like last year's holiday, why should the date be important once it is over? After all, everybody will have to go sooner or later, so it is not a matter of either going now or living for ever.

These rather morbid thoughts did not cause me any great concern. In fact, I felt better for having quietly considered my dangerous predicament. Of course, such serious matters could not be discussed with my contemporaries. It was simply "not done", and our light-hearted apparent lack of concern about the dreadful casualty rate led those remote beings we disparagingly called "bloody earthbound penguins" and "trick cyclists" (psychiatrists) to the false and insulting conclusion that the air crews were "too foolish to appreciate the dangers". The awful possibility of my face being burned off and being blinded, like the young pilots I had seen during my ground training at Torquay, did cause me great concern, and I thought that I would far rather be killed than blinded.

I had a strong premonition that I would be wounded sooner or later, so I started to make some preparations. At night, when nobody would notice, I took to walking about with my eyes shut. After falling over the guy-ropes a couple of times, I decided to keep away from the tents. I counted the number of paces that I dared to take before opening my eyes, and then increased the distance walked each time. One evening I got a bit too daring and collided with a stationary vehicle. The impact was so violent that I thought that the vehicle had run into me, but when I opened my

166

eyes, I saw that it had no driver. After that shock, and as I had no stick, I walked with one arm extended in front of me. My next experiment was to keep my right hand in my pocket and try to do everything, including writing, with my left hand, in case my right hand should become damaged.

I did not think about the possibility of becoming a prisoner of war, until one afternoon when we were called to the flight tent to be addressed by a strange squadron leader who told us that he was a member of "A Force", which I understood to be the branch of the Special Operations Executive that concerned itself with the recovery of shot-down airmen. He started off in hectoring style: "I want you chaps to understand that it has cost ten thousand pounds to train each of you, which is a great deal of money! We are concerned that when men are shot down, they think the war will soon be over, and they make no attempt to get back and carry on flying. Well, I want to tell you that you must make a determined effort to get back. We have people in occupied territory who are able to help you, if only you will make the necessary effort to contact them."

We asked him how we would recognize such people, and if there was a password or recognition symbol. Apparently, we would not be able to recognize them, but they would certainly be able to recognize us. He continued, "If you get captured, especially if you have landed by parachute, you should pretend that you have injured your legs, and then the guards will not be so vigilant. If they take you by train, ask to go to the toilet and then get out through the window." We thought that

167

escaping from moving trains was only for film stars, and we wondered if we were supposed to ask the Germans to stop the train first. "At all events," he continued, "limp and act as though you are in pain, and the guards will not watch you so closely; and then, when you get the opportunity, run like hell! Of course, it is best not to fall into the hands of the enemy at all, but to become what we call evaders. To evade capture you may need to get hold of some civilian clothes, but remember that if you are not in uniform you should retain a minimum of two military buttons, otherwise you can be shot as spies." It then occurred to me that very few of us possessed any such buttons.

He continued, "Another thing you must remember is that while you are an evader you must never betray yourself by whistling, because you probably only know English tunes. When you smoke, you should be careful to hold the cigarette like they do on the Continent, with the finger and thumb, not between two fingers in the English manner. By the look of you lot, you are not likely to betray yourselves by an upright military bearing. Another thing you should know is that men in the Balkans only shave on Sundays. You will not be likely to evade capture very long without help from someone, but it's obvious that you should not approach young people, who are likely to be Nazi sympathizers. It's best to try to get help from elderly clergymen or from other people old enough to remember the futility of war."

That phrase, "futility of war", made an indelible impression on me. I never expected anyone to mention such a thing at that time, and none of us would have dared to use such words. The government had introduced a multitude of wartime regulations, and I thought that to say war was futile might be regarded as the forbidden act known as "spreading alarm and despondency". "The sort of people who will be most likely to help you are prostitutes," he told us, "because prostitutes usually dislike the police and such people; so remember, prostitutes are a good bet!" We tittered at this advice. Most of us had not spoken to a female for many months, and very few of us had any experience of prostitutes. "Well that's one use for our escape money," I heard somebody whisper.

Before every trip, we were handed a waterproof escape kit containing American dollars, which we were forbidden to open unless we were shot down. We had to hand the money back after each trip. After the war, I read that the escape money was fake. The coloured seals on the notes were said to be the wrong colour, and people in possession of them were interrogated after the war in attempts to trace the bodies of missing airmen.

The squadron leader, noticing that we had started a light-hearted discussion among ourselves about prostitutes and escape money, recaptured our attention by continuing, "Always take your revolvers with you, especially when flying over Yugoslavia, because death is preferable to capture by the Ustase." We were shocked to hear that we were being advised to shoot ourselves. He went on to explain, "The Ustase are armed groups who were trained and commanded by German officers to fight against Marshal Tito's partisans, but they have become so badly out of control that the German commanders have been withdrawn and the Ustase are now mainly engaged in terrorizing the civil population. You will know if you are in the vicinity of the Ustase by the evidence of their atrocities, which includes women's breasts being hacked off and their hands being shoved into the cavities. If you see columns of prisoners with German guards, do not join them. The Germans have nowhere to accommodate them. They will be taking them to be shot!"

As we flew over Yugoslavia almost every night en route to our targets, we did not welcome this information about the hazards that awaited us in that country. "But be assured that we have people everywhere who can help you to get back," he went on brightly. "For example, we recently discovered a weak link in an escape chain operating in Rumania. A one-legged woman was taking in Allied airmen and hiding them in her flat in Bucharest, but they disappeared after a while and were not passed on to the next stage in the escape system, so we sent a man over to kill her. We have just got confirmation that he has successfully accomplished his mission and is on his way back, but he has got dysentery, so he is really on the run."

We asked, "If you have got people over there, why can't you give them some sort of identification, so we will know they are genuine?" "No, that's not possible," he told us, "but if you come down in northern Italy, you should beware if you are approached by an Italian corporal who offers to get you through the (front) line in exchange for money. If you go with him alone, he will certainly hand you over to the Germans, so only go in twos. Another thing to remember is that our marine commandos go ashore at isolated locations in northern Italy about midnight once each month during the full moon. They run through the fields and grab anyone they come across. If they miss you, wait in the same place until the next month."

The lecture was terminated when it was time for Red Smythe to brief us for another flight across Yugoslavia. As I prepared my flying-kit, I examined my revolver. I had never fired this one. It was a Colt 45. I looked at the huge hole in the barrel. I did not think I could shoot myself, and I doubted if I would be able to defend myself with it against people who would probably be armed with rifles, so I shoved it back into my kitbag and never took it with me in the air.

The day after the lecture, we looked at the battle order at noon, and saw that we were scheduled to fly again that night. Briefing was to be at four o'clock, so we had nothing much to do for the next couple of hours. Somebody suggested that we could pass the time by playing with our guns — "get some target practice in". I watched as a lad tipped the contents of his kitbag out on the ground between the tents and picked up a revolver. He jumped backwards as the gun fired. Apparently, he had not known that it was loaded and cocked. Fortunately, it was not pointing in my direction. "What are we going to use for targets?" someone asked. "I know! There's a load of empty tins near the kitchen, I'll fetch them." The targets arrived and were lined up along the top of a drystone wall a few yards from the tent lines. We sat on the ground and started shooting at them. Within a short time, a runner arrived with a message from the Commanding Officer. He breathlessly explained, "The CO says that you should appoint a safety officer." We asked him what that meant. "The CO said that one of you should wear a cap and be in charge," he told us. I looked around for the clown who had accidentally discharged the revolver. I noticed that he was not participating in the target practice. "Hey, mush, go and fetch your cap!" I shouted.

After dropping the bombs that night, I gave the usual order, "Close bomb-doors," and then crawled back under the flight deck and stood up in the well. It was the task of Jock, the wireless operator, to open and close the bomb-doors, but this time I saw that they were still open. Jock pulled up the side of my leather flying-helmet and shouted in my ear as he flashed his torch along the bomb-bay, "There's a hang-up — the last one, right at the back!" In the Liberator, the bombs were hung in horizontal and vertical rows on either side of a nine-inch aluminium catwalk, and it was not unusual for the last one to fail to fall off. I knew that the thousand-pound bomb was armed, and as the solenoid unit had fired, it was likely to drop off at any moment; in theory it should have already done so. I clapped my hand on Andy's shoulder and bawled in his ear, "We've got a hang-up — waggle your wings and try to shake it off!" For the next five minutes, Andy did his best, but the bomb refused to budge. The only thing to do was to walk along the narrow catwalk and try to kick the thing off. The space between the upright supports was too narrow to allow me to wear my parachute pack, and I could not carry it because I needed to use both hands to hold on to the flimsy overhead pipes. As I made my way along the slippery catwalk, the force of the slipstream made me almost weightless, and I had difficulty in maintaining my footing. Faint lights twinkled on the ground three miles below me, and I realized that if I slipped I would have no chance of survival. Jock, crouching in the well of the flight deck, continued to shine his dim torch on the bomb. I cursed the fools who had made us put brown paper inside the glass — "so the Germans won't be able to see the light".

As I reached the back of the bomb-bay, I could just see a faint message to the Germans that had been chalked on the bomb by the ground crew — probably addressed to Hitler. I held on tight to the overhead pipes. My fingers and wrists seemed to have turned to jelly. I stood on one leg and kicked at the bomb. It seemed to be stuck solid. We could not take it back to base and land with it on. I had to get rid of it somehow. I began to wish that I had told Andy to stop waggling the wings, as I now hung from the pipes and kicked at the bomb with both feet for what seemed like an eternity. At first, nothing happened and then suddenly it went. I felt as though my stomach had dropped away with it, and I was left hanging precariously from the pipes. My fingers seemed to have lost all feeling, as I somehow managed to get my feet back onto the catwalk. Jock closed the bomb-doors, and I made my way on wobbly legs to the flight deck to report to Andy.

The next time we had a hang-up, we were over Budapest. I was reluctant to repeat the dreadful journey along the catwalk, so this time I remained beside Jock on the edge of the flight deck for a while, hoping that Andy's efforts to shake the bomb off would succeed. No such luck! As I moved to climb down onto the catwalk, Jock shouted in my ear, "Do you want me to go?" I would have given anything not to have to go along that narrow catwalk again, but if he had fallen to his death I knew that I could not have lived in the knowledge that it should have been me.

When we were back at base, Reg could not find his parachute pack. He had left it on the flight deck, but now it was not there. Jock reminded me that when I got down onto the catwalk, something had bumped down and bounced away into the darkness. It was, of course, Reg's parachute. "Well, Reg, all the girls around Budapest will have silk knickers now," Jock told him.

We wanted to keep the intercom clear to allow the gunners to give instructions to Andy to take evasive action in the event of an attack by fighters. The rest of us communicated by shouting above the deafening noise of the engines, directly into each other's ears, although we rarely said more than a dozen words while we were in the air. The gunners spent most trips in lonely isolation, not knowing where we were or if things were going according to plan.

The next time we had a hang-up, and while Andy was trying to shake it off, Reg started to try to climb down out of the mid-upper turret. He could not get down because I was on the flight deck below him, hoping that I would not have to go along the catwalk again. As Reg's boots clattered around my ears, I reached up and thumped him in the crutch to indicate that he should stay in the turret. After we were safely back on the ground at Amendola, I asked him why he had tried to get out of the turret without permission. He explained that he had been alarmed by the aircraft's violent manoeuvres, and when he looked down between his legs he saw that the bomb-doors were open and shadowy figures appeared to be moving down off the flight deck. "I thought you were baling out without telling me," was his plaintive explanation.

During the run-up to the target I was the only one allowed to speak. Even if fighters attacked us, we dared not take evasive action. We were in a concentration of about eighty aircraft, and if we did not maintain a steady course we might collide with one of them. During the bombing run, we were like sitting ducks. The proximity of other aircraft was particularly alarming on full-moon nights. On one such occasion, I could see a Liberator a couple of hundred yards away on our right-hand side, flying at the same height as us. In the bright moonlight, I could clearly read the identification letter on the side of the fuselage. The time came when I had to give Andy a correction to the right, and I knew that the air bomber in the other plane must be also about to move over to the right. As I spoke on the intercom, "Steady — steady — right," I heard Reg's voice shout a warning, "There's a Lib very close on the starboard side!" I ignored the warning, as I knew that the pilot of the other plane, sitting on the left of his aircraft, would have seen us and would correct to the right to avoid a collision, even if his air bomber was a bit slow in giving him the necessary instruction. I continued to instruct Andy, "Right — steady, steady — steady," and as he responded, I saw the other plane move to the right, as expected. Just before take-off for our next trip, I turned to Reg. "Let's have a deathly bloody hush on the bombing run tonight, Reg." He replied, "I'm sorry about that. It was so close and I thought you hadn't seen it."

With so many aircraft over the target at the same time, we must have had quite a few near-misses on nights when there was no moon, but, of course, we did not know about them. I had quite a shock one night when I was just about to press the bomb-release tit and a twin-engined aircraft flashed underneath us, going in the opposite direction. It was silhouetted against the fires on the ground, and I guessed it was no more than about twenty feet below us. As our combined speed was at least six miles a minute, I had no time to recognize the type, but it was probably a German Me 110. If it had appeared a fraction of a second later, my stick of bombs would certainly have hit it. Targets were usually defended either by fighter planes or anti-aircraft cannon, but not both at the same time. Occasionally, we found that enemy fighter pilots were daring to risk not only the chance of being shot down over the target by their own defences, but also the even greater danger of colliding with our bombers.

During my weekly visits to the NAAFI in Foggia, I met more of the lads who had trained with me in South Africa and were either serving on the numerous Wellington squadrons in the area or on the two Liberator squadrons (31 and 34 SAAF). One afternoon, as I looked around the NAAFI for familiar faces, I was particularly glad to see my old friend "Jobbo", who was now a navigator on 70 Squadron. Jobbo proudly announced that he and his crew had acquired a Jeep from some American servicemen. "We got one of our fitters to blot out the American insignia and paint an RAF roundel on the bonnet instead," he told me, "and we have had some new number-plates made up with the same number as the Commanding Officer's fifteen-hundredweight truck, so it's no problem for us to get petrol."

The next time I saw Jobbo, he told me how he and his crew had recently driven several miles out to the coast and found a little village wine bar. After drinking several bottles of wine, they were trying to walk a white line to assess their ability to drive back to the squadron, when several Royal Navy men arrived and joined in the fun. As the sailors' money was becoming exhausted, one of them enquired, "Who owns that Jeep outside?" "It's ours. Why do you want to know?" replied Jobbo warily. He was hoping that the sailors were not about to cause trouble. "Well, the thing is, we're a bit short of cash and we have a Jeep parked outside, too, and we wondered if you would like to buy it off us." A deal was quickly done, and for the equivalent of about five pounds in Italian money Jobbo's pilot acquired his personal Jeep, which became his pride and joy. On one occasion, the Jeep broke down and the British military police helped to get it started. They probably thought that the vehicle belonged to one of the squadron commanders who obtained their Jeeps from the Americans in exchange for half a dozen bottles of Scotch whisky. I assumed that the whisky must have been diverted from stocks intended for the sergeants' mess, as I thought it was unlikely that any one person would have been entitled to half a dozen bottles of such a rare commodity. When Jobbo's crew were eventually posted back to the Middle East, their pilot announced that his Jeep must accompany him on the troopship, or he would not travel. During the ensuing argument with the transport officer, it was discovered that the Royal Air Force in Italy did not actually own any Jeeps, and the vehicle was promptly confiscated.

Until shortly before I arrived on the squadron, flying crews were offered a small tot of rum out of a stone jug while they waited to be interrogated after night-bombing trips. When the front line moved further north the rum ration was discontinued on the grounds that we were no longer in a combat area. "At debriefing there was usually more rum in the Squadron Padre than in the stone jug," remarked Peter Green, a senior crewman. I never encountered the Padre during my time on the squadron, so I presumed that he disappeared at the same time as the rum ration.

Alcohol was usually available in limited quantities in the sergeant's mess, but we did not drink if we were likely to be flying within the next twenty-four hours. On occasions when casualties had been particularly heavy and a "Group Stand-Down" had been announced we declared a "free night" in the mess, and most of us drank ourselves silly — there was really very little else to do on the domestic site during a stand-down. In the primitive shack that answered as the sergeants' mess, with its dusty earth floor, we passed the time, between drinks, by singing rude songs and engaging in rough horseplay.

To my surprise, the Squadron Medical Officer invariably turned up in the mess during a free night. He drank very little, and it was a long time before I discovered the reason for his presence in such drunken company. Apparently, he had been instructed by the Air Ministry to observe the effects of stress on flying men, and to submit a monthly report. He had no difficulty in observing the aircrew officers at close quarters, as he associated with them at mealtimes in the cowshed that they used as their mess, but he rarely had an opportunity to get to know the sergeants, except during our free nights. On our makeshift bar stood a huge tin of evil-smelling anti-mosquito ointment that we rarely used for its proper purpose because it stank so dreadfully and was very difficult to wash off. During the course of the evening, it was usual for some of us to grab an unsuspecting new boy, wrestle him to the ground, drag off his trousers and smother his genitals in a handful of stinking mosquito ointment. The hapless victim fought furiously in defence of his "works", and the harder he fought, the better the sport. Late one night the word went around, "Grab the Doc!" The Medical Officer was quickly overpowered, but to everyone's disappointment, he put up not the slightest resistance when his trousers were being stripped off. Instead of fighting back, as he was expected to do while the dreadful ointment was being slapped on, he collapsed like a dead lettuce. The Doc knew that resistance was futile. He had seen it all before, so he quietly accepted the inevitable and we were denied our anticipated sport. Such an anticlimax! The Doc subsequently wrote in his diary, "Late at night I have experienced great difficulty in attempting to leave the sergeants' mess with any semblance of dignity."

On free nights, we drank whisky until there was none left, and then we unwisely switched to vermouth, vino or Strega. We were not the most experienced drinkers in the world, but we were certainly some of the most fearless. The immediate consequence of a free night in the mess was a phenomenon commonly known as "honking your ring up", followed by a three-day headache and a resolve never to do that again.

On one occasion, a quantity of cans of meat and vegetable stew appeared on sale in the mess. We bought a few cans, and on a night when we were not flying we collected bits of wood for a bonfire, opened the cans and stood them in the embers to heat up. The next morning, one of the new boys approached and asked me, "What were the lads eating around the bonfire last night?" I told him what it was and advised him to nip over to the mess and buy a couple of cans if there were any left. That evening the new boy joined half a dozen of us as we sat on the ground around the fire waiting for our cans of stew to heat up. Suddenly there was an almighty explosion and lumps of burning wood flew up into the sky. We all took to our heels, thinking that some explosive material, such as a photoflash, or a detonator, had been mixed up with the firewood. We eventually realized that the silly new boy had placed his can of stew in the fire unopened. All our open cans of stew were ruined by ash, and the night air was soon filled with appropriately obscene words. Needless to say, the culprit did not linger long enough to experience the full force of our wrath.

Early one evening, I was in the tent assembling my flying-kit and preparing to depart to the airstrip, when a three-ton truck arrived with the estimated number of replacements for those of us who would not survive the night's operation. Guided by past experience, the authorities were usually fairly accurate in their estimate of casualties. We never spoke to the replacements, and hardly spared them a glance. It seemed tactless for them to appear at the domestic site just as we were leaving — perhaps for ever. As the new boys climbed out of the truck, a shout rang out, "Jim! Hey, Jim, are you there? Jimmy Auton, are you there?" It was Johnnie, the "typical fighter pilot", who was such a brilliant bomb aimer that he had been kept back for a few months as an instructor when he finished his training. "Come on into the tent and let's have a quick chat, I'm leaving in a few minutes, so I haven't much time," I told him, as I continued stuffing my escape kit and emergency food pack into my pockets. "How many trips have you done? Is young Blondie on this squadron?" A spate of excited questions proved how thrilled he was to be on an operational squadron at last. He was still the same fast-talking lad — full of typical Cockney humour, but as we talked I became aware of how much I had changed since I had been on the squadron. Johnnie and I were about the same age, but I suddenly felt much older than him. He asked, "What time will you get back tonight?" "I'm not sure that I will be coming back." I did not really mean to say that, and I noticed the look of alarm on his face as he realized that I was not joking.

We were transported to the airstrip at dusk, one hour before take-off time. We had plenty of time to do our checks. I polished the smears off the clear-vision panel, tested the bombsight, loaded the magazine onto the automatic camera and prepared the smoke and flame floats. Then I looked around the dispersal for spare incendiary bombs and empty detonator containers that I would throw out en route. The detonator containers were black with coloured rings and an Air Ministry symbol. I imagined that if such apparently sinister objects were discovered in the street, the Germans would go to the trouble of diverting the traffic and treating them as explosive devices. This way of fooling the enemy had occurred to me when I heard unlikely stories of poisonous sweets having been dropped from German aircraft.

Mac was loading the rear guns and Deaky was sorting out his maps in the front of the aircraft. The rest of us were lying on the ground under the wings, and I was chatting to Andy: "Now when you take off tonight, raise the wheels, not the flaps!" I always said the same thing. It had become a ritual. I did not want to say it, but I felt better for saying it. The lever for the flaps was near the lever for the undercarriage, and to operate the wrong one would have been disastrous. Andy always gave me a wry grin on receipt of my impertinent reminder. Suddenly there was an almighty crashing sound. I leapt to my feet, and without looking back I sprinted as fast as my flying-boots would allow. Reg, having longer legs, was well ahead of me. I shrieked, "What's happened, Reg?" He kept going as he bawled, "All the bloody bombs have dropped off!" I stopped and looked back at the aircraft. There was nobody in sight. It seemed that the crews from all the other aircraft had followed our example and taken to their heels. I cupped my hands to my mouth, "It's OK, Reg, they can't go off!" Out of breath, we slowly returned to the dispersal and found that the entire bomb load of eight thousand-pounders and four five-hundreds had fallen into a heap on the perforated metal planking of the dispersal.

"How the hell did that happen?" I was livid. About ten minutes to take-off time. The trip would have to be aborted! Andy calmly suggested that an American ground crew might come to the rescue. He had noticed them in the distance bombing-up a B17 Flying Fortress, ready for the next day. The Americans arrived with their lifting tackle, and as they set to work on the bombs I looked for the cause of them dropping off. I stood glaring at Deaky through the nosewheel doors.

"Deaky, you must have bloody touched something," I screeched. "I've told you never to interfere with the bombing equipment! What have you touched?" Deaky calmly proceeded to pin the chart onto his table and sort out his navigation instruments. He looked innocent enough, but I knew that Deaky was a born meddler. "You have touched the emergency jettison lever. You are the only one who could have done it!" The main way in and out of the aircraft was through the bomb-doors, and I was horrified by the thought that some of us, or the ground crew, might have been killed in a silly accident. "You must have moved that jettison lever!" I persisted. "Well, I did just wiggle it a little bit," admitted Deaky meekly.

The obliging Americans managed to load all except one five-hundred-pound bomb that had suffered a squashed tail unit. We were a little late taking off, but, thanks to the Americans, the trip did not have to be aborted. For the next few days, poor Deaky was not exactly the "flavour of the month". I had to contradict the Flight Commander and other people who had heard of the incident and assumed that I was the culprit. A few weeks later, Deaky was to have a far worse experience with bombing equipment when he was asked to make up the number in another crew because their navigator was too sick to fly.

I found that I had run out of toothpaste and there was none on sale in the mess, so I decided to make some. I used my spoon to crush some chalk, and mixed it on a plate with a small piece of soap and some salt. It tasted vile, but was better than nothing. I had been trying to sharpen razor blades for several weeks by rubbing them round the inside of my enamel mug. The blades had become so blunt that shaving the top lip was too painful, and like many of the other lads I grew a moustache, and like most of the others, I did not shave at all unless I intended to go into Foggia for a shower.

One afternoon Smythe surprised us at briefing. As we sat in the flight marquee, waiting for him to disclose "the target for tonight", he began, "You chaps are probably doing more than any other branch of the armed forces to win this war." We could hardly believe our ears. Praise! What had got into him? "Yes," he continued, "you are doing a first-class job, but nobody could possibly guess from your appearance what on earth you are supposed to be. I have never come across such a motley shower in all my life. I don't care how you look while you are on the domestic site or in the air, but I cannot have you going into Foggia looking like that. Some of you are not wearing any rank badges, and I have never seen such a selection of footwear." I looked round at the others. Some of them wore grubby white roll-neck sweaters. Trev seemed to be the only one wearing a cap — he was never seen without it. It was battered and it had become so faded by the sun that it was no longer blue, but almost beige. Andy looked like a civilian. He was not wearing one single item of uniform. Deaky was wearing blue battledress with a fancy light-blue civilian shirt that he had bought in an Egyptian bazaar. I wore a purple sweater with a strange brown battledress of a style quite different from anything issued to the British Army. Some people were wearing blue battledress with open-necked khaki shirts. Others wore South African bush shirts and khaki drill slacks. To add to the variety of dress, some people had inherited odd items of clothing from Australians, New Zealanders, Canadians and South Africans who had "got the chop". Several of the officers were wearing suede desert boots, commonly known as "brothel creepers". Some wore Egyptian sandals. Smythe continued, "If I did not know that you were airmen, I would guess, from the look of you, that you were merchant seamen." One of the sergeants stood up: "Excuse me, sir, most of us arrived here with no kit except what we were wearing." "Well, there is no reason for not wearing badges of rank," said Smythe.

We had now had enough of Smythe's nonsense. He seemed to be living in a different world from the rest of us. Everybody began shouting at the same time: "We haven't got any stripes." "We have never had any stripes." "They didn't give us any tapes when we passed out, because there weren't any." "Couldn't we get some stripes from the Yanks?" "The soles of my shoes are worn right through, sir; I have nothing except my flying-boots." "I've only had my tropical kit since I left North Africa." Smythe looked quite baffled. He apparently did not know that we were so short of kit. After conferring with the Flight Commander for a few seconds he announced, "Flying-boots are only to be worn in the air, but you have my permission to wear any other form of footwear on the ground. If you have no badges of rank, chalk them on! You are not permitted to wear American chevrons." He then proceeded to conduct the briefing.

The subject of our appearance was never mentioned to us again, and as we had no alternative, we continued to dress like merchant seamen. I never saw anyone with stripes chalked on his sleeve. A few days later, I met Titch in the Foggia NAAFI. He looked quite comical in brown boots and khaki shorts, a blue shirt and a South African peaked cap without a badge. He had always been a little weird in his appearance. When we were at Bombing and Gunnery School in South Africa, he went through a spell of wearing a sun helmet back to front to shield his fair complexion. In the barrack hut his bed had been next to mine, and I noticed that he kept a framed photograph of a girl on his locker. Some of the other lads used to scoff at him for taking no interest in the local girls and spending so much time writing to the girl who was supposed to be waiting for him to return to England and marry her. "Come on down town with us," they urged him. "It's not good for you to stay in camp every night. We are going to have a few drinks at the Clarendon and then sort the pigs out at the Town Hall dance." At that time, it had been customary for us to refer humorously to all girls as "pigs", although such a word was certainly not appropriate to any of the desirable South African girls whom I encountered. But Titch was implacable in his resolve to remain true to his fiancée, supposedly waiting faithfully in England. "The Yanks will be shagging her rotten while you are not there," we teased him.

Titch had often accompanied me when I hired horses from a woman whose husband was away in the South African army. "I have only ridden my sister's pony at home in England, so I don't think I could manage a huge horse like that," he had told the woman when she brought out two of her "military horses". "Then you had better take the Basuto ponies." And we set off across the veldt on two of the fastest creatures that I have ever encountered. As we went crashing through the bush, I lay flat to avoid low branches, and I felt a gash in the shoulder of the smart civilian shirt I had borrowed for the day from young Blondie. The shirt was ruined, and Blondie was not pleased when he saw it.

We did not have to return to the Air School until the following day, but as Titch would not have anything to do with South African girls, we stood no chance of being invited home for the night, so we went round to the Argyle Hotel. Another aircrew cadet had introduced me to the owner of the Argyle, an elderly Scottish lady who had lived most of her life in South Africa. "There was no harbour when we arrived here from the old country, so we came ashore in rowing boats," she had told me. "You are welcome to stay the night here any time, so long as you let me know before six o'clock in the afternoon, but you must promise not to speak to the other guests. You will have to share a room with a double bed. It will cost you a shilling for the two of you. You will not get a key, but you can come up the iron fire-escape round the back after the front door is locked, and if you make a noise and disturb the guests you will not be allowed to stay here again."

At six o'clock in the morning, the sun was streaming through the net curtains of the large open window. We lay on the bed planning the day's activities. It was already another scorching hot day. Titch asked me, "Have you got any cigarettes?" I replied, "There are some on the mantelpiece." Titch got off the bed and sauntered across the large room. He stood leaning nonchalantly on the mantelpiece as he lit a cigarette. He was stark naked. The door quietly opened and a young bare-footed black girl stood in the doorway, holding two cups. She barely glanced at Titch. He was transfixed with embarrassment, and to my amusement he immediately turned pink all over. The black girl shuffled into the room. As she approached the bed, she murmured, "Your coffee, boss!" I told her to put the cups on the floor beside the bed, and as she turned to go Titch became suddenly mobile — he raced across the room, hurled himself over the end of the bed and disappeared completely under the sheet. "Too late!" I guffawed. "Too late! She's seen it! She's already seen it!"

I had been pleased when I bumped into Titch in the NAAFI at Foggia. He was now attached to a Liberator squadron under South African command, and it was interesting for me to compare experiences with him when we had bombed the same targets. After he had not been seen for a couple of weeks I feared that he might have been killed, and I started to ask men from his squadron if they knew what had happened to him.

They told me that he had received a "Dear John" letter from his girl, informing him that she intended marrying somebody else. He immediately wrote back imploring her not to marry the other man, even if she was pregnant. Titch promised her that if she would wait for him to return, he would marry her and adopt the child. He was sure that if only he could get back to England quickly and talk to the girl, he would be able to convince her that she should not make the mistake of marrying the other man.

Whenever any men were grounded through sickness, Titch volunteered to take their place. In a frenzied effort to complete his forty trips in the shortest possible time, he was trying to fly every night. "He's gone off his bloody head," I was informed. Eventually, the girl wrote, informing Titch that she was not pregnant, but she had simply fallen in love with someone else. Unable to accept that he had been jilted, Titch frantically continued to volunteer to fly every time there was an opportunity. He died instantly, together with fifteen others, when two Liberators collided over Foggia after returning from a night-bombing trip. According to the official records, he had just been promoted from sergeant to pilot officer, but he probably did not know about that.

We heard that the German troops had begun to withdraw from Greece and travel back to Germany through Yugoslavia. During the German evacuation, we intensified our bombing of ports and railway marshalling yards. Our arrival over the target was timed so that the first of the bombers dropped high-explosive bombs, and they were followed up by others dropping containers of what were described to us as "phosphorus and oil bombs". The effect of this kind of attack was particularly devastating. After a short time, the fires on the ground changed from blue-green to red, and it seemed as though the very bricks of the buildings were being incinerated.

Apparently, some of the targets were being selected for us by the Yugoslav partisans, and one morning, after we had carried out a night-bombing attack on a railway marshalling yard, a report from the partisans appeared, chalked on a blackboard in the flight tent, stating how many hundreds of German soldiers had been burned to death while sitting helplessly in the trains. Although I accepted that our actions were necessary to win the war, the details of such huge losses of life made me feel distinctly uneasy.

One afternoon I was summoned to appear before the squadron's relatively elderly and somewhat eccentric Intelligence Officer, who informed me that I had been selected as the member of my crew to carry the "compass button", which looked like an ordinary Air Force brass button, but the top could be screwed off to reveal a tiny magnetic compass. "Now you must promise not to show this button to anyone, huh? Sew it onto your uniform and then, if you get shot down, remove the compass from the button and conceal it on your person, huh?" he told me. "If you get captured, it will be no good sticking it in the obvious place, up your bottom, because the Germans would be sure to investigate that straight away, huh?" I felt distinctly uneasy at the thought of the enemy investigating my rectum, and I wished he had selected somebody else to carry the compass button. This had been my first encounter with the Intelligence Officer, and I was amused by his odd habit of turning every statement into a question by the addition of "huh?", which I understood to mean, "Do you know what I'm talking about?"

I was sorely tempted to copy his habit, but decided not to risk upsetting him by my impudence, as he seemed to be a genial old fellow. I tried to question him about conditions in enemy territory, but without much success. Apparently, such information was secret. I knew that all shot-down airmen who returned through Yugoslavia with the assistance of Marshal Tito's partisans were thoroughly interrogated by British officers of the Special Operations Executive and then warned not to discuss their experiences with anyone else. It seemed to me that our authorities were needlessly obsessed with secrecy, and I wondered why we were denied access to information that would surely have been of use to us if we too were shot down. What I did learn, however, was that Yugoslav male and female partisan soldiers lived closely together, but sexual intercourse was forbidden. In the unlikely event of any partisan woman becoming pregnant, she was shot, together with the man who was thought to be responsible for the pregnancy. "You will bear that in mind, huh?"

I assured the Intelligence Officer that I would not be likely to forget such a vital piece of information. He continued, "If you get shot down and captured by the Germans, you will be sent to Oberursel near Frankfurt for interrogation. You will not be kept there very long unless you start to give them useful information. During your interrogation, they will threaten you, you will hear gunshots, and they will say that prisoners are being shot for failing to co-operate. Remember — you are only to state your name, rank and service number — nothing else. If any airman remains at Oberursel longer than three weeks, we will get to know about it and we will assume that he must be giving them other information, and he will be court-martialled after the war."

I doubted if any of the information that I possessed would be of the slightest value to the enemy. One of the most alarming reports to circulate on the squadron was that Hitler had issued a directive to the German police and military authorities that they were not to take Allied airmen into protective custody too hastily, and they were not to impede the "justifiable wrath" of the civilian population. As a result some Allied airmen were kicked and beaten to death by irate German civilians, and some were shot by the German police.

Deaky and I had only received one flying-badge each at the end of our training, and as no extra ones were obtainable we had both bought observer's badges in a bazaar during our time in Egypt. By this stage of the war observers had been replaced on heavy-bomber squadrons by navigators and air bombers, but as we had both been trained in navigating and bomb aiming we thought that observer's badges, although actually obsolete, were a good substitute for what we should have been wearing. Also, I thought that the word "Observer" might be less likely to provoke the wrath of German civilians, if we fell into their hands, than the term "Air Bomber". The Egyptian badges were actually a very poor imitation of the official RAF versions, and the one that Deaky had bought, being a rather funny shape, was laughingly referred to by others as his "flying arsehole", or as his "flying dog's chuff-box".

Andy continued to fly in clothing that did not indicate in any way that he had any connection with the Royal Air Force. My warnings, that if captured he could be shot as a spy unless he was in uniform or at least carrying a minimum of two military buttons, produced nothing more than a wry grin. Andy was imperturbable and stubborn. My meeting with the Intelligence Officer had made me start to think more seriously about what I would do if, or when, we were shot down. I wrote down all the most appropriate German words I could remember from my schooldays, and formed what I thought to be useful German phrases. I imagined that I might be able to evade capture by pretending to be a German-speaking Belgian or Dutch worker. I did not realize that such people needed identification documents, and it was not until long after the war that I realized how ill prepared we had been for evading capture.

CHAPTER
SEVEN

Supplies for Warsaw

About 4 o'clock one afternoon, we were in the middle of a briefing for the night's bombing trip. Suddenly the start of a violent thunderstorm reminded us all that the end flaps and sides of our tents had been left open. Without a moment's hesitation, we all quickly scrambled out of the flight marquee and raced back to the tent lines. The storm was so violent that the tents were in danger of being blown away. I grabbed the flaps at one end of the tent and was almost lifted off my feet as I fought to lash them shut. As I struggled with the flaps, I became aware that I was standing on a couple of Deaky's neatly folded shirts that had been blown off his bed. The shirts were now covered in my muddy footprints, and as I threw them back on the bed, I noticed that the water seeping through the roof of the tent was stained brown by what had been a thick layer of dust. By this time, we were all soaked to the skin, so we hastily stripped off, grabbed our soap and ran around the tent lines whooping as we washed ourselves in the bitterly cold thunder rain. The sight of dozens of naked men racing about in the open reminded me of how uninhibited we had become since the early days, when men had shyly removed their trousers when preparing for bed, and modestly kept their long shirts on until they had put on their pyjama trousers.

After drying ourselves and changing our clothes, we returned to the flight tent, and Smythe resumed the briefing: "Gentlemen, the target for tonight — another enemy aerodrome in Hungary." We breathed a sigh of relief — not the dreaded Ploesti oil refineries again, and not mining the Danube. The squadron had lost aircraft on both during the previous week.

I later found that rainwater running off my cardboard bed had partially filled one of my flying-boots. There were no facilities available on the squadron for drying clothing and bedding, so I hoped that the next day would be fine, if we lived to see it. We encountered enemy fighters over the target and I saw one of our aircraft shot down, but we were not attacked ourselves.

After debriefing in the early hours of the next morning, I collected my eating irons and aluminium plates from under my bed and wandered off for breakfast. A few weeks previously, a stray bitch had produced a litter of puppies, and one of them, perhaps sensing that I was fond of dogs, had attached itself to me. I saved a little food on my plate each mealtime and shoved it under the bed when I returned to the tent. The puppy always licked the plate so thoroughly clean that I invariably ate my breakfast the next day before I remembered that I had not washed the plate. It was always a great pleasure to find my little Italian dog waiting to greet me each time I returned from a trip.

He was a sort of Labrador-type puppy with lots of soft, loose skin, and we spent many happy hours playing games that he invented. The thing he never tired of was to be thrown up the outside of the sloping tent roof and then to come sliding down stiff-legged. He would always bark excitedly and immediately ask for the procedure to be repeated. Our game certainly did not do the tent roof any good, but his presence was a continual source of amusement and relaxation for me during the most stressful period of my life.

I had been in bed for barely three hours when a runner arrived at the tent flap with the unwelcome news that we were all required to return to the airstrip for a "special secret operation". With nine other crews, we were instructed to fly south to Brindisi — about one hour's flying time away. We had no idea what the special operation was to be. When we landed, about 10.30 in the morning, we found that all the Liberator heavy bombers of the three squadrons in our group were flying in to join us in Brindisi. We climbed into an open three-ton truck with another crew, and I was immediately greeted enthusiastically by "Appy Steve", who had trained with me in South Africa. Appy had always been a very quiet, serious lad and not particularly sociable, but now he became almost boisterous as he cheerfully chatted as though he had found a long-lost friend. The strain of operational flying had certainly had an unusual effect on his hitherto rather gloomy personality.

As we made our way to a wooden hut where we were to be briefed for the special operation, neither of us could have guessed that Appy and his crew would be making a dramatic one-way trip that none of them would ever be able to forget. On entering the briefing room, we saw a huge map on the wall. A pink tape extending from Brindisi to Warsaw caused some mild speculation, but we assumed that it had nothing to do with our special operation. After all, we were heavy-bomber squadrons. We knew that we could not carry any worthwhile bomb-loads to such a distant target. Anyway, the Poles were on our side, so we would not be likely to bomb their capital city. Some joker had pinned up the tape just to fool us, no doubt.

With so many crews present in the room, it was very crowded, and as most of us were smoking, the air was becoming rather foul. We opened some windows, and while we waited, we chatted to old chums from other squadrons. The first question was, "How many trips have you done?" or "Have you been to Ploesti yet?" Eventually an unknown Royal Air Force officer stepped onto a low dais in front of the map, called us to order and quietly disclosed the nature of the special operation. "Tonight you will not be dropping bombs. Each aircraft will carry twelve special parachute containers to be dropped from a maximum altitude of six hundred feet. The dropping zones will be in various specified streets and squares in the city of Warsaw. Each crew will be given details of their particular zone. The contents of the containers will be mainly small arms and ammunition for the Polish underground resistance people who are fighting against the Germans in parts of the city. To ensure accuracy your height of release of the containers must be not more than six hundred feet. To prevent the parachutes being torn off the containers it will be necessary for you to lower your undercarriage and flaps and fly at just above stalling speed. Bombsights will be removed from the aircraft for this operation, as they will not be needed. Take-off will commence at 19.30 hours. Pilots, navigators and air bombers will be briefed in greater detail immediately after this general briefing, and then you will get something to eat. Meanwhile I will now hand you over to a Polish officer who wants to give you some further information."

In profound silence, a Polish pilot moved to the centre of the dais. With a most solemn expression on his face, he commenced to address us in fractured English: "Since thirteen days — these people they fight — if you will not help them — they die." He then went on to explain that since the first of August the Polish Armia Krajowa, the Secret Army of the Interior, had been fighting against the German troops in Warsaw, and after some initial success they had now become desperately short of supplies. We learned that No. 148 Special Duty Squadron and the Polish 1586 Special Duty Flight, operating from Brindisi, had both been making frequent trips to Warsaw and other parts of Poland during the past weeks. A greater effort was urgently required, and that was the reason why the bomber squadrons of 205 Group had now been called upon to help. What he failed to tell us was that both of the SD units had recently sustained unbelievably high casualty rates. His voice cracked with emotion as he described the desperate plight of the people of Warsaw who were counting on our support. From the way he talked — earnestly appealing to us to help his compatriots — it seemed as though he regarded us as volunteers who had some choice in the matter, but we all knew that, as in the case of every flight, we would have to do whatever we were instructed to do. We had no alternative. We gathered that he had made several supply-dropping trips to Poland, and he advised us that we would be safer if we flew over the city at between one hundred and two hundred feet, as the enemy would then have difficulty in bringing the anti-aircraft guns to bear on us. He continued, "But be remembering that the Warsaw skyscraper, the Prudential building, still stands and it has height of sixty metres." I could hear my friends making quick calculations. "Shit! In the dark we'll crash into the bloody thing if we go below two hundred feet," someone murmured behind me. "This sounds a fuckin' sight more hairy than mining the Danube."

I sensed that none of us had any particular enthusiasm for this special operation. We had never before had any contact with the Poles, and we knew very little about their country. The majority of us had still been schoolboys in September 1939 when Prime Minister Neville Chamberlain made his sombre radio announcement that the German government had not heeded a British ultimatum — they had not stopped their attack on Poland, and consequently we were at war. In 1939, the British public's general enthusiasm for the war seemed to be based on a strong anti-German attitude left over from the previous war, rather than a desire to help the Polish people, who were now mixed up in our minds with the oppressed Czechs, Greeks, Dutch, Belgians and a host of other foreigners. The outstanding gallantry of Polish pilots during the Battle of Britain had been eclipsed by other factors, and we knew little of it at the time. In due course, our attitude to the Poles would change from indifference to sympathy and admiration, but for the moment the impending special operation was merely one more step towards the end of our time on the squadron.

The briefing concluded with the alarming information that we would be flying part of the time over Soviet-occupied territory, and that the Russian front-line troops would certainly shoot us if we fell into their hands. "It is safer to be wearing khaki. In blue, you could be mistaken for German airmen. If your aircraft are damaged you must not on any account try to fly eastward and land in the Ukraine." I was glad that I was wearing my strange brown battledress. The rest of us were dressed in our usual variety of "merchant seaman's garb". One man looked as though he was more suitably dressed for a day at the beach than a flight to Warsaw. Peter Green had got up early in the morning and slipped away from the domestic site for a quick trip into Foggia, where he had left some shirts to be washed by the Italians. Although he was aware that nobody was permitted to leave the domestic site until after the battle order was posted on the notice-board, he thought he would not be missed and he would be back before nine o'clock. He arrived back on the site to find, to his consternation, that the rest of us had already left for the Amendola airstrip and the unexpected special operation. By the time he caught up with the rest of his crew, another man had been found to replace him.

The Commanding Officer, Smythe, who happened to be at the airstrip, announced that Peter could take the other man's flying helmet and parachute and fly in the clothing that he was wearing — flip-flop sandals, tropical shirt and shorts — or be court-martialled. Although Peter did not know it at the time, Smythe had already had a man court-martialled in similar circumstances. "If I get shot down, the Germans will think I have come from Africa," observed Peter. Fortunately, for him, his position in the top turret was warmed from the hot-air blowers on the flight deck; otherwise he would have frozen to death without flying clothing.

After we had been fed, we each collected a sandwich containing rather greasy meat that we were to eat on the trip. It was the first and only time that we received "flying rations", and as we expected to be in the air for at least ten hours, we knew that we would need something more than the usual flask of cold tea, brought round by Jock on the homeward leg of each long trip.

At 19.45 hours, we took off from Brindisi's airstrip, which extended to the edge of the sea. I breathed a sigh of relief when we were up in the air. Chatting to locally based airmen, I had heard alarming tales of aircraft running off the end of the runway into the sea. "What do you know about the Polish airmen?" I had asked. "Them? They are all bloody crazy. I've been with them several times. When they get to Poland, they keep flying around flashing their landing-lights on and off to let their friends on the ground know they are there. They are all soddin' mad."

We set course across the Adriatic in bright sunshine. It would still be daylight when we crossed Yugoslavia, and during the entire trip we would have only four hours of darkness. I sorted out my topographical maps and then looked around the plane. It was a fairly recent arrival on the squadron and had been flown on the three previous nights by a pilot named Thyer. I wondered if it had been thoroughly checked over by the ground staff while we were at the briefing. On the way to Brindisi, I had gathered up hundreds of spent brass cartridge-cases and other junk, and thrown it all out of the beam hatches, so I knew that it had not had any maintenance during the few hours while it had been on the ground at our airstrip at Amendola. Would it get to Warsaw and back?

Halfway across the Adriatic I opened the beam hatches on the sides of the fuselage, mounted the guns on each side and then went up to the flight deck to shout in Andy's ear that I was going to test the beam guns. Andy gave me the thumbs-up and I went back through the bomb-bay, examined the supply containers and then prepared to play a trick on Mac, the tail gunner. The beam guns were operated manually, and I had discovered that, as there were no restrictor wires on them, it was possible to fire between the tailfins and the rear turret. I opened fire, and the stream of bullets passed within a couple of feet of Mac's head. In performing this trick, care had to be taken not to shoot the aircraft's tailfins off. I knew that as soon as Mac was able to get out of his turret he would be likely to take a swipe at me for startling him, but that would not be very soon. He would be confined in his dreadful turret for many hours yet.

I gathered up my maps and made my way forward into the front of the aircraft, stopping on the way to pull up the flap of Jock's helmet and shout something into his ear as he sat fiddling with the radio. I never passed Jock without him grabbing my helmet and bawling something into my ear above the deafening roar of the engines. One of his comments on a bombing trip had been, "Into der bunker vee muss go — here komm der pig dog of der RAF," and on another occasion, "Just think of the crumpet you are blowing up!" "Oh no I'm not," I shouted back, "I'm only bombing the men." Both of us would far rather have been safely tucked up with some crumpet on the ground than up in the sky being shot at all night. In the nose compartment, I greeted Deaky, who was poring over his navigation chart. "You OK?" I mouthed. He smiled and raised his thumb. I stretched out on the deck and started map-reading. I was glad that the bombsight had been removed and I had a better than usual view of the ground. With so few hours of darkness, I would be able to map-read nearly all the way to Warsaw. Every quarter of an hour, I fixed our position visually and checked it with Deaky's dead-reckoning.

The weather deteriorated as we neared the Carpathian Mountains, and then we saw planes being shot down in darkness as we reached the vicinity of Krakow. Andy immediately descended to low level, where we would be safer from attack by fighters. We were now too low for map-reading. I crawled back to the flight deck to have a word in his ear. "You are too low for me to get any pinpoints, but we should hit the River Vistula soon, and then it's a straight run up to Warsaw," I shouted. He grinned at me. He had now switched off "George" and was flying the plane manually. I realized that considerable skill and concentration were required to fly the huge plane at such a low altitude in darkness, and I hoped the radio altimeter was working accurately. We soon realized that we were flying along the front line and being shot at by both the Germans and the Russians. As the city of Warsaw came into view, I was horrified to see that it was a vast sea of flames and smoke. I compared the black lines of the main streets with my map, but could recognize nothing. I was angry. They had not told us that the place would be on fire. I asked Andy to gain height so that I would get a better view of the complete town. I could not recognize the designated dropping-zone. We made a couple of left-hand circuits and counted the bridges to try to fix our exact position. We then flew over the centre a couple of times.

It was no use. If I tried to guess the position of the dropping zone, the valuable supplies might land in the fires. We now had the bomb-doors open, and we could smell the smoke from the flaming city. As we continued to fly back and forth, the fires showed no sign of abating. We skirted around the perimeter of the city, and I noticed that the suburb of Zoliborz, north of the last of the bridges, was relatively clear of flames, and I remembered from the briefing that the area was in the hands of the insurgents. I guided Andy into position, and at a height of five hundred feet, with an indicated airspeed of 140mph, I released the containers into an open space. Fortunately, none of them hung up. Bomb-doors closed, wheels up. We gained a little more height, retracted the flaps and set course for base. We had been over Warsaw for fifty minutes, flying through continuous tracer flak and machine-gun bullets. How did they miss us? We saw other planes being shot down over the city. It was not until later that we learned that one of them was from our own squadron, piloted by McRae. As his aircraft exploded, one man was flung out without a parachute. He fell about two hundred feet into the soft mud of what he at first assumed to be the riverbank. He had in fact, landed on the bank of a lake in a municipal park. As he lay there, dazed by a head wound, some German soldiers rowed out in a dinghy to pick him up. As they crossed the lake, he could hear the German anti-aircraft gunners cheering when they hit another of our planes. He was the sole survivor of McRae's crew, and the British authorities needlessly informed him later that the other members could not be individually identified. They were eventually interred in a communal grave.

We headed south, dodging the enemy fighters around Krakow and climbed over the Carpathian Mountains. As we recrossed the River Danube, I reached for the topographical maps and prepared to get a visual fix by leaning out of the beam hatches. I was so tired I could scarcely keep my eyes open. Apart from a couple of hours' sleep on Sunday morning, I had been awake for two days and two nights, and now it was early on Monday morning. I called Deaky on the intercom, "Deaky, do you want a pinpoint?" "No, it's OK, we're on track," he replied. I prided myself on my map-reading capability, and normally I would have told him our position, just to show off, but in my weary condition I was content to do nothing.

It did not seem long before we appeared to be crossing the Adriatic coast. We should be back at base in about fifty minutes, I thought. Within ten minutes, Deaky's plaintive voice came over the intercom, "Jimmy, can I have a word with you?" I glanced out of the hatch. We were already over land! What the hell had gone wrong? I scrambled through the bomb-bay, crawled under the flight deck and stood up in the nose compartment. It was daylight and I could see Deaky with his mouth wide open and tears dripping off his chin. He bleated in my ear, "I don't know what country we are over." I grabbed all the topographical maps and flopped down on the deck. There was no cloud. Good visibility. It would not be long before I sorted the problem out. But to my consternation, I found that we had no maps that corresponded with the ground below us. "Let me see your log," I said. As I started to look through his dead-reckoning calculations, Deaky insisted, "I got a good pinpoint on the Danube, I don't know what's gone wrong." I checked the calculations from the Danube. In theory, we were exactly where we should have been, but when I looked out, I saw that we were obviously lost. Deaky's face was ashen. He looked totally exhausted. I crawled back under the flight deck to report to Andy. Jock was busily reassembling the radio, which had been on fire. Bits were spread out on his table. "The fookin' Gee box has packed up, too," he growled. "We're up shit creek without a paddle." I did not need to explain our predicament to Andy, it was obvious to him, but he looked as untroubled as always.

As I chatted to Andy, Smudger, the flight engineer, stood up and pushed past me to check the visual fuel gauges behind the bulkhead. "What's it look like? Are we OK?" I asked him. He shook his head: "Empty!" He tapped the gauges. "But we are still flying, how much time have we got?" Smudger was as placid as Andy. I had never seen him look worried. "When the gauges show empty there is no way of knowing. It could be just a matter of minutes." He went back to his seat and scribbled in his log. I stood behind Andy. It was five o'clock in the morning, bright sunshine — not a cloud in the sky. I tapped Andy on the shoulder and pointed down to the ground on the port side. We were about to pass near to an airfield, and aircraft with black crosses on the wings were clearly visible. Junkers 52 transport planes — no danger to us, but if we attempted to land then the airfield defences might open up on us. Peering ahead, I saw that we would very soon be heading into mountains, and I noticed in the valley below us a long straight road. I lifted the flap of Andy's helmet and shouted excitedly, "You can put down on this road — it's plenty wide enough for a landing. That's what I would do, if I were you." Andy shook his head. "I think we'll press on."

I could not believe it. We were out of fuel — lost — heading into the mountains. I half-heartedly tried to remonstrate with him, but Andy was not to be persuaded. "We'll press on," he repeated. I felt faintly sick. We cleared the mountains, passed over stretches of land and water, and then we were unexpectedly over the open sea. Andy immediately descended to about fifty feet. "Tell the others to prepare the emergency kit and get ready to ditch," he told me. I went back and told Mac to get out the emergency water supply, fishing tackle and other stuff, and then I returned to the flight deck. The sea was perfectly calm — not a ripple on the surface. The aircraft had a large rubber dinghy. We were going to be OK. We could just flop down onto the water when the engines cut out. I noticed that Jock had at last finished rebuilding the radio, and it seemed to be working. He suddenly jumped to his feet, clapped one hand to the earphone of his helmet, gesticulated and jabbered excitedly. I stared ahead and saw that we were flying towards the coast — a runway — by coincidence it was Brindisi. We touched down and turned off the end of the runway. The engines spluttered and stopped. We would not have had enough fuel to fly round the circuit if the runway had not been clear. Safe at last. We had been in the air for eleven hours and forty minutes.

Wearily, we climbed up the steps of the control tower and told the Duty Pilot who we were. A bowser was sent out to refuel the aircraft, and we flew back to Amendola, where our interrogation was carried out in record time, as we were the last crew to return.

We tried to eat something before we flopped down on our makeshift beds. After a night off, we were briefed to fly to Warsaw again, but this time the containers were prepared at Amendola, and our dropping-zone was in the woods on the outskirts of the city. In the absence of fires, it was not difficult to find the dropping-zone, and as we swooped in low through a hail of machine-gun bullets. I thought, it would only take one single shot in the head to kill me.

Remembering the Polish pilot's advice, we descended to just above the treetops as we approached the clearing in the woods where I had to release the supplies. To my surprise, a lone soldier stood swinging a lantern from side to side. If I had known him, I could have recognized him — we were so close. I later discovered that his companions had wisely remained safely out of sight beneath the trees. By the time we returned to Amendola, we had lost so many aircraft that a group stand-down was declared, and we had a few days on the ground. One afternoon, we and the other survivors were transported to No. 240 Wing Headquarters a short distance away, and there we assembled in a marquee. Nobody knew why we were there until an officer with a walking-stick hobbled into the tent and introduced himself — Air Marshal Sir John Slessor — the Air Officer Commanding-in-Chief — the most senior Royal Air Force man in Italy. We were interested to see that he wore pilot's wings, and we listened intently to what he had to say. "In view of the very high casualty rate, I feel that I should explain why these operations were carried out in support of the Warsaw Uprising. The Prime Minister, Winston Churchill, has recently been here in Italy, and he said we could not stand idly by while the Poles are fighting for their liberty, because, after all, it was on their account that we entered into the war. There were no other aircraft available, and that is why the squadrons of 205 Group were called upon." He appeared to be slightly tearful as he went on to express his regret for the extraordinarily high casualty rate. I felt distinctly embarrassed by his obvious sincerity. We were not accustomed to any such display of compassion. Not one of us spoke; we stood there in sullen silence until he left the tent. The incident was not discussed. We had other concerns.

As the days passed, the full horrors of the Warsaw operations began to emerge. The Polish flight had lost 160 per cent of its established strength. No. 148 RAF Squadron had been reduced to only one officer pilot, and the Liberator squadron under South African command had sustained appalling casualties after two nights' operations. Of our aircraft that had reached Poland, ninety per cent had been shot down and others had returned with dead and injured men on board. We had lost our Flight Commander, Squadron Leader Liversidge, and most of our most senior aircrews. Trev, being one of the most experienced survivors, was promoted to the rank of acting flight lieutenant. He was now our Flight Commander, aged twenty-two. I never saw him smile again, and I think he never left the domestic site, except when he had to fly.

Appy Steve's story was horrendous. His very experienced South African pilot had, without warning, jumped out by parachute and abandoned the rest of the crew to fend for themselves, after the plane had been badly damaged by flak over Warsaw. Luckily, the job of flight engineer was being carried out by a young South African lieutenant, Bob Burgess, who had recently qualified as a pilot, although he had never flown a Liberator. Bob struggled to keep the plane in the air, and gave the others the option of parachuting to safety. When they found that he was going to try to keep flying until daylight and then attempt an emergency landing, the others decided to stay with him in the crippled machine as it drifted, almost uncontrollably, in circles, eastwards into the Ukrainian airspace that we had all been warned not to enter. Bob had never sat in the left-hand seat or landed a four-engined plane, so the chances of survival looked extremely bleak. The plane had lost all hydraulic power — no flaps — no brakes. At daybreak, he saw a concrete runway, but it was completely unusable as it had an enormous crater in the middle. Nearby was a large ploughed field, and by a miracle Bob managed to get the huge machine down without any casualties. To his horror, he then saw that he had narrowly missed an almost invisible, rust-coloured tractor. The crew fired off red signal-cartridges, and people arrived from the nearest village

— a man mounted on a horse and armed with a sword, a lorry-load of female soldiers and then a man who had visited the United States and who assumed that the crew of the Liberator were Americans. Eventually, Bob, Appy, and the others reached the safety of the British Embassy in Moscow. Many of their friends were less fortunate, and their corpses lie in the cemeteries of Krakow, Prague, Budapest and other distant places.

Another South African pilot, Jack van Eyssen, managed to keep his burning plane in the air long enough for his crew to bale out a few miles from Warsaw. By the time he jumped out, the fire had spread to three of the engines and part of the fuselage. His top gunner, George Peaston, landed by parachute on the roof of a building occupied by Polish soldiers of the Armia Krajowa, who took him the next day to see the remains of the plane. Two men were dead in the wreckage, and another lay a few yards away with a partially opened parachute. Jack van Eyssen had landed by parachute some distance away, and immediately set off eastwards, using the Pole Star as a guide. He figured that he might reach Lublin, walking at night and hiding during the day. He lay in a ditch at the side of a road and peered at the passing trucks. Some of them were American-made vehicles and he assumed that they were driven by Russians. He was about to hail one of the trucks when a horse and cart came into view, driven by a Russian officer. He shouted and the cart stopped. Jack tried to explain in a mixture of English, Afrikaans and German that he was a South African Air Force officer. The Russian showed no interest in that. "How old are you?" he enquired. Jack told him. "You are not as old as me, why do you have grey hair?" asked the Russian as he turned the cart off the road into a field of tents. "I stop here," he said. "Goodbye." Jack would not be dismissed so easily: "No, not goodbye. I want to speak to your Commanding Officer." As the Russian dismounted from the cart Jack followed, and they both entered a tent. "Commandant!" said the Russian, pointing to a large man sitting at a table with a group of others. Jack explained who and what he was. The Russians seemed faintly interested. He then asked them for something to drink. He had not had anything to eat or drink for many hours. The Russians now produced a bottle of vodka and proposed a toast to the Red Army, followed by Marshal Stalin, Winston Churchill, President Roosevelt and Jack himself. Jack feared that he would not survive so many drinks on an empty stomach, so he pleaded for water and food. "Water not good — vodka very good!" they told him. Eventually Jack convinced them that he really did need water and it arrived in a rusty kettle and tasted awful. Then a large dark sausage appeared, with some coarse brown bread and a large knife. Jack was among friends. In a matter of weeks, he was back on his squadron in Italy after rejecting an offer of repatriation to South Africa.

CHAPTER
EIGHT

Sorrento Leave

The group stand-down was soon over. Replacement aircraft and crews arrived, and we resumed bombing of railway marshalling yards, harbours and troops. We hoped to get a few days' leave if we were to be sent to Warsaw again. Men who had survived Warsaw were now being shot down over other targets. It seemed certain that we would not reach forty trips. Talking to men in the NAAFI at Foggia, I discovered that the Warsaw flights had demoralized everyone — even the men who had not participated. I heard that a gunner on Jobbo's squadron had jumped out of the rear turret and run away from a Wellington that was about to take off. "We were partly to blame for telling him what a rotten target it was, and that we would be lucky to get back," Jobbo told me. "A few days later we discovered him in Foggia and persuaded him to come back to the squadron with us, because he had merely been declared 'absent without leave'. He had flogged all his kit, so we all scrounged some more for him. He said he had been waiting every day until the NAAFI was about to close, and then hiding in a cupboard all night. The Commanding Officer did not punish him, but then he

215

buggered off again, and this time he's been charged with 'desertion in the face of the enemy' and sentenced to ten years' penal servitude."

Young Blondie's crew had been saving up to go on leave. The money was hidden in their tent. They all knew where it was, and one of their gunners deserted and took it with him. When the rest of the crew eventually went on leave, they stopped for tea at the NAAFI in Naples. To their surprise, they came across the missing gunner. While several of them kept him talking, one slipped quietly away to fetch the military police. While he was being dragged away in handcuffs, Blondie was hitting him all the way out of the NAAFI. They would not have turned him over to the police if he had not taken their savings.

The authorities began to compel aircrew officers to attend courts martial of men who had deserted or refused to fly. Obviously, the authorities expected the witnesses to come back from the trials and alarm the rest of us with warnings about the dire consequences of desertion and refusal to obey orders, but I never met any aircrew officer who had attended a court martial and did not sympathize with the accused.

Wandering through Foggia, I came across a young aircrew officer wearing blue uniform, but without a cap. "How are you doing?" I greeted him. He replied, "I'm under close arrest." I did not know much about "Air Force Law" and the difference between open arrest and close arrest, but I told him I did not think that he would be allowed out if he was under close arrest. "Anyway, what have you done?" He replied that he had shot an American during a session in a wine bar. "What, badly?" "Yes, he's dead." "Why did you shoot him?" "Well, we had had quite a few drinks and he said something disrespectful about the British Empire, and I had my revolver in my pocket, so I shot him." "No wonder you are under arrest, but I'm surprised that you're allowed to go out into town." "Well, they haven't grounded me, I'm still flying." I presumed that the authorities, being so short of pilots, were delaying court martial proceedings until he had done his forty trips — if he survived that long.

We had not been warned that the weather would be so bad during the Warsaw flights. We heard later that half of the aircraft had turned back due to navigation difficulties and technical trouble. Both of the planes that our crew had flown were shot down on the following nights. Hailstones as big as golf balls had fallen in the Foggia area and penetrated the upper and lower surfaces of the wings of an Avro Anson that the top brass had been using as a runabout. It transpired that weather reports concerning the route to Warsaw were obtained via London, and they were always out of date.

We were now engaged in bombing to support the invasion of the south of France, and the bad weather continued. One stormy night we took a huge load of propaganda leaflets to throw out. The leaflets were secured in strong brown paper. I opened a packet and read one of the leaflets. It was in the form of a German-language newspaper, entitled *Luftpost* — Airmail. It was aimed at German soldiers in France, exhorting them to surrender and assuring them that they would be immediately transported to safety in Canada. There were illustrations of beer-drinking German soldiers sitting on the veranda of a log cabin, grinning at the camera. "Come and join us!" was the caption in German. I had broken my thumbnail opening the packet. My fingers were numb from cold. I was angry at the thought of German soldiers being offered safety and comfortable living quarters while we would be returning to our disgusting conditions on the squadron. I raised the hatch in the floor, and without opening any more of the packets I pushed them all out together. If the Germans wanted a comfortable life in Canada, they could open the packets themselves.

The next day a member of the ground staff, a leading aircraftsman, approached a group of us as we stood around the notice-board waiting for the battle order. "If any of you would like to learn Italian I can give you lessons in the afternoons when you are not flying." From his quiet, cultured manner of speaking, we knew he was a proper teacher. At every opportunity, we assembled in the flight tent for Italian lessons. No teacher has ever taught such enthusiastic pupils. We were hastily learning the language in preparation for the time when we might be lucky enough to get away on leave and practise on the Italian girls.

One afternoon our teacher advised us not to talk to local people. The only local people we ever saw, except for those in Foggia, who rarely had anything to do with us, were the old men who came down from the mountains on donkeys about once each month to sell us tomatoes, water melons and eggs. We rarely had an opportunity to talk to any Italians, but why on earth, we wondered, was he warning us against talking to local people? He then patiently explained, "It would not be advisable for you to fall into the habit of talking like them, because they do not conjugate their verbs." He did not seem to realize that our only purpose in learning the language was to communicate with girls, if we lived long enough to get away on leave. Conjugating might then be uppermost in our minds, but certainly not in relation to verbs.

Each day, as we scanned the battle order, we were dreading a repeat of the Warsaw trips. Morale on the squadrons was at a low ebb, but surprisingly our Medical Officer reported to the contrary in his official diary. Evidently, he decided to tell the higher authorities what he must have assumed that they wanted to hear. However, the commander of the South African squadron, very sensibly, made a more accurate report on the true state of his own aircrews' morale.

One morning Andy told me that our crew had been granted nine days' leave, and I quickly prepared to get away for what I feared would be the last holiday of my life. Jock and Smudger planned to make their way north to seek Smudger's brother, a sergeant in the Gordon Highlanders, somewhere in the front line. After hitch-hiking on military trucks, they were riding on an Army petrol bowser during the last stage of the journey when they casually asked the driver how far they were from the front. He replied, "We are already in the line now. The nearest German troops are on the

high ground over there." The two airmen hastily
thanked the driver for the lift and scampered away from
his hazardous load. Smudger had no accurate
information about his brother's whereabouts — he just
knew that he was somewhere in the front line that
extended across the full width of Italy. Disregarding the
sections of the line occupied by the Americans and by
the Poles, they eventually found the Gordon Highlanders and were permitted to talk to Smudger's brother for
only about half an hour. They were then told to make
themselves scarce, as the Gordons were preparing for
an attack, and they had no wish to be burdened by
"two crazy airmen who had travelled so far just to say
hello".

To our surprise, Deaky had announced that he did
not want to go on leave. He preferred to stay on the
domestic site and save money. "What are you saving
money for?" we wanted to know. "To get married to
Eunice," he replied. We knew that Eunice was his
childhood sweetheart, but would she still be available
for marriage when Deaky returned home — assuming
that he survived the war — which seemed unlikely? I
doubted it. The "Dear John" letters were arriving thick
and fast — even the married men were getting them.

Our pay was only about five pounds per week, minus
stoppages, and it was paid in "occupation currency".
The Italians were skilled forgers, and a great many
of the notes were worthless. From time to time, the
Allied authorities arranged for minute alterations to
be incorporated into the design of the notes, but
the forgers soon followed suit. Most Italians were

understandably loath to accept paper money, so most of us converted our pay into more acceptable barter goods such as cigarettes, soap, chewing-gum, chocolate and canned food, whenever such scarce items were available in the sergeants' mess. By the time we went on leave we each had a sizeable bag full of such items.

As Deaky could not be persuaded to join us, we set off without him in a three-ton truck for an overnight journey across Italy. Jock and Smudger left us as we passed through Naples, and the rest of us continued through astonishingly beautiful coastal scenery to our destination — Sorrento. After life on the desolate Foggia plain, Sorrento seemed to be the most wonderful place on earth, with sun, warm sea, wine bars and an abundance of girls. I resolved that the entire remainder of my life on earth would be crammed into nine hectic days and nights of debauchery in Sorrento, and then I would have to return to the squadron to be killed in the air. Since the Warsaw flights, I had become fully convinced that a very early death was inevitable. I had no future, so I had no worries. My fate was sealed. Nothing mattered except the immediate pursuit of pleasure. It was as though I had been granted a temporary release from a condemned cell on "Death Row".

We registered at the Minerva, a small hotel that had been commandeered by the Air Force to accommodate aircrew men on leave. I parked my few belongings on one of the multi-tiered bunks, and decided that I would not be spending any of my time there. The hotel was supervised by Alan, a young pilot officer who had been mistakenly thought by the authorities to have finished his tour of operations on a Spitfire squadron. In fact, he had only recently arrived in Italy, and had not yet served on an operational unit. Alan was quite content to wait quietly until the error came to light, as it did in due course.

My first morning in Sorrento was spent swimming in the sea and becoming easily aroused by a multitude of enticing girls who did not seem to have much on, even when they were dressed. Most of the afternoon was spent with Mac and others sitting outside a café in the main square, guzzling far too much vermouth to the non-stop sound of violins and accordions playing Neapolitan music. Meanwhile, two of our crazy lads had hired a rowing-boat and decided to row out to sea until they lost sight of "bloody Italy". When they returned to the shore some hours later they found that the boat had drifted with the current and they were several miles from their departure point, so they had a long walk back to Sorrento.

I wandered alone through the town, and was repeatedly urged by local youths to patronize places that offered "eggs a chips". Other youths were touting on behalf of females. Each approach was the same: "Hey, Joe! You like-a-fuck-a-my sister? Nice-a-girl. Nice-a-clean-a-bed!" Apparently, all Allied servicemen were called "Joe", and Sorrento was fully geared up to satisfy all their most urgent needs. I noticed a shop with the name "Prophylactic Center" neatly painted on the large fascia board. I was not familiar with the word prophylactic, so I wandered in to find out what it was all about. The jovial Italian Army corporal in charge of the place explained that it was a venereal disease clinic. He offered me a handful of condoms. I was surprised to notice that they were of Italian manufacture and each packet contained instructions for use in Italian. They had been intended for issue to Italian troops. I wondered if the Pope knew about that. The corporal chuckled, "I suppose-a-give only three. You wanna all night session, okay, I give-a-more, is okay!" He tilted his head on one side, shrugged his shoulders, and extended his hands to the side with palms upward. I understood his gesture to mean, "So what the hell — it's not my money!" I thought it would be ungracious of me to spurn such generosity. I pocketed half a dozen free condoms and went on my way.

Early in the evening, I selected the cleanest of the wine bars and settled down to practise my Italian language on the staff. Eggs, chips and a bottle of red wine were ordered from the serving girls without difficulty, but as they were too busy with their work, I then gazed around for somebody else on whom I might practise. A youth was collecting up glasses and empty bottles from the tables. As he came near me, I greeted him in Italian, and asked him a few simple questions about his name, his age and about the middle-aged couple that I could see through the open kitchen door. He immediately replied in halting English that he was Franco, the fourteen-year-old son of the house, and a keen student of English. He told me, "I wanna go in America after war finish. My uncle live much long time in America — since before war. I like talk with you now

— practise English conversation. My teacher — Italian man — not much good accent, I think." The old people were his mother and father and the family had owned a "place for make alcohol" before the war. "You mean a vineyard for growing grapes — making wine?" He shook his head: "No, not vineyard — big factory for make brandy and spirit and Champagne and things. When soldiers come — terrible — it all burnt in fighting. Family only have bar now and much work — very hard."

I told him that I would make a bargain with him: "You say everything to me in Italian and English and I will say everything in both languages to you. We can correct each other's mistakes and both learn something, OK? But first I will ask you something that I want to know — who is that pretty girl over there — talking to your parents — is she your sister?" I realized that I had consumed rather a lot of wine, but I told myself that I was not actually drunk. In my slightly befuddled state, it seemed to me that the young lady in question was the most desirable creature in the whole world — long straight black hair — olive skin — bare legs. I must talk to her. "Rosa? No, she not my sister," replied Franco, "but I tell you — one moment — I get *dizionario*."

Franco was gone for a couple of minutes. I hoped that the young woman would still be in the bar when he returned. He came back armed with a rather tattered Italian-English dictionary. "She similar like cousin," he told me. "She daughter from cousin from my uncle's wife. How you say in English?" The relationship was too complicated for me to work out. "You have a very big family. Maybe we would say in English that she is your second cousin, but I am not sure. Please go and tell Rosa that I would like to talk to her and I want to invite her to drink something with me — maybe cognac. Then you stay here and help me, if she does not understand everything." Franco shook his head slowly. "Is no possible she talk with you. She no talk with soldiers. She no go with soldiers. She say she married." I was puzzled. "She says she is married! Is she really married?" Franco shielded his mouth and whispered, "Husband — doctor on ship — ship finish — kaput — all men finish — dead. We much cry. We wear the black clothes, but Rosa no much cry — no wear the black clothes — she say, is possible he no dead — is possible he come back sometime. Rosa no like speak with other man." I could well imagine the turmoil that must have been caused when the Italian forces, defeated in the south of Italy, changed sides, while those in the north remained allied with the Germans. After the collapse of the military command structure, no doubt, it would be difficult for relatives to find out whether their men were dead or alive. "Tell me, Franco, where was the ship sunk?" Franco whispered, "Ship was in harbour at Bari. Much big explosion. Everybody know all men dead. Only Rosa say possible husband not dead — possible he come back."

I wondered if poor Rosa was unable to accept the fact that her husband was never coming back to her. Was she to live like a nun for the rest of her life? Perhaps not, if I could manage to have a word with her. I watched as Franco gave my message to Rosa. Her eyes flickered in my direction, but she made no sign of being interested in me. It had been a long day. I decided to stagger back to the Minerva and then see what the morrow brought forth.

The following day I had breakfast in the dining room. During my few days' leave I wanted to forget all about operational flying, but that proved impossible, surrounded as I was by other aircrew men — all with their own horror stories of life on the squadrons. One of the most common topics discussed was the problem of so-called "hang-ups" — bombs failing to drop off, necessitating repeated runs over the target with the consequent danger of collisions each time planes circled and rejoined the congested bomber stream. One night a crew made seven runs over the target because none of the bombs would drop off. They tried the usual waggling of the wings and other things, but they were still unable to get rid of the bombs, so they brought them all back and landed with them on — a very tricky procedure. During a period of about twenty weeks, my own squadron's crews reported that they had experienced hang-ups on fifty-nine occasions. The worst hang-ups involved mines. The ones situated at the rear of the bomb-bay were slung off centre — that is, they were not hung from their centre of gravity. If an aircraft landed with the mines on board, the aircraft's deceleration would cause the mines at the rear to tear themselves free and cartwheel down the fuselage, taking everyone and everything with them. Every air bomber's nightmare was being on the narrow catwalk in the dark, over the open bomb-doors, without oxygen or parachute, kicking at hang-ups.

Aircraft instrument failures, engine failures, gun-turret failures and problems with the oxygen supply were frequent irritations. On one occasion, over the target, our aircraft was hit by shrapnel in the reduction gear of one engine. We returned on three engines, and when we were only a few seconds from touchdown another engine on the same side unexpectedly cut out. Andy managed to land in the dark, and we all walked away from what we considered to be a good landing in the circumstances. I heard stories of replacement Halifax aircraft being flown out from England and found to be already overdue for major overhauls, so they had to be rejected due to lack of adequate local servicing facilities. Some of the Halifaxes had odd engines and worn-out tyres. There were no suitable tyres in Italy, so the crews who had brought the planes from England had to take them straight back. Some old Short Stirlings, obviously salvaged from aircraft dumps in England, were found to have grass growing in them! Others broke down and had to be abandoned on the way to Italy.

I wondered how many men were being killed due entirely to the clapped-out condition of the aircraft — not by enemy action. As we lingered over breakfast, I related an incident that had occurred one evening, just after we had taken off and were climbing up to our predetermined altitude before setting course. I was listening out on the radio as other aircraft were calling base to report technical difficulties. I heard the pilot of

227

a Wellington complain that his aircraft would not climb, and he wanted permission to land. He was instructed, "Jettison fuel until you are able to reach your operational altitude and get as far back as possible on return!" As I listened to the radio conversation, it had seemed obvious to me that the Wellington pilot and his crew were being given a death sentence. They would have to attempt to climb over the Alps to a target in France. If they had been permitted to land, the crew and the plane would certainly have survived to fly another day. "Callousness and stupidity combined with blind obedience," I muttered to myself. "Why the hell doesn't he ignore the fools on the ground — land and risk a court martial?" I knew that Gus, young Blondie's pilot, had turned back one night after his aircraft had been severely damaged by flak over Yugoslavia. On returning to base, he explained to the Commanding Officer that the damage was such that there was a possibility that the tail unit would break off, so he had turned back to save the lives of his crew. He was told severely, "You should only begin to consider the safety of your crew after you have achieved your objective — not before. You should have disregarded the damage and attempted to reach the target!"

I recalled how Jasper and his crew were taking off on their first operational trip. Their heavily overloaded Liberator managed to become airborne, but then crashed back onto the runway. The bombs wrenched themselves off their mountings and shunted forward through the fuselage, killing four of the crew who were sitting on the flight deck. Jasper and the other two survivors suffered burns, but managed to get out before the plane exploded. Nobody was blamed for the accident. Another Liberator pilot had an almost identical experience, but without fatalities, when his aircraft dropped back onto the runway after being airborne for some distance. The very next time Jasper was attempting to take off at night, in a different Liberator, the plane suffered a complete electrical failure.

Rather surprisingly, some of us, especially the pilots, expressed a liking for the Liberators, but I considered the ones we had were death traps and totally unsuitable for use as night-bombers. Nobody in authority ever mentioned to us the possible reasons for aircraft failures, and the aircrews did not usually discuss the subject, but now we were far away from the squadrons — we had time to think and we had time to compare unpleasant experiences. We knew that our Liberator squadrons were seriously short of spare parts, and even items such as nuts and bolts were scarce. We had heard that when the Liberator squadron under South African command urgently needed a welding set, a search was made among the civilians in Foggia. An Italian with a suitable outfit was eventually found, and the South Africans offered to buy it from him. He refused to accept payment in Allied occupation currency, but he agreed to let them have it in exchange for a quantity of Air Force boots. What a way to run a war! I felt sure that the German forces, or the Italians for that matter, would have commandeered whatever they needed, not bartered with the civilians. I had no doubt that the friendly American Air Force technicians at Amendola would have gladly given us, free of charge, all the spares we needed for our clapped-out Liberators, but to prevent that happening the High Commands had craftily arranged that we shared the landing strip with American B17 Fortresses, not Liberators.

After breakfast at the Minerva, I went sightseeing in the town, and discovered an Opera House where the San Carlo Opera Company was presenting *La Traviata*. I booked a seat for that evening's performance, and after spending a few hours drinking with the lads, I returned to the Minerva and smartened myself up in the civilian-style bush shirt and slacks that I had bought at a gents' outfitter in South Africa. We had been permitted to wear such good-quality kit in South Africa, and without a cap or Air Force insignia we had looked like civilians. Fortunately, my kitbags had arrived from South Africa a couple of weeks before my leave, so I no longer looked like a shipwrecked sailor. In the warmth of the Mediterranean evening, I stood outside the theatre waiting for the doors to open. I watched Italian men arriving in rather tired evening suits. The ladies wore elegant gowns that had seen better days. I was, at first, rather surprised that people had bothered to dress up in wartime, but I quickly became impressed by the civilized charm of the occasion. Inside the theatre, I saw that people were obtaining opera glasses from the cloakroom, and I decided to get some in case my seat should turn out to be too far back from the stage. To my surprise, I was handed a huge pair of what seemed like submarine commander's binoculars. It appeared that the more elegant small opera glasses were being handed only to the ladies.

When I found my seat, I realized that I would not need the binoculars, because I was in the centre of the front row of the stalls. I soon discovered that I was seated directly behind the orchestra conductor, and so close to him that I could see little of the centre of the stage until he raised his arms. I felt rather foolish, sitting there with the huge pair of binoculars on my lap, but I dared not put them on the floor for fear that they would be stolen. Waiting for the curtain to go up, I decided not to waste the money that I had paid for the hire of the binoculars, and I used them to stare at the musicians in the orchestra pit. One of the lady violinists was well worth looking at, and I wondered if I stared at her long enough, she might react favourably to my obvious interest in her. After a while, she noticed me staring at her, and after looking embarrassed at first, she soon put on a very hostile expression. During the intervals, I amused myself by using the binoculars to examine the members of the audience in the seats behind me — paying special attention to the women.

To my surprise, I discovered Rosa from the bar, sitting a few seats away from me with another attractive young woman. I observed that Rosa had also noticed me, and I wondered if I might manage to speak to her after the performance. When the two women left their seats I tried to get ahead of them in the foyer, but I lost sight of them in the crowd. Suddenly I felt a tap on my shoulder. I turned and saw the young woman who had been sitting with Rosa. "*Buona sera*," she said, "I am Maria. I am the friend of Rosa. Please, if you come with me, I take you to the apartment where Rosa lives." As I accompanied her, I asked why Rosa was not walking with us. "Maybe I will tell you later, but not now, or maybe Rosa will tell you," she replied, somewhat mysteriously. After a few minutes, we reached a typical Italian apartment block with the distinctive smell of Italian cooking — music blaring from open windows and loud voices echoing round the courtyard.

"This is where Rosa lives. My boy-friend and I have been invited for supper and Rosa wants you to make up a *quattro* — how you say — a foursome," Maria informed me. As we entered the building and climbed the concrete stairway in almost total darkness, disturbing thoughts fleetingly occurred to me. I was alone in a strange neighbourhood. Was this a trap, using the girls as bait? Perhaps the Italians were about to beat me up and rob me. When we reached the second floor, I saw Rosa and Maria's boy-friend waiting for us in the light of an open door. They greeted me in Italian and informed me that the young man, a cook by trade, had prepared the food while the girls were at the theatre. We sat down to supper immediately. I very soon decided that the way Rosa looked at me and her whole manner indicated plainly that she was not merely interested in me as a guest to make up the foursome at supper. While we sat drinking vermouth after the meal, I promised to bring, on the next occasion, some of my barter goods — cigarettes, chocolate and canned meat — to repay their hospitality. They were obviously delighted by the suggestion, and I felt pleased that I had already succeeded in "getting my feet under the table" by the second day of my leave.

It was quite late when Rosa's friends left the apartment, and she then asked me to help her to draw the large curtains in the adjoining room. She stood on a rickety chair and climbed on top of a large radio-gramophone to tug at the curtains. I quite unnecessarily warned her not to fall, and held her bare legs. As she stepped down from the chair, she tripped and fell into my arms. It had been far too long since I had been in contact with a girl, so I needed no greater invitation to spend the night with her.

After temporarily satisfying my lust, I asked her why Franco had told me she was married. She explained that pretending to have a jealous husband was her way of avoiding unwelcome advances from the multitude of inebriated Allied servicemen who visited the bar. "I'm not *stupido*, I know he's dead," she told me in a mixture of Italian and broken English. "More than one year 'usband dead and now today you here — first time another man in my bed. When Franco said me what you speak about me, I am very glad. I already notice you looking at me. I'm thinking I like you, but is no possible talking with you in the bar, so is fortunate I'm seeing you in the *teatro* this evening."

While we lay there smoking the customary post-coital cigarettes, I gazed at her beautiful nakedness and hoped she was telling me the truth. I did not relish the thought of an irate husband bursting into the room. I then asked her why she had told her friend Maria to

233

approach me, and why she had not waited and walked from the theatre together with us. She explained that girls seen with Allied servicemen were usually stopped by the Carabinieri, Italian police, and instructed to report to the police station the next day. They were then compulsorily registered as prostitutes and required to attend a venereal disease clinic every month to be examined and have their registration card stamped. "I could not risk that happening to me, so I did not want to be seen with you." I was puzzled. Why was Maria not frightened to be seen with me? I wanted to know. Rosa sighed and explained that Maria and her boy-friend had got to know some American soldiers — good boys — Italian Americans — their grandparents were originally from Naples. Maria often met them with her boy-friend, because the American boys were bringing cigarettes and tins of Spam to exchange for *vino*. One day Maria's boy-friend was too busy, working, so she went to meet them without him. The police saw her talking to them in the square and they made her register as a prostitute.

"It does not matter so much, because Maria's boy-friend knows she is not *prostituta*, but if they made me register I would lose my good — how you say *reputazione*. Sorrento is a small place. People have long memories. I would not be happy to live here after the war if they thought I was a bad woman. Now you know why I cannot be seen in the street with you."

"It must be humiliating for Maria to have to attend the clinic for examination," I suggested. "Of course," she replied, "every month she has to wait almost half a day in the clinic with terrible bad girls. She is prettier than them, and immediately after the doctor's examination the sergeant of the police always asks her to sleep with him, but she will never do it, so to punish her, because she refuses to sleep with him, he makes her wait until all the other girls have had their cards stamped before he stamps hers." I now guessed why there were said to be as many as 47,000 prostitutes in the nearby area of Naples. Most of them were probably decent, half-starved girls who had found they were able to tap a ready source of food and other scarce commodities by associating with Allied troops, and had consequently been forced by the police to register as prostitutes.

During the remainder of my time in Sorrento, I returned to the Minerva only for breakfasts, a shower and a change of clothes. My days were spent in swimming, lazing on the beach and drinking wine with the lads. Each evening I visited the bar for a meal that was invariably served with a free bottle of wine and followed by a bilingual conversation with young Franco. My ability to speak Italian was improving rapidly. In the bar, Rosa merely acknowledged me with a brief smile, but I was not allowed to show any familiarity while she was working. When she left the bar, I followed her at a discreet distance and entered the apartment, where she invariably greeted me excitedly in rapid Italian, as though we had been parted for years.

Rosa liked to speak to me in English, which she had learned entirely from books while she had been studying to be a "*farmacista*". Her English, spoken as rapidly as her Italian, was accompanied by violently expressive hand gestures. Almost every word was mispronounced, and she never used an English word if a similar-sounding Italian word existed. One night she began to talk about her husband. "Very good man — very good look," she began with a torrent of words, "but after one — maybe two time — he no make the sex; he say is *non possibile* no more. I say *perche*? Why is *non possibile*? I say he no love me. He say, sure he love me, but only is *non possibile* the sex. I very miserable."

She went on to explain that she became convinced that she must have been the one at fault. Maybe she was simply no good in bed and that was the reason why he could not perform. "Did you not sleep together before you were married?" I asked. She explained that Italian men might well sleep with numerous other women before marriage, but they usually did not sleep with the woman they intended to marry, because they liked to think that their brides were virgins. She went on to explain that after her husband's death she became anxious to find out if she really was useless as a sexual partner, but she did not want to have anything to do with local men, because "they have empty head with big mouth". She had been perfectly willing to form a temporary liaison with me, because nobody would find out about it, and if the experiment should prove to be a sexual failure, it would not be such a catastrophe as another unsatisfactory marriage. "So you have used me for a sex test," I said. She snuggled up to me: "*Si*, is good *esperimento* — is good *successo*, no?" Success it certainly was. There was definitely nothing wrong with Rosa. I felt sympathy for her unfortunate late husband. Nights in bed with the enthusiastic Rosa were both exhausting and instructive. "Now you are not always in such big hurry, I will show you how to do it in a way that is better for me," she told me. A few days later, when she announced in English, "Always my night with you is full with pleasure," I knew that her totally uninhibited tuition had not been wasted on me.

On returning to the Minerva one morning, I learned that the military police had been there in the middle of the night searching for deserters. As I was missing from my bunk, they left an instruction for me to report to an officer in the nearby Hotel Vittorio. Full of vermouth, I cheerfully reported to the officer in question at about 2 o'clock in the afternoon. He was a kindly-looking, softly spoken Scotsman, very solemn and old enough to be my father. He began in grave tones: "You were not there when the Red Caps checked on people at the Minerva last night. I suppose you were sleeping on Italian premises — with a girl, no doubt." I proudly told him that I was spending my nights with a lovely Italian girl. "She is absolutely beautiful and very sexy — a young widow — twenty-five years old — well educated — a qualified pharmacist — from a very good family." He sighed and mournfully shook his head. "I suppose you are on leave from an operational squadron. Oh dear, I do worry about you boys." The vermouth was beginning to take effect, and I had difficulty in suppressing a fit of the giggles. I had

237

survived two of the dreadful Warsaw flights and several trips to Ploesti. We had lost ninety per cent of our crews and I was still only halfway through my tour of forty operations. I was unlikely to survive longer than a few more weeks, and it seemed that this man was merely worried about my morality. I looked at him closely. He was dressed in khaki battledress with no distinguishing badges. I was puzzled — he did not strike me as being an officer of the military police. I noticed that he wore a black tie, and I then guessed that he was an Army padre of the Church of Scotland. If I had guessed that earlier, I might not have given him such a full and frank account of my nocturnal activities. I never saw him again.

My time with Rosa was helping me to recover from the stress of life on the squadron. I was now beginning to feel mentally relaxed. Before my leave, I had often awoken in a sweat and with pounding heart, having dreamt that I had fallen asleep in the air. After fumbling around in the darkness to assure myself that I was, in fact, in my makeshift bed, I had then lain awake, smoking cigarettes for hours. Occasionally, while flying at night, I had an uncanny feeling that somebody, who should not be in the plane, was hovering behind me. The feeling persisted until I switched on my flashlight and assured myself that nobody was there. I never mentioned this to anyone on the squadron, but I later discovered that it was a common manifestation of neurosis among aircrew men.

My genuine fondness for Rosa surprised and slightly troubled me. I had not expected anything more than a brief sexual interlude, but she had quickly become an important part of my life and I regretted that my time with her would soon be over. Another thing troubled me. Some of her relatives lived in northern Italy — in areas that we were regularly bombing. I hated the thought of being involved in the killing or maiming of people like her. I had become accustomed to the sight of Italian civilians with obvious signs of war disablement, but that did not greatly disturb me, as I did not know any of them personally. Since the early days of the war, we had all been encouraged by British government propaganda to despise Italian people — generally referred to as "Wops", or "Eyeties" — in an attempt to dehumanize them. Now, I found that my association with Rosa was causing a change in my attitude to my part in the war, and I began to feel uneasy about further bombing of Italian targets.

All too soon, my time in Sorrento came to an end. I told Rosa that I would be leaving the following day, and we spent a final night in energetic copulation. I told her that if I eventually returned to the disposal centre, along the coast in Portici, I would try to visit Sorrento again. She slowly ran her fingers through my hair and pouted like a small child. "I like you — much *simpatico*. You go — no good! *La guerra* — no good! *Aeronautica* — no good! I see you never again!" I feared that she was right in thinking that she would never see me again. As I got dressed, she lay naked on the bed. In the early morning sunlight, she looked so

239

beautiful and I longed to stay with her. "If only the senseless bloody war would end today," I muttered to myself. "*Arrivederci, Rosa, ciao!*" Her eyes were like wet black cherries. The three-ton truck was due to leave for Amendola in half an hour.

I hurried back to the Minerva. The other lads were waiting outside by the truck. They cheered when I came into view, and I noticed the look of relief on their faces. I was too late to get any breakfast, but luckily, they had packed some bread and salami to eat on the journey. Our grinning driver gave me a knowing wink as I climbed into the truck. It was now farewell to Sorrento — we were going back to the war.

CHAPTER
NINE

Supplying the
Partisans

It was early morning when I entered our tent and found Deaky sitting quietly on his own. I was eager to tell him all about the delights of Sorrento, but first I asked him, "What have you been doing while we have been away? You ought to have been with us, not hanging about here by yourself. You must have been bored to bloody death." Deaky's worried look told me that something had gone wrong. It appeared that he had foolishly allowed himself to be persuaded to fly as a substitute for a navigator who had fallen sick. "Why the hell did you do that? You silly sod," I berated him. "Never volunteer for anything! If you had got the chop, we would be stuck with a bloody sprog navigator for the rest of our tour. Anyhow, what sort of a trip did you go on?" Deaky replied wearily, "It had to be aborted. We took off and got up to about six hundred feet, but the aircraft wouldn't climb any higher, so the skipper told me to jettison the bomb-load. I set the switches on 'safe', but three of the bombs went off. They fell not far from the domestic site. Huge lumps of turf and stones were blown up into the plane. All the oxygen containers exploded. It was a terrible mess. We crash-landed at Tortorella. It was lucky that nobody got hurt. It shook me up, I can tell you."

I stared at him incredulously. "Christ all bloody mighty! You should have known better than to drop the bloody bombs live. I've shown you often enough how to set the switches so the bombs won't go off. What a balls-up! Six hundred feet with a full fuel load — bloody hell — it's a miracle you weren't all killed. What did Trev [the Flight Commander] say about it?" Deaky explained that later investigation had absolved him of all blame. Apparently, the ground crew had run short of the standard wire fusing links, so they had improvised by making up some substitutes, which had become jammed tight in the solenoids of the release gear, and so the bombs were unable to be dropped without them exploding. I wondered how many other potentially lethal improvisations the ground crews were being obliged to undertake due to the chronic shortage of spare parts.

As we wandered over to the field kitchen to see what Glad was preparing for lunch, I saw one of the aircrew lads approaching — wearing nothing but flying boots, khaki shorts and a cocked hat. "Hi there, Napoleon," I greeted him, "where did you get the hat?" He replied at great length that he had snatched it off the head of a member of the Carabinieri police in Foggia and run off down the street with it. The policeman had chased him, and several other Italians had joined in the pursuit. "I dodged around a corner into an alleyway. There were some derelict cars there and I jumped into one and ducked down. I heard them all run past, then I waited a few minutes and ran back the other way. Not a bad souvenir, is it?"

Within the next few days, a couple of his friends appeared in American officers' peaked caps that they had "liberated" during a visit to the shower baths in Foggia.

The atmosphere on the squadron had undergone a marked change since we had been away on leave. So many new crews had arrived — we were among strangers. We had very little in common with the sickly, pale-faced replacements, many of whom had come straight out from England and were unused to the dreadful living conditions to which we had long been accustomed. The continual threat of further flights to Warsaw hung over us like the sword of Damocles, and morale suffered in consequence. Announcements from the Air Officer Commanding-in-Chief and others appeared on the squadron's notice-board in praise of our efforts, but they served merely to annoy us. We read that "only well-trained crews of the highest calibre" could have made the trips to Warsaw. The High Command seemed unaware that many of our men had arrived on the squadrons with woefully inadequate preparation. The squadron's Medical Officer reported the case of a flight engineer who had suffered a breakdown and was unable to continue flying. He noted in his official diary — "What could be expected of a man who had only two and a half hours' previous air experience?" To our disgust, a senior officer compared us with the men of 617 Squadron who had flown from England to bomb the German dams. We strongly resented the comparison. "We flew to Warsaw repeatedly, whereas the 'Dam Busters' only made one trip to the dams, and sustained far fewer casualties than we had over Poland," I heard one of our pilots grumble. "He should have compared our Warsaw flights to the charge of the soddin' Light Brigade. That would have been a bloody sight more appropriate."

Seeing men in flying kit returning from Amendola one morning, we asked them where they had been, and they explained that they had been with an official film crew, acting the part of men who had flown to Warsaw. "But you buggers never flew to Warsaw!" I heard someone shout indignantly. The "buggers" replied, "All you blokes were in bed so we were told to pretend that we were you." High dudgeon reigned among the men, who thought that the makers of such fake documentary films deserved to be lynched.

Red Smythe disappeared without any explanation being given to us, and I thought at first that he might have been killed. A new commander arrived — a group captain who had never seen a shot fired. He had dropped down to the rank of wing commander in order to get what the Americans termed "some combat time". For several weeks, we neither saw nor heard anything of this new boy, and even after he had plucked up enough courage to emerge from the shadows, he remained as remote from us as his predecessor.

Our spirits were slightly raised one day by the announcement that the Polish government-in-exile had awarded us the Cross of Valour. Soon afterwards, I was helping to sort through someone's kit when I came across a pair of striped braces that he was going to discard. We cut up the braces, sewed pieces onto our uniforms to look like medal ribbons, and then hitched a lift into town. The few Warsaw veterans in the NAAFI did not need to enquire what the "medal ribbons" were. One of them asked me, "When did that come through?" and after a few minutes, there were no "Warsaw men" in sight. They had all returned to the squadron to collect their non-existent awards. The only people who laughed at the joke were those of us wearing the bits of striped braces. The others were not amused by our hoax.

As time went by and nothing further was heard about the Polish medals, I concluded that the British authorities had used the announcement as a temporary morale booster — a deception for encouraging the new boys. However, I was wrong in my assumption. In fact, the British authorities had informed the Poles that only specified individuals would be permitted to receive the award. When the Poles asked to be given the names of the relevant individuals, our squadron nominated only one man, who subsequently told the Commanding Officer, "I cannot accept this award because I never flew to Warsaw." He got the reply, "Nothing to do with me, sergeant, it's a foreign award — we didn't give it to you." Several years later the Commanding Officer remarked to me, "The Adjutant had submitted the name. He never did anything right!" Being immature and childish enough to think that medals were of great importance, we remained disgruntled until the Polish authorities eventually invited us to submit our own names to them directly, and to produce our flying-logbooks as evidence. Medals were then presented to those of us who had survived long enough to receive them.

As soon as the squadron had assembled sufficient replacement aircraft and crews, we resumed flying, and every time we flew over the front line, Jock pointed to the flashes of the guns on the ground and shouted to me, "Look, that's the real war down there!" I knew what he meant. The Prime Minister, Winston Churchill, during his visit to Italy, had said that the fighting men should receive a ration of beer, but the men of the heavy-bomber squadrons did not get any because we were based in an area that was too far from the front line. Apparently, the chair-bound warriors of the General Staff considered us to be in the same category as non-combatants. A similar situation arose later in the year when the night-time temperature fell below freezing level and we asked for more blankets. The authorities declared that, due to a world shortage of blankets, only the fighting troops in the line were to get extra ones. Consequently, we had to wear the kapok-filled, quilted, inner suits of our flying-clothing, not only to fly in, but also to sleep in — not the best of arrangements in the absence of laundry facilities. Some of the ground staff airmen, having no alternative, slept in their grubby working clothes, and according to the Medical Officer the result was a nasty outbreak of boils.

Our activities had now been extended to include not only bombing but also the dropping of parachute containers of supplies to Marshal Tito's partisans in enemy-occupied Yugoslavia and to partisans in the north of Italy. The parachute containers were dropped, as in the case of the Warsaw flights, from very low-level — usually 200 feet — with flaps down and flying at just above stalling speed. Occasionally we flew alone to remote areas where partisans awaited us with dropping-zones indicated by bonfires at night or marked by white parachutes laid out on the ground in daylight. The German troops were never far away, and we knew that if our arrival time over the dropping-zone was not punctual the brave people on the ground would be in even greater danger. One of the great hazards of supply dropping was caused by the people on the ground choosing dropping-zones in mountainous areas that were inaccessible for aircraft flying at low level. When we were briefed for yet another of these "special-duty" operations, we were astounded to hear that eighty aircraft were to arrive at the same time over a valley into which they were to descend several thousand feet in darkness. The valley was short and narrow. We would have to attempt to corkscrew down into it. We listened in silence as we learned what was to be expected of us. Suddenly, a voice from behind me bellowed at the briefing officer, "It's impossible. In fact, it's suicide! Don't you know it takes five miles to circle a Liberator?" The valley was less than two miles wide. I craned my neck to see who had been brave enough to object to the stupidity of our superiors. It was Gus, young Blondie's pilot. "And what about the danger of collisions when so many aircraft are there together?"

The briefing officer and his cohorts huddled together in earnest discussion. "To avoid collisions, you had better put your lights on as soon as you arrive over the valley," was their decision. As we arrived at the valley, the sky became filled with circling aircraft with their port and starboard lights on, and within a few seconds three were shot down. The rest of us switched our lights off and started to attempt the impossible descent. The illuminated dropping-zone was incredibly close to a sheer cliff face, and as I lost sight of the dim horizon above it, I was instructing Andy to attempt almost vertical turns in pitch darkness. A string of parachute containers suddenly appeared suspended so close in front of me that I could see their vague shape. Fearing that the parachutes would become entangled in our propellers, I screamed at Andy to keep turning tighter, and then I released our containers, without caring that we were several miles from the designated dropping-zone. That night I repeatedly ran through my complete vocabulary of swear words as I cursed the people who had set us such a hopeless task.

There were now two main topics of conversation at the NAAFI in Foggia. Most men who had not yet been granted leave were keen to hear about our adventures in Sorrento. Some of the new boys were more interested in accounts of the dreadful Warsaw flights, and I began to experience a smug feeling of superiority whenever they asked me about the subject. I was surprised to learn that not everyone had chosen to spend time in Sorrento. Some of the more adventurous lads had called at nearby American Air Force bases and found that it was possible to get a flight on one of the many freight planes shuttling to and from such destinations as Algiers, Malta or Sicily. They were banned from taking flights to Britain because men had been known in the past to report sick at home to prolong their leave. Others had delayed their return by announcing to the authorities before the end of their leave that they would have no official means of transport back to Italy — knowing that by doing so before they were due back they were committing no offence. Since Rome had fallen to the Allies many of the Catholic lads had gone there, but they had not been officially permitted to stay in the city overnight, so they had spent a great deal of their time dodging the military police as darkness fell. Peter Green and his crew of sergeants decided to spend a day climbing up Vesuvius — a hazardous undertaking, as the volcano had recently erupted and there were pockets of lethal gas on the slopes. They were on their way up when they passed a junior British Army officer, who upbraided them for failing to salute him. They listened in silence to his indignant rebuke and then walked away — still not having saluted. What he did not know was that nobody on our operational squadron saluted officers, and it was an unwritten rule in areas like Foggia, where British and American officers outnumbered our non-commissioned aircrew men, that saluting was abandoned, and consequently the aircrews had quickly forgotten the silly ritual. "Obviously a newly commissioned non-combatant pongo," someone observed. "I wonder if the poor buggers with the Army in the front line have to keep saluting each other while they are under fire!"

Quite a few of the lads had visited the ruined Roman city of Pompeii, where one of the attractions was the brothel area, with its well-preserved display of vulgarity. Some Italian men — self-appointed guides — were showing a party of American Army women the ruins, but deliberately avoiding the brothel. The women obviously knew they had not seen everything, and they asked the guides, "Isn't there anything else to see? Our friends have been here and they told us there was more." The crafty Italians shook their heads. "We are not allowed to show anything else to ladies. No, it is not permitted. That is not for ladies." The American women were persistent. "We wanna see everything, d'ya hear?" "Aw shit, Mary Lou, give 'em some more o' them goddam liras — we ain't got all day to stand here jawing." Having achieved their aim of extracting more money from the women, the Italian "guides" showed them around the ancient brothel area. There were squeals of delight and, "The folks back home ain't never gonna believe this!"

I was loath to relate intimate details of the time I had spent with Rosa, but I was inquisitive about how the others had occupied themselves. Many of the quieter lads had hardly ventured out of the Minerva at all. "What? With all that Italian crumpet available in the town — you might never get another chance!" They explained that there were tea-dances on the hotel terrace in the afternoons and plenty of local girls attended. I remembered that I had returned to the hotel one day while a tea-dance was in progress. The master of ceremonies was conducting an elimination dance. "Every man with blue socks get off the floor," he shouted, and then, "Every man with black shoes is eliminated." The last couple left would get a bar of chocolate — a great prize. The girls were very disappointed when their partners were eliminated. During the interval, the men collected plates of cakes that were set out on a large table, and offered them to the girls. Instead of taking one cake and eating it, every girl produced a paper bag and shovelled in as many cakes as possible to take home with her. The rapacity of the girl contrasted remarkably with the politeness of the airmen. "Excuse me, would you care to dance?" I overheard Andy ask one of them. As I guffawed, he gave me a well-deserved shove, and I very nearly fell over the railings of the terrace into the street below.

Ginge had an amusing experience, which was not funny when it occurred. He was in bed with a young woman when about midnight the loud stamping of Army boots on the concrete stairway heralded the arrival of the military police. The girl whispered in alarm, "It's the Red Caps — quick, hide in here," as she pushed him through the large double doors of what he thought was a cupboard. When his eyes became accustomed to the darkness, he discovered that he was out on the second-floor balcony overlooking the street, and he soon became aware of the dark shapes of people walking on the pavement below. The doors were fastened on the inside and he was marooned. Completely naked, he squatted down in the corner of the balcony until about twenty minutes later, when the girl let him back into the room and announced that the Red Caps had departed. "I don't know why she shoved me out on the balcony," Ginge told us. "I suppose she must have thought I was a deserter and she was protecting me. While I was outside I remembered that my uniform was draped over the back of a chair in the room with all my documents and money in the pockets, and I wondered if she was ever going to let me back into the room or if the Red Caps might take my clothes away with them."

It was in the NAAFI that I first heard the horrifying account of an SAAF navigator being suspended for four hours by his parachute lines underneath the belly of a Liberator as the plane returned from an attack on Ploesti. The man had jumped out over the target after the aircraft had been damaged during an encounter with an enemy Ju 88. The Liberator had become very difficult to handle when one engine and part of the starboard wing was shot away. The pilot first became aware of the navigator's absence when he asked for a course to steer for base and got no reply. The pilot succeeded in bringing the crippled Liberator back to base, but when preparing to land, the crew found that the nosewheel was jammed by a section of the navigator's parachute that was caught on the nosewheel door. They opened the bomb doors and attempted to pull their colleague in, but the force of the slipstream made this impossible, so they cut the parachute free and allowed the body to fall to the ground a mile from base. Incidents such as this seemed more tragic than casualties directly caused by enemy action.

Occasionally, the Commanding Officer and another officer would arrive in a Jeep a few seconds before take-off time, and hand over a mysterious figure who was to be given a signal to jump out at a specified place (usually a map reference) en route to our bombing target. The parachutists, of unknown nationality, always assumed to be men and referred to as "Joes", were not to be spoken to, but merely tapped on the shoulder when it was time to jump out through the large hatch in the deck at the rear of the bomb-bay. I was always fearful that the "Joes" might be dropped in the wrong place, and it was only later that I learned something more about them — that some of them were women, and many of them carried hundreds of gold sovereigns. Years later General Wheeler told me about his own experiences. After four abortive attempts, he was dropped in Albania to try to persuade the partisans to fight against the Germans instead of each other. The Royal Air Force parachuted in supplies of sabotage materials, including some explosive coal that was intended to be loaded onto the tenders of locomotives. "There was just one snag — there was no railway in the vicinity," he told me, "and I had difficulty in preventing the partisans from using the coal on their camp-fires."

CHAPTER
TEN

Hospital!

As we approached the end of our operational tour, we hardly dared to hope that our luck would hold out. I tried to make sure that Deaky always remembered to wear his "lucky" shirt. On the two occasions when he had not worn it, the trips had nearly ended in disaster.

Andy appeared to remain as placid and imperturbable as ever, but Jock and I became increasingly intolerant and quick-tempered.

As the weather turned cooler, the mosquitoes became less of a pest and the swarms of locusts that had daily devoured the cook's vegetables now disappeared. The Medical Officer reported that the leaking drums of used oil placed in the nearby river had provided a film of oil on the surface to control the mosquitoes.

Once again, the food rations failed to arrive, and the cry went up, "Oh, come on, Glad, make us a marmalade tart!" Miraculously, Glad was able to make marmalade tarts of about a foot diameter on his improvised field-kitchen apparatus if he had the necessary ingredients. A catering officer from GHQ Cairo visited Foggia and reported that the food supplied to the squadrons was "adequate and of good quality". We guessed that he must have dined with the Americans. He certainly did not show his face on our squadron.

On returning to the domestic site after a bombing trip, we were riding with Johnnie Rush's crew in a three-ton truck, and I noticed that one man had not removed his leather helmet. It was unusual for anyone to keep a helmet on after leaving the aircraft, and I wondered who this man was. At the domestic site, the "odd bod" wandered away to the tent lines instead of accompanying the rest of us to debriefing, and then I realized that it was Glad, the cook. I was amazed that he should have risked his life unnecessarily. "Boredom, pure bloody boredom!" explained Glad. "I had volunteered for flying duties on enlistment and the interviewing officer asked me if I knew how to make a rice pudding. Thinking the question was part of the general knowledge test for potential aircrew, I went into great detail about how to make a rice pudding, and the next thing I knew was that I had been enlisted as a cook. I never wanted to be a cook and the job bores me stiff. I know that after the war nobody will ever believe that I have done any flying, and some people think I must be a damned fool, but I don't care."

To our surprise, an announcement was made that each trip to Warsaw would be counted as two, and that meant that if our luck held out we would reach forty within the next few days. We waited anxiously to hear what the next target would be. Knowing that we were so near to completion placed an unexpected strain on us. For the first time since we'd arrived on the squadron I started to think tentatively about the future — it looked as though there might be a future after all, but none of us dared to tempt fate by talking about the matter.

The squadron now had more crews than aircraft, so we were not flying as frequently as previously. We scanned the battle order each day, hoping that our crew would be listed on it, and were dismayed when we were not. The stress of waiting was beginning to tell on us.

One day a couple of us decided to kill time by attempting to walk across country to Foggia. Such an undertaking would have been out of the question a few weeks previously because the soles of my shoes had been worn right through. In the early days I had always taken them with me in the air — tied to my parachute harness — in case I was shot down, but I had stopped doing so when they needed repairing. Needless to say, there were no shoe-repairing facilities on the squadron, so I had cut out some pieces of cardboard and put them in the shoes until I was lucky enough to find a civilian cobbler in Foggia, who cut some leather off the flap of an old saddle and mended the shoes for me in exchange for a packet of cigarettes. As we walked over the bleak Foggia plain, we came to a solitary little boy who was tending a flock of sheep, miles away from any sign of habitation. In the absence of any other form of shelter from sun or rain, the boy was carrying a neatly furled black umbrella that would not have been out of place in the City of London, but looked odd in the hands of a boy who was dressed like a scarecrow. We stopped and tried to joke with him about the umbrella until I noticed that he was trembling with fear. He was obviously terrified of us. I tried to explain in Italian that we were not Germans. I pointed to myself and said, *"Inglese — non Tedeschi."* He was not reassured, and seemed very close to tears. I wished that we had a bar of chocolate to offer him, but then doubted if he would have dared to accept it from us. In his eyes we were, no doubt, the sort of brutes in uniform who needlessly slaughtered innocents like him and his mother. The terrified child had made me feel ashamed at the thought of the atrocities that he might have seen being perpetrated by men looking similar to us.

We met an aircrew man in the NAAFI who told us that he had discovered a family who agreed to do his washing for him in return for some soap and an occasional tin of corned beef. A couple of weeks later they invited him to stay for lunch, and he was interested to find out whether they would make the corned beef into a warm meal like hash, or serve it straight out of the tin. In fact, they did not serve the corned beef that day. Instead, a tray of little cooked birds, the size of sparrows, appeared out of the oven. "I looked at their poor little carcasses and imagined the way they would have been happily chirping and hopping around," he told us, "and I just couldn't eat any of them." It then occurred to me that I never saw a cat or a dog in the town, so I assumed that they had all ended up in the pot.

★ ★ ★

It was a Tuesday morning, and immediately after breakfast, the battle order was posted on the notice-board. I was glad to see that we were on it, but I felt uneasy when I learned that we were to carry out a bombing operation in daylight, instead of under cover of darkness. "Don't try to emulate the Americans. They have been highly trained in formation flying — you have not," we were warned at briefing. "Fly in a gaggle. Don't risk collisions by getting too close."

We had often expressed respect for the precise way the American pilots flew in very close formation so that the gunners could bring the maximum number of guns to bear when enemy fighters attacked their day-bombers. We did not fly in formation at night because most of the time we could not see each other in the dark, but we were sure that loose formation flying in daylight would not be beyond our capability. "The cheeky bastard!" I heard an Australian voice growl. "As the Yanks are so shit-hot in daylight, why are we being sent on this trip instead of them?" We all knew that the Liberators with their tinted Perspex and glaring reflector sights were not ideal bombers for use at night. We also realized that the modified planes that we flew were less suitable for use in daylight than those flown by the American squadrons. All the Royal Air Force's Liberators were converted on arrival at Amendola so that they could carry a heavier bomb-load. This meant that the front gun turrets were gutted and the ball-turrets under the belly of the aircraft were removed. Ammunition for the remaining guns was not excessive, and the fuel load was always kept to the minimum. The Americans carried two gunners to operate what we called the "beam" guns, but we didn't, so those guns were usually unmanned. With only half as many crew members and fewer gun turrets, we knew that we were far more vulnerable in daylight than the Americans. "Once again we are the ones who get the shitty end of the stick," I heard somebody groan.

It seemed to be a fairly routine form of briefing until we were told, "On this daylight operation you will have a fighter escort." We had never had a fighter escort before, and we were delighted at the prospect of being accompanied by a squadron of RAF Mosquitoes. To our surprise, the briefing officer announced, "The escort will be provided by the *Regia Aeronautica*, the Italian Air Force." The pronouncement produced laughter and cries of derision from the majority of the crews. "What use will they be? A crowd of bloody Wops! They'll piss off at the first sign of opposition." The briefing officer was indignant. "I can assure you that these men, serving under Royal Air Force operational command, are the cream of the Italian Air Force. They are all very experienced fighter pilots. They will rendezvous with you over the Yugoslav coast and escort you to within sight of the target. After you have left the target area, they will escort you back to the coast." Someone whispered, "That's if the bastards ever turn up." The briefing officer continued, "There is one thing you should be aware of — any Germans that you may encounter en route are likely to be flying the same type of aircraft as the Italian escort." There were groans and muffled comments from the crews. "Typical!"

"Another soddin' balls up!" "How the fuck are we going to know which ones are the Germans and which are the Italians?" "Oh why worry? Let's just shoot at every bastard that comes within range!"

After briefing, we streamed out of the flight marquee and made our way back to our tents to collect our "eating irons" — aluminium plates and chipped enamel mugs. Heavy rain had caused the trampled earth between the tent lines, the flight tent and the so-called cookhouse to resemble a ploughed field. The ground inside the tents was sodden and our blankets were perpetually damp. As there was nowhere else to put my parachute pack, it spent most of its time on the damp ground under my makeshift bed. There was no parachute (maintenance) section on the squadron, and the parachute had not been repacked since it was issued to me several months previously, and as it became ever more dilapidated I often used the handle of a spoon to poke protruding sections back into the cover. I was concerned about the effect of damp and doubted that the parachute would be of any use in an emergency. Long after my time, the parachutes were eventually sent for repacking in Foggia, where, according to the Commanding Officer, some of the packs were found to contain paper instead of parachutes.

In the absence of any other footwear suitable for wet and muddy conditions, most of us were obliged to wear our flying-boots all day. The departed Wing Commander Smythe would certainly not have been pleased, but the new commander did not seem to be at all concerned.

As we sat eating our lunch of dehydrated potato and unidentifiable stewed meat, our talk centred on the chances of the Italian fighter escort putting in an appearance in the right place and at the right time. We had learned that most Italian events were typically postponed until "*domani*", and it seemed that tomorrow seldom came, so we had little faith in the reliability of the Italian Air Force. But as we reached the Yugoslav coast, to our surprise the Italian pilots did, in fact, arrive at the rendezvous point on time, and not only did they escort us to the target area, they continually circled in the intense flak over the target throughout the raid. Their display of reckless bravado was obviously intended to impress us, and it certainly had the desired effect. Before leaving us, they put on a brief but spectacular display of aerobatics.

At debriefing back at Amendola, one of the "second-tour" lads related how his previous squadron had encountered opposition from the Italian Air Force during the desert campaign in North Africa. "We found they are never any good in defeat, but they are always shit-hot so long as they have good aircraft and are on the winning side." Some of us expressed regret that we had no opportunity to meet these "shit-hot" Italian pilots personally. They had unexpectedly gained our respect and admiration. We later found out that the Italians were serving under Royal Air Force operational command at Brindisi. They were serving together with pilots of the Croatian Air Force who had also recently

261

changed over to the winning side. Surprisingly, under the same RAF control were a squadron of Yak fighters of the Soviet Air Force and a squadron of Russian Dakotas. The Russians were engaged in the support of Communist partisans in the Balkans, and were paid in US dollars at an even higher rate than the Americans.

I awoke before dawn on Wednesday 8 November. After several attempts with damp matches, I managed to light the hurricane lamp. There was ice on the can of water in the tent, and my damp towel was crisp with frost. It was nearly a week since I had shaved with my blunt razor blade, ordinary soap and icy water. Having failed to prise open the frozen cap of the water can, I thought that I would have to remain dirty and unshaven until I next had the opportunity to visit the shower baths in Foggia. At the shower baths I would, as usual, sort through the "trash can" to find a razor blade, discarded by the Americans, that might have another shave left in it. My little Italian dog had jumped onto the bed during the night and burrowed under my two blankets. His warmth was always welcome, but not his fleas.

The rapid onset of winter was making life on the squadron increasingly miserable. Sleeping in a flimsy tent on a sheet of cardboard without a mattress was taking its toll. A few days before, when I found that I could not raise my left arm without pain, I sought the advice of the Medical Officer. I explained that I was having difficulty in crawling under the flight deck to the front compartment, dragging my parachute pack and portable oxygen bottle. His only comment was,

"Perhaps you have been sitting in a draught." He offered me no treatment. His main function seemed to be the convincing of the sick that there was actually nothing wrong with them. I remembered how the "Doc" had appeared at a briefing during a widespread outbreak of gastro-enteritis. "Don't wait until the last minute before take-off and then report that you have a dose of diarrhoea — I need at least half an hour to stop it!" he had told us.

The condition commonly known as the "shites", or "gyppo tummy", was not always caused by Glad's catering. The open-air lavatory buckets were always swiftly occupied immediately after every briefing for such dreaded targets as Ploesti. I noticed that the Doc usually kept well out of the way on those occasions. He obviously had instructions from on high that when a "maximum effort" was called for (meaning that all available aircraft and crews were to fly), nothing whatsoever was to be allowed to prevent a man from taking to the sky, so long as he was still breathing. As a result, many men flew when it was quite obvious from their appearance that they were ill. Some callous mirth resulted from the plight of one of our young pilots who had suffered the agony of diarrhoea during the bombing run. After engaging "George", the automatic pilot system, he attempted to scramble from his seat as soon as the plane was clear of the target area. It was too late. He sank back into his seat and the rest of the crew had to share the resulting stench for several hours. We noticed, particularly among apprehensive "new boys", that fright often had a remarkable effect on bowel

263

function, and this led to the expression "a touch of ring twitter" being commonly used to mean a state of dread.

The battle order was posted very early in the morning, and I was glad to see that our crew was listed. I studied the details of the weight of bombs, fuel and oil to be carried, and concluded that it would be a relatively short trip. If the Warsaw trips really were to count double, as we had been told, we would certainly finish within a week. "Just today's trip and then we have only two more to do. We are going to make it!" I said to Deaky at breakfast, and then I immediately regretted having said that. We had never discussed our chances of surviving, and I feared that I might be tempting fate by making assumptions. Deaky made no reply. He stared gloomily at his breakfast of lukewarm reconstituted powdered egg. "Don't fail to wear your lucky shirt, and we'll be okay," I quipped.

Today's target was to be a small, but important, town — a road and rail junction in Serbia. We assumed that the Yugoslav partisans had suggested that it should be bombed as it was said to be full of German troops on their way back to defend the *Heimat*. It was to be another daylight attack, but this time we would have no fighter escort. "On this occasion you may choose your own aiming point. The whole town is the target," we were told. "Bombing altitude is to be ten thousand feet or below the cloud base." This was the only time that we were to carry out indiscriminate bombing of a town. Our previous targets had been mainly airfields, railway marshalling yards, harbour installations and oil refineries.

At the time, I was totally unaware that Allied politicians had decided upon a campaign of area bombing of German towns in what proved to be a futile attempt to sap the morale of the civilian population, and that Air Marshal Harris, the head of Bomber Command, had agreed to oversee that grisly task. I am glad that I was never called upon to take part in the campaign of "terror bombing" of civilians, as I fear that I might not have found sufficient courage to face imprisonment for refusing to obey orders. Doubtless we were fortunate in that Harris had no jurisdiction over our squadrons in Italy. "What's he like?" I had asked some of the new boys from England, who had recently been transferred from a squadron under Harris's command. "We call him 'Butcher' Harris," I was told. "All he cares about is getting at least thirty trips out of everybody. He does not give a shit for anything else. He never visits any of his squadrons. He is not interested in the aircrews." I then guessed why we, in Italy, had to make do with ancient Wellingtons, clapped-out Halifaxes and second-hand Liberators, instead of the greatly admired Lancasters that were at Harris's disposal. We were not under his command, so he had no interest in us.

We approached the target area and began to descend. "Ten thousand feet or below the cloud base?" I bawled in Deaky's ear. "That's a bloody joke. It looks like ten-tenths right down to the deck. I can't see a thing. Another cock-up by that twat of a Met man!" Andy continued to descend. From his position, he was blind to whatever might be immediately below and

265

ahead. Surrounded by about eighty others and flying in dense cloud, there was a danger that we might come down on top of another plane. I lay on the deck and stared out through the clear-vision panel. I could see nothing. I felt the turbulence that was usual in thick cloud — or was it buffeting from the slipstream of another plane? I had always hated blind flying. Abruptly, we broke through the cloud base into clear visibility. The altimeter showed five thousand feet. The area was mountainous and the ground seemed remarkably close. I quickly got a pinpoint, using my topographical map, and commenced the run-up to the target. There were no other aircraft in sight and no bomb bursts. It looked as though we were first in.

We still seemed to be losing height as I gave Andy the necessary corrections to bring us over the centre of the town. I hastily scribbled pencil notes on the margin of my target map, for use at debriefing — "No activity on the ground — No motor transport — Railway line — No trains". I was relieved to note that the town seemed deserted. I pressed the bomb-release "tit" and watched the bombs falling at pre-set intervals. Each bomb had a kind of organ pipe fitted to the tailfin to emit a terrifying shriek as it fell. I scribbled the time "12.00 hrs". I counted every bomb as it came into view and noted its point of impact. The first four hit the centres of large buildings, the next one fell between two buildings and the next one the middle of a road and rail junction. Watching such destruction at fairly low level, in daylight, was fascinating. Would this prove to be our easiest trip so far — a "piece of cake" in our childish jargon? I knew that Jock would be jerking the lever of the bomb-doors to keep them open, and watching the bombs fall away. Eight thousand-pounders. Luckily, no hang-ups. I gave the usual instruction to Jock over the intercom, "Close bomb-doors!"

We were due to turn left immediately after bombing. I called to Andy on the intercom, "High mountains to port — hold this course for half a minute!" Mac chimed in with the warning, "Flak very close astern!" A sudden whoosh of air and the whole of the bombing equipment disappeared from in front of my face. The nose of the aircraft had shattered into a thousand pieces. I knew that I had been hit. It seemed as though my head had been blown off, but I felt nothing more than a blast of air. The switch for my microphone had disintegrated in my right hand. I instantly thought that the plane might be crashing, and I struggled up on to my knees to look at Deaky. My blood was gushing onto the deck, and the look of horror on Deaky's face spoke volumes. He seemed to be unhurt, and he was pressing his fingers to his throat microphone as he jabbered on the intercom. He would be telling Andy what had happened to me. One of the engines had been hit and had to be feathered, but that was not too serious. We were not crashing. Although I was not dead yet, it would not be long — I was losing so much blood, I would surely bleed to death.

I still felt not the slightest pain, and I thought I had read somewhere that in the case of very severe injury, like the loss of a limb, the body goes into shock and no pain is felt. It was a few seconds after twelve noon on a

Wednesday. It was not the right time to die! My vision was starting to fade as I wriggled under the flight deck and got up on my knees in the well. Jock was already opening all the first-aid kits on the carpeted floor of the flight deck. His face was a mere pale pink blob. I seemed to be looking at him through a pane of frosted glass. My right arm hung limply and the hand seemed numb. I raised my left hand to investigate the damage to my face and head. To my probing fingers, the right side of my face felt as though it had become transformed into a mass like raw meat. A shard of Perspex, longer than my finger became dislodged from my right eye and fell to the deck. Jock immediately started to bind up my complete head and both arms.

I felt a prickling sensation in the left side of my chest. My clothes were hanging open. I fumbled with my left hand, pulled out the hollow nose-cap of an anti-aircraft shell that had penetrated my chest and handed it to Jock. He shouted in my ear, "It's got words on it — must be your name." He then hauled me up onto the flight deck, and I slumped against the bulkhead. Jock sorted through the first-aid kits and found a small collapsible tube. "I'll give you a shot of morphine," he shouted in my ear. My lower jaw was not working properly, but I managed to mutter that I was not in pain and did not need any morphine. I made the effort to ask, "Andy okay?" "Yes, nobody else has been hit." Ignoring my protestations, Jock shoved up my tattered sleeve and jabbed the morphine needle in to my arm. He then repeatedly blasted pure oxygen into my face as he shouted, "I've sent a signal — there'll be an ambulance waiting for us. We should be back at base pretty soon." I wished he would stop talking to me. I just wanted to be left alone. Never before had I felt so utterly exhausted.

We trundled to a halt in the dispersal, and as soon as the bomb-doors were opened our ground crew scrambled aboard and lifted me gently off the flight deck and out through the bomb-doors. I was carefully propped up against a pile of blankets on a stretcher, where I sat waiting for further attention. I heard Jock telling someone, "I tied a label on him showing the time when I gave him a shot of morphine, but perhaps morphine should not be given when there's a head wound." An unknown voice called out, "Carry him around to the front of the aircraft, so he can see the damage!"

I would have liked to know the exact extent of the damage, but I could barely see, and as I sat waiting I wondered why I was not being loaded straight into the waiting ambulance. After a further delay of several minutes, I became aware of Smudger's gruff tones as he threatened the members of the medical team. "What's the bloody delay?" he bellowed. One of them replied that they were sorting through the remnants of the first-aid kits and one pair of scissors appeared to be missing. Infuriated, Smudger lifted one of the medics off his feet and flung him away from the plane. Then he bawled out, "I'll do the lot of you stupid bastards, if you don't get him into that ambulance right now." The hunt for the missing scissors was immediately abandoned, and I heard Andy telling the others that he was going with me. As we set off for the military hospital in Foggia, Andy murmured sadly, "And it's my birthday today." It was his twenty-second birthday. I felt sorry that the day had been spoiled. There would be no celebratory piss-up in the mess. "Your birthday — it should be mine," I whispered, "I'm the one who's got a present." I was still twenty; I wondered if I would reach twenty-one.

Andy accompanied me into the operating theatre, where I was laid out on a table. Everything seemed so impersonal. I was glad that Andy was there with me. Nobody else said a word to me. The medical team talked about me as though I were either deaf or already dead. A woman's voice said, "I think he must have been quite a good-looking boy." I felt my tattered clothing being cut off. Two pairs of khaki shorts — two pairs of trousers — two shirts — two Air Force woollen pullovers — one civilian pullover — two battledress blouses. The escape pack of silk maps and American dollars and the emergency pack of concentrated food tablets that I had carried in the inside pockets of my battledress blouses were riddled with shrapnel. I was stripped down to the pair of "long johns" that I had borrowed for the day from Mac. My watch had been shot off my wrist and the compass button had been shot off my shoulder. I was given an injection in the arm.

I slowly regained consciousness to find that I was in a hospital bed. I explored with the fingers of my left hand. My head and the upper part of my body were bound up like an Egyptian mummy. Only a small part of the left side of my mouth and my left eye were not covered. I could make out the vague figure of a woman in white standing at the next bed. I tried to cough to attract her attention. As she turned to me, I croaked, "Can you tell me if they have had to cut off my ear?" She then asked sharply, "What are you in for?" I replied, "I have been wounded and I wondered if the doctors have had to take off my ear." In the same abrupt manner, she said, "You will have to wait and ask the day staff. I know nothing about you." From her reply, I guessed that it was night time. I thought how foolish I would look if I had only one ear — and what about my nose? I could feel nothing through the bandages. I thought I would rather be without an eye. A black eyepatch would not look so bad, but to be without a nose! I felt sick at the thought.

Early in the morning, a figure in Air Force uniform leant over me. I could see that he wore pilot's wings. "How are you feeling?" he asked. "You had a load of shrapnel and Perspex in you. The metal has all been removed, but there was not enough time to take out all the Perspex. The trouble is that Perspex doesn't show up well on the X-rays." Thinking that this pilot must be another hospital patient, I asked him, "How do you know so much about me?" He replied, "I'm the surgeon who operated on you." I had not expected a surgeon to be also a pilot. I was glad that he had something to do with me. I felt that he was one of us, even though he was non-combatant. He assured me that I still had both ears and most of my nose. "Your right eye has been pierced. The anterior chamber has collapsed and lost its fluid, so you will have to remain flat on your back for a month while we treat it. On no account are you to sit up." I was surprised that he did not ask me any questions about the incident, but then thought he must have seen many cases like mine. I never saw him again.

A nurse appeared, raised the dressing from my damaged eye and dropped some cold liquid in. "You are very lucky," she told me, "you are being treated with this new penicillin." I did not feel lucky. "It's very cold. Do you think you could warm it up?" I asked her. She answered haughtily, "Certainly not. It has to be kept in a refrigerator. You will be treated with penicillin every hour."

I wished that I felt well enough to enjoy the luxury of being at last in a proper bed with crisp clean sheets and a pillow. I slept most of the day and night — being awoken only for the hourly eye treatment and for feeding. A man who told me that he was not a trained member of the medical staff, but just an aircraft hand on general duties, had the task of feeding me with a small spoon. I was able to poke the food off the spoon into the exposed corner of my mouth with the little finger of my left hand. I had very little appetite, and as he fed me with what I thought was diced carrot, I told him, "I don't want any more of that carrot, thanks." He answered, "It's pineapple," and I then realized that I had lost not only most of my vision, but also my sense of taste. I was very soon to find that my sense of humour became another casualty.

"I want you to pay attention! I have something important to tell you." An officious female's squawk abruptly startled me out of my doze. "Just listen to me. I want you to understand that while you are in this hospital your rank counts for nothing. You are just another patient, that is all. Remember, your rank counts for nothing here!" I wondered why on earth she was berating me in such strident tones. After all, I was a mere sergeant, the lowest aircrew rank, not a general or a bloody admiral. I was incapable of responding to her unexpected outburst. I would have liked to point out to her that I was feeling very ill and that although I did not expect sympathy, I did not need to be subjected to her bullying tirade. "Nasty bitch," I muttered under my breath. I was soon to discover that her brusque manner was common to most of the nursing staff. "You have developed dermatitis around the eye," I was told accusingly, one morning. "It will have to be treated with penicillin cream." Later I overheard some talk about conjunctivitis and tests for allergy being carried out on the other eye. Within a few days, I was totally blind, with both eyes covered by dressings. The nurses reacted with obvious annoyance when I asked questions about my condition, so I stopped asking them anything.

Being blind, I had no sense of the passing of time. I seemed to drift constantly between sleep and consciousness, rarely able to distinguish night from day or one day from the next. Still lying flat on my back, I felt myself being lifted out onto a stretcher and carried to a different ward. I heard someone mention "cross-infection in the ward", and assumed that I was now being transferred to somewhere more sanitary. After two weeks of total blindness, my left eye was uncovered and I was relieved to find that I could see reasonably well with it. After four weeks of lying motionless on my back, I had the dressing removed from the other eye, but with it I found that I could merely distinguish between light and darkness. I thought, one eye that functioned was far better than none at all, and my spirits improved considerably. Eventually I was allowed to sit up in bed. Using a bedpan while lying prone had proved both awkward and humiliating.

Attracting the attention of the staff had also been a problem, and it still was so, even when I could sit up. There was a male nursing orderly who often scooted through the ward, and I preferred to ask him to fetch a bedpan, rather than asking one of the females. "Not now, not now, I'm busy. I'll bring one as soon as I can," was his invariable response, as he rushed past my bed. "I'll shit the bed, if you don't get a move on," I threatened, after he had kept me waiting until I was in agony. Getting a bed-bottle was equally difficult, so I made sure that I had one "on standby" in the bed at all times. I eventually realized that the man was deliberately and sadistically exercising his power over me, and I decided to teach him a lesson. My opportunity came one evening, after he had kept me waiting for a bedpan for about an hour. As he passed by the foot of my bed, I let out a mournful groan and made a peculiar hissing sound. His curiosity caused him to fall into my trap. He came close to me. I continued to hiss and then mumbled unintelligibly. He leant over me, and immediately he was close enough I managed to use my left hand to grab him by the windpipe, twist his head so that it was trapped against the bed, and proceed to choke him. I was surprised that I could muster so much strength in one arm. "I keep asking you to fetch me a bedpan," I reminded him. He eventually wrenched himself free, leaving traces of the skin of his throat under my unusually long fingernails. I had no difficulty in getting bedpans and bottles promptly after that episode.

I was now allowed to have visitors. Andy told me that after he had left me at the hospital, he trudged through the town to the Manfredonia road, where he waited in the rain for a lift on the back of an open lorry. When he arrived back at the domestic site, he was reprimanded for accompanying me to the hospital instead of reporting for debriefing with the others. The good news was that the crew was declared "tour expired" — being one man short, they did not have to do the remaining two trips. Within a few days, they were posted away. They had survived against all the odds and so had I.

The news that I was in hospital spread quickly, and old friends began to call in whenever they could get in to Foggia. Johnnie displayed his typical Cockney humour: "One in the mince pie and one right on the old pumper. Cor blimey, you nearly had it!" Young Blondie arrived with a present. "Here's that shirt I promised you," he told me dismissively. In fact, he had never promised me a shirt, although, of course, he knew that I had no clean clothes, but I believe he felt that bringing me a present was a sentimental act — a sign of weakness — something to be glossed over and disguised by superficial banter. "See this nailfile, I borrowed it from your black pig in PE and kept it," he joked. "She was not black — she just had black hair," I explained to the other visitors. "By the way, Blondie, do you ever get any mail from your cross-eyed pig?" I had never seen any of Blondie's girl-friends in South Africa, but I frequently pretended that I had. Blondie replied indignantly, "She was not cross-eyed!" I whispered to the others, "Yes, she was. I don't know why he denies it. A squint can sometimes be quite attractive in a woman."

On their next visit to the hospital, my visitors told me that the Commanding Officer had arranged for the dogs on the domestic site to be shot. When asked the reason, he had replied with just one word, "Hygiene." I had never considered hygiene to be a factor that had ever troubled the people who were responsible for our disgusting living conditions — the leaky tents — no water main — no electricity — no beds — no more than two blankets each — no proper lavatories — no toilet-paper — no wash-house — no facilities for washing and drying clothes — no storage facilities for flying-clothing and parachutes — no decent cooking facilities — no official transport into town for a shower. I thought of the number of times I had returned from an exhausting and dangerous trip and the joy of finding my little doggy friend waiting to greet me in the early morning of what might well be my last day alive. I felt sad and angry to learn that my little dog and six others had been shot. I wished I had the opportunity of telling the Commanding Officer how foolish it was to destroy the beneficial effect that the dogs had on the morale of the aircrews. I doubted if I would get such an opportunity. I supposed that the Commanding Officer had no interest in me as the weeks passed without any official communication from the squadron, but I was wrong. Shortly after my period of total blindness, an official visitor appeared. He sat on the next bed, and from his manner I guessed that he was either the squadron's Medical Officer or Adjutant, but I could not distinguish his features. His head was merely a pink blob, without eyes and mouth. After a few minutes of small talk, he announced, "I'm pleased to inform you that you have been awarded the Distinguished Flying Medal."

At that moment all the anger and resentment that had been simmering for so long came to the boil, and it was as though I could hear a recording of my own voice growling, "I don't want the thing. Tell them to stuff it up their arse!" My visitor was shocked into silence. I repeated, "Tell them to stuff it up their arse! What I need is some clothing, not a bloody medal." He muttered something about hoping I would soon be feeling better, and went away. I now felt tremendously relieved. I had needed to let off steam, and I had made the only form of protest available to me. Some days later, Blondie came bouncing into the ward and greeted me with, "See you've got a gong then!" I did not want to discuss the matter, and I replied that I knew nothing of it. He continued, "It was on DROs, and all the lads know about it." I did not bother to tell him about my encounter with the Medical Officer. "What else is new?" I wanted to know. "Well, there were a couple of Italian bints [girls] living in the sergeants' lines until the Squadron Commander found out and got rid of them." I presumed that he had not ordered them to be shot like the dogs. "Souvenirs from Sorrento, perhaps," I said.

One day, as I lay in bed, I realized that I was getting better when I started to take notice of the Italian girl who was bending down to sweep the floor beside my bed. I was enjoying my blurred view of the backs of her thighs when she suddenly snapped into an upright position and looked behind her. "What's wrong?" I asked her in Italian. She told me, "It is very, very dangerous to bend down." I wanted to know why. "They creep up behind me and touch me, and sometimes they grab me and turn me upside-down, because they say they want to find out if I am wearing knickers made out of hospital linen." I wondered who "they" were, and guessed that she must have been molested by the hospital staff.

I was waiting for my dressings to be changed when I was startled by a shrieking female, "Lie to attention, lie to attention!" It sounded like the woman who told me that rank did not count. She sped up and down the ward, "Lie to attention, lie to attention!" I wondered what had got into her. She paused by my bed and screeched, "You are to lie to attention immediately!" I muttered, "What does it mean?" She replied, "It means lie flat on your back — legs straight — feet together —

head straight — both arms straight down by your sides, above the bedclothes." It had been a long time since I had even been ordered to stand to attention, and I had never heard of anyone being required to lie to attention. "What for?" I asked. She explained that the officer in charge of the hospital was approaching on his round of inspection, so I must do as I was told — "Lie to attention!" I responded by putting one bandaged arm above the sheets and the other one inside the bedclothes. I bent one leg so that my knee stuck up in the air and slowly wriggled until I lay diagonally across the bed. "Lie to attention!" she bleated again. "Can't do it!" I grunted, and then I muttered under my breath. "The silly bastards will want me to put on a cap and salute lying down next." Some weeks later, when I was allowed out of bed, I truculently stuck my hands in my trouser pockets as the boss man made his inspection. I was wearing flying-boots and one of the battledress blouses that I had worn in the air. The battledress and the flying-boots were stained with dried blood. I did not like being dressed in such a fashion, but I had no alternative. I was preparing to react belligerently if told to stand to attention. The officer was carrying a riding crop and whacking the side of his trousers as he approached me. I was ready for an altercation. To my surprise, he greeted me cordially, asked me about my condition and seemed to have a genuine interest in my replies. I took my hands out of my pockets, made an effort to stand up straight and chatted to him about my injuries. It would be a long time before any other military doctor showed comparable sympathetic interest in me.

After about six weeks in bed, I had been horrified to find that I was at first unable to walk. I was weak and my balance seemed to have been upset, but that phase soon passed, and I was able to walk along the corridor a couple of times each week to a room where operations were performed on my right eye. Minute pieces of metal and Perspex were removed from the eyeball under local anaesthetic, and then a small piece of wood was dug out. "Was there any wood in the plane?" I was asked. The matter puzzled me until I remembered that I always propped the wooden box for the astrocompass against the hot air pipe to stop the air blowing into my face during the bombing run. The box must have been shattered in the explosion.

I was told that an eye in such damaged condition had never been saved before. "Thanks to the use of penicillin, the eye has not had to be removed, but you will never again be able to see with it." The other eye was now fully recovered, but I had another problem — I had no short-term memory. I could not remember events from day to day. I took to scribbling notes on bits of paper, and when I came across them later, the only way I knew that I had written them was by recognizing my handwriting. I decided not to tell anyone about my amnesia, and hoped that it might be just a temporary condition, although it must have made other patients conclude that I was rather weird. I was walking through the corridor one afternoon when I saw a sergeant pilot whose face seemed familiar; I stopped him and asked him if he had been on my squadron or at any training units at the same time as me. I told him, "Your face is so familiar, I'm sure I have seen you somewhere." He grinned at me as he replied, "You sat opposite me at breakfast this morning."

Christmas came and went quietly. Jobbo arrived with a large bag of sweets and two bottles of wine. A young woman from ENSA, the organization for entertaining the troops, sat on the next bed flashing her legs at me. I guessed that she was doing her bit for victory. No doubt she was pretty, but I could not see her face clearly. "What's happened to you?" she asked. I told her, "I was hit by flak." She then asked me what flak was. I thought everybody knew. In time, I would find out that I was quite wrong in that assumption.

At a distance of two beds away from me was a South African black man of the Cape Corps. He never had any visitors, and I was inquisitive when he received some mail. By throwing a packet of cigarettes to him, I made contact. He took one cigarette and started to get out of bed to bring the packet back to me. "I don't think you're allowed up. Just throw it back," I told him, but he obviously could not throw anything at a white man, so he padded over to my bed and handed me the packet. I was able to find out that his letters were from his woman at home in the tribe. "She can't write herself, but somebody in the tribe writes for her," he told me. I would have liked to know the contents of the letters, but I did not like to ask. I did, however, discover what had caused him to be admitted to hospital. Some

Italian youths had allegedly hit him on the head with a bottle and cracked his skull. "I will get even," he told me, "I'm a truck driver. I often drive through a narrow tunnel. When I drive through the tunnel, they have to stand close up against the wall. I'll get them." I was concerned that he might very well get the wrong ones, but I realized that he nursed a grievance against Italians in general, and it would be futile for me to try to dissuade him from trying to get even.

One day I learned that the man in the bed at the far end of the ward was a wounded German pilot. I was keen to practise my schoolboy German on him, so I asked him a few questions, and was surprised that he did not want to tell me anything other than what I already knew: that he was a German and he was a pilot. I later realized that he was sticking to the rules — name, rank and number only.

To relieve the boredom, I began to interrogate all the other patients in the ward. Most of them had far more interesting stories than mine. One pilot officer had jumped out of his crippled Spitfire and his parachute had caught on the side of the cockpit and opened. His shoulder was being smashed against the tail as the plane went down, and he was temporarily blinded by glycol streaming back from the engine. His squadron colleagues watched him going down attached to the plane, and when it exploded on impact with the ground they flew back to base and reported that he had been killed. What they did not know was that the parachute had torn itself free a few seconds before the crash, and he had drifted onto some telegraph wires that broke his fall and saved his life. Fortunately, he was on the right side of the front line. He got a lift on a horse-drawn cart to a field hospital, and the same day he was flown to the base hospital in Foggia.

A pilot with a fierce black beard was in for observation. After being shot down on the wrong side of the line, he had been taken care of by an Italian family that ran a bar frequented by German troops. The family provided him with some civilian clothes so that he could do menial work in the bar. As he could not speak either German or Italian, he pretended to be dumb and slow-witted when the Germans were present. "I became quite popular with the German soldiers. They often bought me wine and gave me cigarettes. I stayed there a few months until the Allied troops arrived, but as I had grown this black beard, I had difficulty in convincing them that I was an Englishman," he told me.

I was surprised to find that British casualties were arriving from Greece. Greek insurgents who had fought against the Germans since the start of the war, and who had been supplied with guns and ammunition by the Allies, were now trying to prevent the British from restoring the monarchy. One patient had been shot as he walked down the stairs of a building. The bullet had entered his mouth and come out of the back of his neck.

An aircrew wireless operator from my squadron was hopping around the ward on crutches. I knew what had happened to him. A lump of shrapnel had gone right through one thigh into the other when the plane was riddled with more than a hundred holes over the target. The Australian pilot managed to bring the plane back to Amendola, and as our crew stood waiting for the next crew to land and join us on the truck back to the domestic site, we were horrified to see one aircraft with its lights on coming in to land while the damaged plane without lights approached from the opposite direction. Both planes touched down at the same time and raced towards each other. We knew that the runway was too narrow for the planes to pass each other, and we expected to witness the most awful crash from our view at right angles to the runway. To our amazement the planes did not crash. We jumped into the truck and chased after the damaged plane and found that it had landed on the unlit "dirt strip" that ran parallel to the runway. The pilot had guessed the position of the dirt strip, which was in complete darkness, and landed without lights, flaps and brakes. We knew that a Liberator landing without brakes could run for about seven miles, but as we chased after the plane, its nosewheel burst and brought it to a halt. All the crew members, being aware of the danger of fire, managed to scramble out, and after waiting a few minutes to ensure that it was safe to do so we climbed aboard to inspect the damage by the light of our torches. The engines had been damaged and the radio had been on fire. The front of the plane was badly damaged so that the pilot was exposed to the cold and his feet had become frostbitten. In the front compartment, there was a hole as big as a bucket a few inches above the navigator's seat.

"Where the hell were you when that happened?" I asked him. I knew that if he had been sitting in the seat, he would have been chopped in half. At first, he could only exclaim in his strong South African accent, "Shit man — shit man! Shit, look at that!" After his excitement eventually subsided, he was able to tell me that he always lay down on the deck beside the bomb aimer to see what was going on during the bombing run, and he was lying down when the damage had occurred over the target. All the way back to the domestic site the navigator repeated, "Shit man!" He had had a lucky escape and was obviously in shock.

One or two of the hospital patients were soldiers who had been wounded in the line. One of them told me that he had a leg wound that he was deliberately keeping open so that he would not be sent back to the front. He told me, "I shut myself in the bathroom every couple of days and rub soap into it and then bandage it up again. I'm not going back in the bloody line." I was surprised that he told me his secret.

I had my own secret, of course — the amnesia. I hoped to return to flying duties eventually, and I thought it wise to say nothing that might spoil my chance of retaining my aircrew status.

One day a three-ton truck arrived at the hospital and took me back to the domestic site to collect what remained of my kit. To my surprise, the driver told me that he had also been wounded. "Got a lump of shrapnel in the arse when an aircraft blew up on the runway," he told me. "I'd delivered the crew to the airstrip and waited to see them take off. When the Lib crashed, I ran to it, thinking I might be able to pull somebody out. When the plane burst into flames I ran away, and I was just diving into a slit trench when the plane blew up. That's how I got the shrapnel in my arse." I realized that it must have been the occasion when Jasper's Liberator crashed and half the members of his crew were killed.

The atmosphere on the domestic site was depressing. The whole area was a sea of mud. In miserable drizzle, a few men wearing groundsheets were squatting on the lavatory buckets in the open. I noticed that some of the crews had made shacks out of the cardboard sections of crates in which overload tanks had been delivered to the American Air Force. The shacks reminded me of the natives' shantytowns in South Africa.

I quickly collected my kitbag and returned to the hospital. I now had a greatcoat and shoes, and a few days later I was glad to be told, "You ought to go out for a walk." I had been issued with a pair of steel-rimmed sunglasses with leather dust-shields on the sides, such as had been used by troops in the desert. I could not keep my eyes open without the sunglasses, but I felt foolish going out with them on in a snowstorm. I decided to go to the NAAFI. There was nowhere else to go. I stood in the street by a fountain that I recognized, and then I realized that I had no idea where the NAAFI was. I wandered around to see if I came across it, but without success. My memory was worse than I had realized. I hastily retraced my steps to the hospital, fearing that I might forget where that was if I stayed out any longer. I decided never to go out of the hospital again. As I got undressed in the evening, I noticed a large buff-coloured envelope, bearing my name, attached to the end of the bed. I tipped out the contents — my X-rays. I had never seen X-ray pictures before, and I was interested to see how clearly the shrapnel showed up. A piece of metal about the size and shape of a bullet was in the right side of my head, and a similar piece was in my chest. As I had a four-inch scar with stitch marks on my chest, I assumed that the shrapnel had been dug out from there, but I wondered if the metal had been removed from my head, and thought, at any event, it was not surprising that I suffered some loss of memory. I questioned one of the nurses and was told sharply that I had no right to meddle with the X-ray pictures — they were there for the doctor's use and I was not to touch them again.

After two months in hospital in Foggia, I was transferred to a hospital on the other side of the country at a place called Torre del Greco, where I stayed for another month, and then I was discharged and sent to the familiar disposal centre at Portici. I had no money, so I applied for what was called a casual payment, only to be told that I was not due for any money. "As a matter of fact, you owe us fifty pounds," the pay clerk told me haughtily. I was surprised in view of the fact that I had not received any money for over three months. Had they charged me the cost of repairing the damage to the plane, or, more likely, had someone else been drawing my pay for three months while I was in hospital? I would never find out.

In Portici, I was interviewed by a senior medical officer, who asked me, "What do you want to do now that you are out of hospital?" I replied that my only interest was in flying, so perhaps I could become a bombing instructor. "I'm recommending you for repatriation to the United Kingdom," he replied, "your vision isn't up to aircrew standard." I explained to him that when using the old CSBS only one eye was required — the same as when using a rifle; and with the modern Marl 14 bombsight, it didn't matter whether the bomb aimer used one eye or two. He was not listening. "I'm recommending repatriation," he repeated. "You must remain on twenty-four-hour standby to leave by air." I was dismayed; I protested that I did not want to return to the United Kingdom. I was not ready for my parents to see me looking like this. I had not yet come to terms with my appearance. I had deep red and blue scars on my face, a white scar like a cataract on my eye, the swollen eyelid hung down in an ugly fashion and I had no right eyebrow. I was ashamed of my appearance, and I found that I was continually trying to hide the right side of my face behind my hand. My memory was improving, but I had slight difficulty in using my left hand, which I kept in my pocket to disguise the problem. I was in a mess and I needed time to recover my confidence. Sorrento was not far away, and although I was on twenty-four-hour standby for repatriation by air, I would have risked slipping away to see Rosa if I had not been so ashamed of my facial disfigurement.

I noticed that the detention centre was still in operation at Portici, and a couple of my earlier acquaintances were locked up in there. Elderly Italian men in shabby clothes and women and children with malnutrition sores on their bare legs still queued silently in the courtyard, waiting to get a share of the swill. One little boy crouched on the ground and started to eat his precious portion, when two older boys who had just arrived snatched it out of his hands and ran off. In the dining-hall, I tried to persuade the men sitting at the next table not to stub their cigarettes out among the remnants of food on their plates. They looked surprised. There was not much sympathy for the Italians. I had watched nuns trying to beg money for children from Allied soldiers, and heard them being told, "Don't ask us. Go and ask *Il Papa* to give you some of the gold out of the Vatican. He's got plenty."

CHAPTER
ELEVEN

Back Home Again

It was now February, and the little amount of war news that we heard was not encouraging. So-called "pilotless planes" were said to be attacking London and the south of England. I imagined such planes to be as big as our Liberators, whereas they were merely the size of one bomb. Time passed slowly as I waited, one day at a time, for the plane back to England, which never came. After waiting four weeks for a plane, I finally boarded a ship, instead, and my kitbags, marked with large red crosses, were carried on board for me. My expectations of a pleasant voyage and a bed in the ship's sickbay were dashed when I found that no sleeping accommodation was provided, and I had to sit on a wooden bench at a bare table for two weeks, wearing all my clothes, including my greatcoat. As the weather was stormy, I did not venture on deck, except when the sirens sounded to announce submarine alerts, and on those occasions I shivered in the rain on the open deck, hoping that I would be spared a watery grave.

When the ship reached our secret destination, Liverpool, customs officers came aboard and spent twenty-four hours thoroughly searching the ship and its passengers. I cannot imagine what they expected to find. Many men had been abroad for three or four years, and were anxious to be reunited with their wives and families. In view of the troops' impatience, I would not have been surprised to see the customs men thrown overboard. When we were finally allowed ashore, I had to carry my own kitbags with their Red Cross markings and struggle onto a railway train. I travelled to London and reported to the Air Ministry, where I was given a pass allowing me to go on five weeks' leave, reporting each week for medical examinations. Nobody offered me any money or asked me if I had anywhere to go. I was probably the only man off the troopship who was not glad to be back in England; I was not looking forward to my mother's reaction to my wretched physical appearance.

My parents had a house in Hillingdon, west of London, so I had somewhere to stay that was not too far from the Air Ministry's medical centres. My father, a senior officer in the Royal Air Force, was quite obviously disappointed that I was not a commissioned officer like the rest of his relatives. He had served in the Air Force ever since he transferred from the Army at the end of the previous war, and he was now based at the Enemy Equipment Research Unit in Harrow. I learned that he occasionally flew over to the Continent to pick up German equipment for investigation. He looked aghast at me in my strange brown battledress, worn-out black shoes, un-ironed blue shirt, faded blue cap with a badge of entirely the wrong size that I had bought in a Cairo bazaar, and exclaimed, "Good Lord!

Haven't you got a proper uniform?" I knew that I looked like a scarecrow, and I felt like a fool. My mother's hysterical outbursts did not help matters. She was mainly concerned that I was so seriously underweight. I discovered later that the doctors had described me in their notes as a case of severe physical debility, and I then wondered why I had been dumped in the aircrew disposal centre at Portici for a month, instead of being given convalescent leave and some decent food.

On the morning after my arrival at Hillingdon, one of the "pilotless planes", now known as V1s, or doodlebugs, flew low over the house making a noise like a tractor without a silencer. When the engine stopped, I shouted to my mother, "What shall we do?" She calmly continued pegging the washing on the clothes-line. "You can't do anything," she replied. A few seconds later the sound of an explosion and a plume of smoke indicated that the flying-bomb had landed not far away in Greenford.

Shortly afterwards several loud explosions were reported by the Ministry of Information to be gas mains exploding all over London. My father told me that they were Germany's new secret weapon, the V2, and although many hundreds of the V2 rockets were expected to fall on London shortly, the Air Ministry had advised their staff not to evacuate their families from London as any such exodus might cause panic among the civil population. The arrival of the rockets certainly caused me to feel panicky. I wondered if I had returned from active service abroad to be bumped off at home with mother and father.

Every week I travelled by underground train to visit the Central Medical Board, and on each occasion as I came out of the station I noticed that another of London's buildings had disappeared. We had clearly not won the war yet. I soon realized that I was not being examined by what I termed "proper doctors". Each week I was interrogated by men in white coats who were solely interested in my mental state. "Are you interested in girls?" I was asked. "What sort of girls are you interested in?" "Do you dream?" "What do you dream about?" I considered that the whole process was a waste of time, and made a few flippant replies, all of which were painstakingly scribbled down in longhand by my interrogators.

I was still hoping for a return to flying duties, so I tried to make light of my physical problems. In addition to severe stomach pains, I had another problem that I did not wish to disclose. I found that I could not sit down quietly and talk to people for more than a few seconds. In a confined space, I felt compelled to pace up and down or go outside; otherwise, I would feel like screaming and smashing up the furniture. I dared not discuss this problem with anyone, and I hoped that it would improve in time. After several encounters with what I guessed to be psychoanalysts, I was given a reduced medical category, which meant that I was grounded and could serve in the United Kingdom only. I was dismayed that my flying career had terminated. I was twenty years old.

Upon my next visit to the medical centre, having nothing further to lose, I disclosed that I was suffering severe stomach pains and passing black stools. "That's a natural reaction to having stopped flying," I was told. "Don't think about the stomach pain, and it will go away." I left the medical centre and called at a restaurant for a meal. My left hand was still not working properly, and my fork wavered on its way to my mouth. Out of the corner of my good eye, I noticed a woman at the next table nudge her companion to draw his attention to me. I felt angry, and would have liked to stick the fork into the two of them. Of course, the stomach pain did not go away, and eventually I suffered a perforated duodenal ulcer and severe haemorrhage.

At the end of my five weeks' leave, I was instructed to report directly to an isolated unit on the east coast. I was unhappy about the prospect of a mundane job on the ground, but I soon discovered that I would not lack excitement. The Royal Air Force believed in simply telling people to do a job, but not how to do it. Although I was still merely a sergeant, I was given the title Bombing Range Safety Officer, responsible for practice bombing, rocket firing, air-to-ground gunnery and gunnery instructing. Then I was given the rather more hazardous job of bomb disposal, without any prior tuition. Most of the bombs I dealt with weighed either 250 kg or 500 kg. In my spare time I cycled around the locality on a little bicycle, meant for one of my staff of airwomen, and warned the inhabitants that they should not make "frivolous and irresponsible" complaints about cracks appearing in their ceilings.

On one occasion, I was preparing to blow up a large sheet-steel container of small anti-personnel bombs. I instructed my squad of half a dozen airmen to open the container so that I could place an explosive charge inside. No sooner had the container been opened than one of the bombs seemed to leap out like a frog. It had a sprung diaphragm on the nose and a little parachute tucked into the tail. I immediately took to my heels and sprinted a couple of hundred yards, before stopping for breath. "When we saw you take off, we knew we ought to get the hell out of it pretty smartly, Chiefy," the airmen told me. I started to explain that the bombs would not explode until the parachute in the tail had opened and pulled a safety pin out of the side of the bomb. "Then why did we run away?" they asked. "I ran because I was shit scared, but I know they won't go off while the safety pins are in, so let's go back now and blow the bastards up," I replied. We slowly returned to within about twenty yards of the bombs, and the airmen listened quietly while I tried to convince them and reassure myself that the bombs really would not imminently blow us all to kingdom come. They looked doubtful, but they had to do as they were told. I was in charge.

The war in Europe ended, and our great wartime leader, Prime Minister Churchill, made a triumphant speech, praising the munitions factory workers and others who had contributed to the defeat of the

Germans. He seemed to gloss over the efforts of the men who had carried out the mighty strategic bombing offensive. Perhaps he forgot us, or perhaps he was following the growing trend of public opinion that had begun to turn against people like us as soon as we were no longer needed.

By this stage of my Air Force service, I was a flight sergeant with "time promotion" backdated one year, so I should actually have been a warrant officer. One morning as I was preparing to blow up some more bombs and crack some more ceilings, I was handed an official communication informing me that, as I had been declared unfit for flying duties, I had lost my aircrew status. I did not qualify for further "time promotion" and I was reduced to half pay, but I could retain my flying-badge. My rate of pay would now be ten pounds per month. I was working seven days a week so long as the weather was suitable. I had not had a day off for months. In view of my hazardous duties and low pay, the Air Force certainly had a bargain.

Every few months I was required to attend a medical board, but I could not see the point of that, as I was obviously permanently disabled. I travelled from early morning until late one night to attend such a board. "Well, how are you?" I was asked. "About the same," I replied. After a cursory eyesight test, the medical officer declared, "I think it's best to leave you with the same medical category — not fit for flying — fit only for ground duties in the UK. You will certainly never again be fit for flying." I had not expected any other decision but I felt that the words "not fit for" were degrading. It was like being told, "You are not fit to lick my boots." Since early childhood, physical fitness had been a coveted sign of superiority, and passing the stringent physical examination for flying personnel had been a proud achievement. Vanity and conceit made even the mere wearing of glasses a matter to be scorned as a horrible sign of weakness. During morning parades when we were at training schools the corporals would shout, "Fall out the sick, lame and lazy!" Any aircrew man who reported sick was suspected of either swinging the lead (malingering) or being not tough enough to stand the pace. Pride had caused many an aircrew man to keep going when he really should have been on the sick list. I was now relegated to the miserable ranks of the inferior, and I felt embittered.

Although I did not yet know it, my battle with the doctors was only just beginning. My final medical examination in the Royal Air Force was unbelievable. Six months before I was due to be demobilized, I was summoned before a medical officer whom I had never seen before. As I stood before his desk, fully clad with my cap and greatcoat on, he surprised me with the words, "You should have had a medical board last year, but as you did not have it I'm giving you one now. You are A1." I immediately burst out laughing: "I don't think you can do that without examining me, and as a matter of fact, I did have a medical examination last year." He opened a file and replied, "There's nothing in the file about it. I don't know why you say you had an examination last year. What do you allege happened?" I told him that although I would have preferred to retain my aircrew status, I was grounded permanently on half pay and my medical category was A4BH. He pointed to his rank insignia and replied impatiently, "I am a squadron leader. I am competent to conduct medical boards and you are now recategorized A1. That's all, you can go now." A few weeks later, I was offered a commission in the Royal Air Force Regiment. I was told, "You will be a pilot officer [the lowest commissioned rank] with an immediate posting to Aden." I knew that the Arab terrorists (or freedom fighters) were struggling for independence, and I had no intention of getting involved in that conflict, but I asked the interviewing officer, "When is the medical examination?" He replied, "There isn't one. It is not necessary for you aircrew men. We know you are okay." I did not bother to point out that I was not an aircrew man. He rattled on about armoured cars and infantry. I was not paying attention. I had decided to leave the Air Force at the first opportunity, so they would simply have to manage without me in future.

Shortly before I was due to be demobilized, I took a couple of days leave and visited an engineering factory in the Midlands, thinking that I might secure an offer of employment. The personnel manager interviewed me: "Now tell me, what have you been doing in the war?" he asked. I thought what I had been doing was pretty obvious, as I was in Air Force uniform with medal ribbons, wound stripe and flying badge, but I answered politely, "I have been flying in the Royal Air Force." He replied offhandedly, "That's really not a great deal of use to us, is it? We cannot pay you men's wages for doing boys' work." Although my immediate reaction was an overwhelming desire to punch his smug face, I realized that he was right. My wartime experience in the Air Force was of no use to a potential employer. It was time to stop secretly picturing myself as the wounded hero returned from the war. I was a useless member of society and it seemed that society owed me nothing. It was time to grow up, forget the past and start a new life.

CHAPTER
TWELVE

Coming to Terms With the Post-War World

The Royal Air Force took back its uniform from me and gave me a cardboard box of civilian clothes instead. I put on the trilby hat. I had never owned such a hat before, and I joined several other self-conscious men as we looked at ourselves in a mirror and laughed at the ridiculous spectacle. As I walked out through the gates of the demobilization centre at Uxbridge, a rather shifty-looking character offered me a couple of pounds for my cardboard box of clothes. He was making the same approach to every newly discharged airman. Civilian clothing was strictly rationed, and the black market was eager to welcome us. I offered him the hat, but he was no more interested in it than I was. As I crossed the road and made my way to the railway station, I remembered how as an eight-year-old child in Uxbridge I had seen men in shabby raincoats shuffling along the gutter, playing musical instruments, while another man rattled a collecting-box at uninterested passers-by. I had run back home to ask my mother why men with the same medals as my father were begging in the street. She explained that they were unemployed ex-soldiers of the Great War. Now, about thirteen years later, I too was an ex-serviceman with an uncertain future, and as I stared into the same gutter, I wondered if anything had changed. I would soon find out. My humbling interview with the personnel manager had resulted in a job as a workman in the engineering factory, at a wage of six pounds per week. After much searching, I found lodgings near the factory with a Mrs Pippin, a rather sour old widow. "What time do you want breakfast?" she asked me on the day before I was due to start work. When I said, "Seven o'clock," she shrieked, "So you are a workman! I only have professional men as lodgers. If I had known you were a workman, I would not have taken you. My previous lodgers were gentlemen on the staff — in the drawing office. They had breakfast at eight o'clock." My southern accent had fooled Mrs Pippin into assuming that I was a gentleman. It was obvious to me that I would get the boot as soon as a proper gentleman appeared on the scene.

I reported at the factory at seven-thirty on Monday morning in the middle of a fuel crisis. The workmen were all wearing their overcoats as they stood at their machines and workbenches. I was to be a lathe operator, but as I pointed out to the chargehand, all the lathes were occupied. "Don't worry about that," he told me, "we're sacking four hundred on Friday. You can work on the fitters' bench until then." My workmates with their northern accents were highly suspicious of me, and clearly suspected that I might be "one of them

301

bloody management trainees" instead of a genuine workman. It was clear that class prejudice was not solely a prerogative of the upper classes. I was interested in finding out what life had been like for the men in reserved occupations who had been engaged on essential war work in the factory. One of the fitters told me, "You needn't think it was much fun for us here. It was bloody awful — what with overtime and night shift, fire-watching duty and Home Guard duty." I found out that he had been a lieutenant in the Home Guard — a kind of drinking club, from what I could gather. He had married a well-paid girl who worked in a munitions factory, and between them they had saved enough money out of their high wages to start buying a house. As he was only a little older than I was, I concluded that he was more fortunate than he realized. I did not bother to tell him what the Air Force had paid me for night duty.

I seemed to have little in common with my fellow workmen, and I wondered if any other ex-servicemen might be around. "You see that bloke over there with the millwrights? He was a pilot in the Air Force," I was informed. I doubted it. Surely, nobody else would accept such menial factory work. I looked at him in his greasy boiler suit. "Are you sure he was a pilot?" I asked. "He doesn't look much like the type." My informant replied, "Well, he's supposed to have been a pilot, but he's a bit of a weird lad, he never says a word to anyone. Go over and see if you can get anything out of him." I approached him cautiously and introduced myself. He told me his name was Doug, and I was delighted to find that he had been a pilot on Wellingtons in the Far East. At the end of the war, he had been given the solitary task of single-handed evacuation of all his squadron's aircraft. After flying each plane for hundreds of miles, he had returned to the squadron by train to collect the next one. The duration of the train journey was two weeks. No wonder he had lost the habit of talking to people.

He was in lodgings in the same street as me, and we began to meet occasionally for the odd drink together in the Spotted Cow. After he had been to see his parents in Bridlington one weekend, he told me how he had stopped to listen to a man on a soapbox urging people to take a sightseeing flight in a light aeroplane. The man pointed at Doug: "Now you, sir, yes, you, sir, what about taking a flight? I'm sure you would enjoy it!" "No thanks," replied Doug. "I've had one."

Doug and I were kicked out of our respective digs at about the same time. I had not been getting on very well with Mrs Pippin. I was studying engineering design each evening with my textbooks and papers spread out on the dining table. While I was busy, Mrs Pippin was surreptitiously turning down the gas lamp until I could hardly see. "The gas pressure always gets low at this time of night," she would lie to me. She resented me studying. "What are you doing that for?" she asked. "I suppose you are trying to get a better job?" I confirmed that she was right. She pursed her thin lips and nodded slowly, "Oh yes, I thought so." Not only was I misleading people with my deceptive southern accent, I was apparently intending to step out of my class. Mrs Pippin was fiercely proud of her working-class roots, and she did not wish to have any truck with the likes of me. "My husband was a steelworker all his life — a union official and proud of it," she informed me with an indignant sniff.

When Mrs Pippin announced that her mother, aged ninety-five, had just died, I commented brightly that I thought the old lady had had a good innings, but Mrs Pippin told me that the bereavement had come as an unexpected shock, as her mother had been in such good health, and my comment was in bad taste. Mrs Pippin went away for the funeral and stayed overnight. She did not approve of wireless sets, so she never used hers except as a plant stand, but I liked a little background noise while I was studying, so I bought batteries and got the set working in her absence. When she returned home about nine o'clock in the evening, I was sitting at the dining table with my textbooks. The gaslight was burning brightly on full power and there was a rare fire in the grate. Gracie Fields was belting out the words of a popular song, "Now is the hour for us to say goodbye." Mrs Pippin rushed across the room and almost wrenched the knob off the wireless set in her haste to switch it off. It had rained, and the black dye of her hat was trickling down her face. She looked comical. With a look of disapproval, she quickly took away the ashtray. She then shovelled a big lump of coal out of the grate, took it through the scullery and threw it out in the back yard. "We won't be up much longer," she told me. The next day she told me that she had decided to stop taking in lodgers, so I must move out.

My attempts to find alternative private accommodation were unsuccessful. My father was in India, assisting the Viceroy, Louis Mountbatten, in the dissolution of the British Empire. I was on my own with nowhere to live. In similar circumstances, some men were trying to rejoin the armed forces — often at lower rank and pay. Others vowed, "I would not even join a Christmas club after that bloody lot." My own feelings were that nothing could ever be as bad as what I had experienced on the squadron — nobody was shooting at me — I was alive, and things could surely only get better. I went to the local Labour Exchange and stood in a queue with returned soldiers and redundant munitions workers who were seeking employment. When I got to the front of the queue, I explained to the clerk behind the counter that I already had a job, but nowhere to live. I could see he was relieved that he did not have to explain once again how local factories were laying men off and jobs were scarce. "Here is the address of an industrial hostel, built by the Ministry of Aircraft Production for war workers," he told me. "Now aircraft production has stopped and the workers have been cleared out, the accommodation is at our disposal. I will give you a note to take round there. Have a look at the place and let us know if you want to move in there."

I found that the so-called hostel comprised a collection of asbestos huts, each divided into rooms for two, and a separate hut that served as the cookhouse and canteen. The place had a layout similar to an Army camp, but with better accommodation than anything that had been provided for the troops. I was allocated a room with an Irishman who worked locally as a labourer, laying railway lines. Fortunately, he was always out in the evenings, so I could devote my spare time, undisturbed, to my engineering studies. The cost of accommodation included breakfast and an evening meal in the canteen.

It was in the canteen that I discovered that the other residents and the cooks were either what the authorities termed "stateless persons", or "displaced persons", who had been allowed into England after release from German concentration camps or they were slave workers who had been taken from their homes and transported to German factories. Their countries of origin were Poland, Lithuania, Latvia, Czechoslovakia and other former enemy-occupied territories. Few of them could speak much English, so their common language was a form of "concentration-camp German". They seemed reluctant to talk about their experiences, as though they were ashamed of their pitiful situation — as though they were themselves partly to blame for what had happened to them. My knowledge of German eventually enabled me to elicit from them sickening accounts of wartime atrocities perpetrated by the Nazis. I noticed that some otherwise attractive young women had deep, unsightly scars on their legs, which they explained were the results of cruel muscle-grafting experiments carried out by the Nazi doctors in the concentration camp at Auschwitz. These young women had been seriously damaged by cruel and humiliating radium experiments on their reproductive organs.

From the Poles at the hostel I learned what the Air Force had not seen fit to tell us. I learned that while we were dropping supplies to the beleaguered people of Warsaw, our Soviet allies were already in the suburbs on the other side of the River Vistula. The mighty Soviet army had deliberately halted its rapid advance and waited for the inevitable collapse of the uprising due to lack of adequate Allied support. The uprising lasted sixty-three days, and a quarter of a million of Warsaw's inhabitants were killed during that time. The German army had actually been in retreat until the Soviet army halted its advance and gave the Germans an opportunity to attempt to carry out Hitler's instructions to kill all Warsaw's inhabitants and demolish the city. Women and children were lined up and machine-gunned to death. Flamethrowers were used to incinerate people cowering in the cellars. Drunken troops of a German penal battalion, after capturing a distillery, raped the patients and staff of a cancer hospital. Before the uprising eventually collapsed, starving people were reduced to eating dogs and meat hacked off the carcasses of horses that lay fly-blown in the streets. Men and women soldiers of the resistance army were down in the filth of the sewers into which the Germans were lobbing hand-grenades. After the uprising collapsed, the disarmed remnants of the resistance forces were transported to Auschwitz and other concentration camps.

Hearing horror stories from people who had been on the ground, while I was in the air above Warsaw, made me feel uneasy about my reluctance at the time to be involved in the hazardous Warsaw flights. I wished we had known what exactly was happening on the ground. If we had known about the immense scale of the German atrocities, we would have had more sympathy with Warsaw's Poles instead of assuming that they were foolish for not waiting quietly for liberation, as most of the people of Paris seemed content to do until our troops appeared in the vicinity. We would have felt indignant if we had known at the time that the French Resistance had received ten thousand tons of supplies during the war, but the far larger and better-trained Polish underground forces, that our airmen were belatedly attempting to help, had been sent a mere six hundred tons. In accordance with the British government's sickening policy of appeasement of Stalin, Anthony Eden, the British Foreign Secretary, had secretly declared that the Poles should be deliberately kept short of supplies and given "only enough for sabotage purposes, otherwise they might attack the Russians".

Understandably, the Western Allies were fearful that the Soviet Union might arrange a separate peace with the Nazis and allow them to close down the Eastern Front and turn their full force against the West. Stalin had to be appeased at all costs. When the Polish Ambassador, Count Edward Raczynski, and his chief of staff reported to Prime Minister Churchill that thousands of Polish airmen and soldiers were threatening to go on hunger strike in protest at the lack of adequate support for the Warsaw Uprising, he replied, "We do not need the Polish battalions now."

Our few Air Force survivors of the Warsaw flights were told personally by our AOC-in-C, when he talked to us in Italy, that Churchill had said we should not stand by idly while the people of Warsaw were desperately struggling for survival, because we owed the Poles a debt of honour.

A "Debt of Honour" — such hollow words. When we flew to Warsaw, we had not known that the fate of the Poles had already been sealed by an agreement with Stalin that the Soviets would control Poland through a post-war Communist puppet regime. We had not known that while our men were being shot out of the skies over Poland, not only our German enemies but also our Soviet allies were preventing Polish resistance forces in outlying areas from coming to the aid of the Warsaw insurgents. We had not known that Stalin had broken off diplomatic relations with the Polish government-in-exile when the unlawful massacre by the Soviet regime of thousands of Polish officers at Katyn was disclosed to the world. We had not known that Stalin had closed the airbases in the Ukraine at the start of the Warsaw Uprising in August to prevent us from using them. The American airmen, flying shuttle-bombing missions from our base at Amendola, had been able to land in the Ukraine right up to the end of July. We had not known that our Soviet allies were deliberately shooting at us over Poland to prevent us from reaching Warsaw because they were in dispute with the anti-Communist Polish government. We did not know that our flights to Warsaw in aid of the Poles had been declared by the British Chiefs of Staff to be futile well before they took place, or that Prime Minister Churchill had disregarded this military judgement. We did not know that it did not really matter whether we dropped our supplies in the correct place or not. The uprising was doomed from the outset, and the sacrifice of our airmen was a futile gesture that would have no bearing whatsoever on the outcome of the war.

At the end of the war, the British government followed Stalin's lead, and withdrew diplomatic recognition of the Polish government-in-exile in London that had placed its thousands of soldiers and airmen at our disposal throughout the war, and recognized instead the Communist government that had been foisted on the Polish nation by Stalin. The Polish gold that had been brought to Britain by the government-in-exile was then handed over to the Communists. No Polish troops were permitted to participate in the triumphant "victory parade" through London. Bevin, the new British Foreign Secretary, arranged for a note to be given to the Poles who had fought alongside our troops. The note thanked the Poles for helping us to win the war, and told them that they should now return to their own country, "Because there is nothing for you in Britain or in the British Empire, despite what Churchill might have led you to believe." He also told them that in accordance with an agreement made with the Communists, all Poles who returned home would be perfectly safe "so long as you are not criminals". Poles who went back were immediately branded as criminals by the Communist regime, arrested in their hundreds and persecuted for having served in the West. Many people were either beaten to death, sentenced to be executed without trial or tortured during long terms of imprisonment. Most of the Poles who had served with us in the West would not live long enough to see the freedom for which they had fought so gallantly throughout the entire duration of the war. The Warsaw flights, with our casualty rate of thirty per cent per night, represented my worst operational flying experiences, and although I wished to put all memories of the past behind me, I could not resist an overwhelming compulsion to discuss the Warsaw Uprising repeatedly with the Poles at the hostel. I did not talk to them about my own experiences, as they seemed so insignificant in comparison with theirs.

Andy had remained in contact with me by letter ever since we had both left the Air Force. His first letter had informed me that he had been awarded the Distinguished Flying Medal, and he thanked me for being such a valuable member of his crew. I could not bring myself to tell him how, in a fit of rage, I had spurned such an award.

In common with all other ex-servicemen, I was required to register with a civilian "panel" doctor. The doctor took the trouble to see me personally. "I might as well check you over while you are here," he told me. After examining me, he said, "I don't know what's happened to you, but you are in a hell of a state." I explained that I had sustained multiple wounds while

I was flying, and he exclaimed, "Then you ought to be getting a war disablement pension!" I replied that I would not qualify for such a pension, because I had been declared A1, albeit with my cap and overcoat on, shortly before leaving the Air Force. He scribbled some notes and then told me, "I will get some forms and fill them in for you, and then you sign them and send them off to the Ministry of Pensions." He added indignantly, "They should not be allowed to get away with this sort of thing. It's absolutely disgraceful!"

A few weeks later, after receiving a summons to attend a Ministry of Pensions medical board, I reluctantly took a day off work without pay. I had no expectation of a satisfactory outcome, and felt sure that I was wasting my time and money in attending the examination, but a few weeks later a letter from the ministry informed me that I had been awarded a war disability pension of nine shillings (45p) per week. The letter also advised me that this was an interim assessment, and that my case would be reviewed in due course. Nine shillings per week was a derisory amount, and I was disgusted to note that all war disability pensions were linked to the recipient's former military rank. This discrimination made me wonder why, for instance, an officer's amputated limb should be considered more valuable than that of an ordinary soldier. In due course, I received another letter from the Ministry of Pensions telling me that my pension was being discontinued; I was offered the sum of £25 in final settlement. I could appeal against this decision, in which case I would risk losing not only the pension, but also the final settlement. I found that many of my disabled contemporaries, not wishing to suffer the humiliation of further medical boards, took the final settlement, but I decided to appeal.

The Ministry of Pensions Medical Boards always followed the same pattern. The two medical officers sat behind their desk and looked down their noses at me as though looking at something the cat had dragged in. "Go into the cubicle," I was instructed, "take off all your clothes and come out here." I knew their game. A naked man should be subdued, rather than truculent, in their presence. I obediently undressed and stood stark naked on the cold linoleum, waiting for them to look up from their scribbling. They sat there feeling, no doubt, vastly superior in their suits, collars and ties. One of them got up and slowly walked around me. "Well, where is it?" he asked impatiently. "Where is it?" I assumed that he was looking for evidence of my disability. "Where's what?" I asked meekly. "Well, what's happened to you?" he snapped. "I was hit by anti-aircraft shrapnel," I told him. "Ahha!" he said triumphantly. "Looking up when you shouldn't have been!" I thought to myself, Now I've got the supercilious bastard. He has assumed that I should have been in the air raid shelter. Being naked had not inhibited me. Enraged, I bellowed at him, "No, I was not looking up when I shouldn't have been. I was up there! You see, you simply can't have a fucking air raid unless some stupid bastard is up there!" He jumped back, startled. "Why don't you read the bloody file?" I shouted. "Then you will know what's happened to me."

He scampered back to safety on the other side of the desk and sat down. "I'm sorry, I'm sorry," he stammered, as his face reddened. "You needn't apologize. That is not the most stupid bloody question I have been asked. I've stopped saying I was hit by flak, because you people don't seem to know what that is." I had narrowly avoided saying "you bastards" instead of "you people". He hastily fumbled through the pages of the folder containing my medical documents. Still completely naked, I stood waiting defiantly for the next stupid question. "Thank you, that's all," he said, "you can get dressed and go now. We will be writing to you in due course." The other medical officer looked up from his scribbling and gave me a slight, wry grin. I guessed he had enjoyed his colleague's embarrassing encounter with me.

In due course, I received a notification that the interim assessment of my war disablement pension would be extended for a further period of two years. Shortly before another encounter with the Ministry of Pensions doctors, I was undergoing treatment by my panel doctor for a respiratory disorder, and the treatment was causing my fingers to tremble slightly. A Ministry of Pensions doctor, whom I had not seen before, dealt with me in the usual high-handed manner: "Hold out your hands and spread the fingers wide." I did as he told me, and then he blurted out, "Good God, man, your nerves are in a dreadful state! Have you always been like that? Why don't you get something done about it?" I made a supreme effort to control my temper. The next time I saw my panel doctor he asked me, "How did you get on at the Ministry of Pensions examination?" I told him what had transpired. His face turned crimson, and he jumped up from his seat and paced rapidly back and forth, as he shouted, "You should have punched him straight in the face. Of course you were all like that — all the pilots were like that and all the bloody submarine commanders, too." He continued, "He was taking unfair advantage of his position. How dare he speak to you like that! You should have hit him in the mouth." I had not dared to do so. The war had left me with a violent temper, and I knew that if I had hit the man once, I might not have been able to stop. "Well, I suppose it is their policy to try to humiliate us, so that we won't keep coming back and claiming war pensions," I said. "It would have been cheaper if we had been killed outright instead of merely being wounded and coming back to make a nuisance of ourselves."

Having heard that the government might consider giving financial grants to some war veterans to enable them to obtain professional qualifications, I made the necessary applications for interviews. The interviews were conducted in an atmosphere quite similar to that of the Ministry of Pensions medical boards. I was asked brusquely, "What were you studying before you joined the Air Force?" I answered, "I studied mathematics in order to pass the aircrew entrance exams." I was asked, "So, were you not already studying for a professional qualification?" I explained that I was only seventeen when I joined the Air Force. "At the time it appeared that we were losing the war, so there seemed to be no point in thinking about a profession. Our towns were being bombed by the Germans, and I thought that by joining the Air Force I could help to stop the war." The expressions on the faces of my inquisitors seemed to say to me, "You poor simpleton!" I suggested that if I were granted enough to live on for two years — long enough for a full-time course to gain the Higher National Certificate in mechanical engineering, I would pay back the money. "I don't want anything for nothing. I do not expect you to give me a free gift — just a loan. When I start work again after two years, you can deduct instalments out of my pay like income tax." They told me haughtily, "We only give grants to people of professional status."

By the time of my third unsuccessful attempt, I was sick of the discourteous manner of the civil servants at the interviews. When one of them was particularly disparaging in his remarks, I let fly with a torrent of invective before slamming the door on my way out. His colleague scurried after me and jumped in the lift with me. He shook me warmly by the hand. "Thank you for doing that," he said. "I have to sit there, day after day, listening to him being rude to people like you. So far, you are the only one who has told him off. He thoroughly deserved what he got today. You really let him have it! It was a pleasure listening to you."

I returned to the hostel and sat eating an evening meal in the dining hall with Doug, my fellow factory worker. In the general hubbub from the ex-concentration camp victims, I told him about my unsuccessful attempts to secure a government grant. He had not tried to get one. We were both having difficulty in becoming integrated into civilian life in an industrial area where most people had been in reserved occupations throughout the war. "They think we are bloody fools for joining up," I said, "and I'm beginning to think they're right." Doug sighed, "You just can't talk to civilians. It's no good trying to tell them anything — they would never understand."

I made my way back to my room in the asbestos hut. There was no table in the room, so I removed the large mirror from the dresser and laid it flat to use as an improvised drawing-board. I very rarely went out in the evenings. I always worked on my engineering studies until around midnight. I was determined to get away from the stink and grime of the factory as soon as possible. I was equally determined never again to ask the government, or anyone else, for a loan. All the energy generated by my aggressiveness, anger and bitterness was now to be channelled into the struggle for a successful career. Meanwhile, Andy was also having difficulty in finding suitable employment. For a time, he worked as a "foot in the door" insurance man, before becoming a social worker. I could not bear to lose contact with him. Through him, I remained in contact with the other members of our crew. We were all struggling to survive as civilians in an unfriendly environment now.

During the time when I was engaged on bomb-disposal duties on the isolated east coast, I had spent some of the long summer evenings helping a local farmer with his haymaking. Understandably, my keen interest in his attractive sixteen-year-old daughter met with his stern disapproval. At the time, she was still attending grammar school, and he hoped that she was destined for better things than being associated with an airman of the "here today and gone tomorrow" variety. "How do you imagine that he will be able to keep you in the manner to which you are accustomed?" I tended to sympathize with his opinion.

By the time we married, she was almost twenty years old and I was still a poorly paid factory workman. I now had an even greater incentive to make a success of my life. We moved to London, I got another job as a factory worker and continued my part-time engineering studies on the kitchen table. I was now also perfecting my knowledge of German and learning Russian. Every moment of my spare time was spent in studying. I was obsessed with the idea that it was necessary for me to become more successful than the men of my age who had stayed at home during the war.

Three years after leaving the Air Force, I secured a position at the government's Armaments Design Establishment as a member of the aircraft cannon design team. I reported to the chief designer on my first day: "I am actually a production engineer. I don't know anything about the design of aircraft cannon." He replied, "But I understand that you were flying in the Air Force!" I pointed out that I had also been shot, but that did not make me an armaments designer. He then told me that I would be working on the development of a revolutionary type of gun. Nobody knew much about it. It was to be based on a German prototype, found in a burnt-out train. He ran through the firing principle, and I was surprised to find that it was a mechanical gun. "When I was flying, we were sometimes followed by Ju 88s with a dull red light in the nose," I told him. "We thought the red light was some kind of a homing device and that when the Ju 88 was close enough to us the two Me 109s accompanying it would attack us. Rocket-firing aircraft also attacked us. Why don't you design some kind of a predicted rocket-firing gun instead of a mechanical gun?" What I was suggesting was a heat-seeking guided missile, although such words were not yet in use.

My salary was a mere £325 per annum, but I was now a real gentleman with my own soap, towel and mug. The main attraction of the job was the very long leave periods that I could use for studying, and I had one free day each week to attend technical college. I used a large part of my salary to pay for private language tuition. My German tutors were two hard-up German Jewish émigrés who were studying for university degrees. I also learned to speak Russian from the well educated daughter of a bank director who had fled from Russia during the October Revolution. She now needed to supplement her laundry employee's wages, and I needed a native teacher.

Not wanting a secure, but low-paid, job for life, I soon gave up armaments designing and took a succession of jobs to widen my experience of production engineering; and then, in 1953, when I had been out of the Air Force for six years, I took my first big step into the unknown world of international trade. After an interview entirely in German, Curt Rockwell engaged me to work in the German department of his thriving machine-tool import-export firm. "What exactly is the job?" I asked him. He told me, "The job is what you make it."

I was given a desk and a load of files in German. Nobody told me what to do, but fortunately, the Air Force had accustomed me to being "thrown in the deep end". By the time I left, eight years later, I was in charge of the German department with its staff of German émigrés. I also had control of the company's advertising and exhibitions. All correspondence with our German and Swiss suppliers was in German. We had an endless stream of visitors from Germany, and sometimes, after an exhausting day's work, I found that it was easier to stay in German than to switch back into English.

I often travelled to British factories with German service engineers who spoke no English. The service engineers, from various parts of Germany, spoke their local dialects, which I soon learned to understand. For obvious reasons, I always asked them if they had served on the flak guns in Yugoslavia during the war. From the ex-Nazis and the anti-Nazis who had served in the German forces I gained a better understanding of the futility of the war.

I often heard people say that there can be no winners in war, but it seemed to me that certain people had profited hugely from the misery and sacrifice of others.

It seemed that the winners were politicians and military men in exalted positions that they could never have reached in times of peace. Others who profited included the munitions manufacturers who operated on the "cost plus profit" basis, and then, later, the men who became rich by dealing with cheap debris of war such as unwanted aeroplanes, scrap metal and other surplus war materials. For many years, the film industry's tycoons would continue to profit by turning the horrors of war into fictitious entertainment for the masses. It seemed that the war's main losers, of whatever nationality, were the people who had done the fighting, the innocent and the bereaved — sadly, society seemed once again to have made fools of them all.

Finding that my knowledge of German had vastly increased my earning power, I now decided to seek a job where I would be able to use also my knowledge of Russian, and I began to look around. I soon had the good fortune to secure a position with ABMTM, one of Britain's leading international sales organizations, at double my previous salary. The chief executive was a wealthy eccentric by the name of Michael Stipelman. A Russian by birth, he had brought all of his considerable fortune to England at the time of the Bolshevik Revolution. After qualifying as a medical doctor in Odessa, he had decided not to pursue a career in medicine, but had become an engineer instead. Stipelman was eighty-three when I first met him. He told me, "I have no intention of retiring. Retirement would kill me. I have never needed to work, because I have plenty of money. Look at these cufflinks —

321

diamonds and sapphires — I designed them myself. I thought an engineer should certainly be competent to design a pair of cufflinks. Normally, there would only be gems on one side, but I had plenty of stones, so I have them on both sides of each one. Of course, such cufflinks would usually be only for use with evening dress, but I never go out at night, so I wear them all the time."

My title was "Overseas Travelling Representative". No such position had previously existed in the fifty years since the organization had been founded. Once again, it was a case of "the job is what you make it". I could travel all over the world at will. I had no fixed financial budget. I spent as much of the organization's money as I thought reasonable. Stipelman told me, "When you are abroad, you should always travel first class and stay in the best hotels. People who do not know us may ask you where you are staying, and it enhances the prestige of the organization if you are staying at the most expensive hotels." Nobody told me what to do or where to go. Each time I returned from abroad, old Stip, as his underlings commonly called him, would merely ask me where I planned to go next. We would then spend an hour or two in his room, speaking in Russian. The word "office" was never used — the employees worked in "rooms".

Due to his eccentricity, conversations with Stipelman were fascinating. He asked me, "When you have a haircut, do you take your own brush and comb and towel?" I told him that I did not, and he said, "I always go to the barber on a Thursday, and I sit next to Lord

So-and-So. I always tell the barber to wash his hands before he starts. Last week he said he had just washed them, and I said I had not seen him do it, so would he please wash them again."

Stipelman's afternoon tea was never placed on his desk — perhaps for fear that a visitor on the other side of the desk might accidentally cough or sneeze in it. The tea, served in an elegant bone-china cup, had to be placed on the mantelpiece where it should have been out of harm's way. As I chatted to him one afternoon, he rang for the tea lady and told her, "Kindly take the tea away and change it. Mr Parkinson was here a little while ago. He placed his bowler hat on the mantelpiece, and I fear he may have passed it over the tea." The tea lady turned to me, sighed and raised her eyes to the ceiling. I attempted to keep a straight face.

After returning from an overseas trip late at night, I arrived at the offices at about half-past-nine the following day. Stipelman was slowly making his way up the staircase to his room. As I caught up with him, he turned to me and said, "I am taking my holiday this week." I asked him if he was going away. "Oh no, no!" he replied, "I am just starting work half an hour later than usual each day."

Having received no indication of what might be expected of me, I made up my own mind about what needed to be done. I first toured the dozen or so factories of the organization to learn about their products. Then I travelled around the world, appointing new agents and investigating any of the old ones who were ineffective. Once I had done that, I decided to visit all the places where I had dropped bombs or parachute containers of supplies during the war, and this required trips behind the Iron Curtain. In those days, no tourists travelled behind the Iron Curtain, and visits were only possible by obtaining business visas. No representatives of other British firms were travelling to the Communist-controlled countries, and as a German- and Russian-speaking Englishman I was at first regarded as something of an oddity by the officials of the state trading organizations.

To my surprise, I was soon able to secure huge orders for plant for the manufacture of tractors. I quickly recognized the vast untapped market in the developing countries of Central and Eastern Europe, so I changed my title to Export Sales Manager, engaged half a dozen young production engineers, made them into export salesmen and added the necessary clerical staff to my team. I proceeded to do whatever I chose, on the assumption that my authority could be regarded as unlimited until such time as I might be told otherwise. Within a short time, I found that the Communist authorities allowed me to travel freely anywhere I wished, so I frequently flew to Vienna, hired a large Mercedes car and toured the factories behind the Iron Curtain for a month at a time. The organization's volume of export business increased enormously. I was becoming one of the country's most successful export executives, and my salary increased accordingly.

Sixteen years after the end of the war, I returned to Italy, opened a branch office in Milan and staffed it with English-speaking Italians. I chose a serious and dignified Venetian named Asteriti as the office manager. During my monthly visits to the Milan office, I only spoke Italian to people such as hotel porters, waiters and taxi drivers, and I noticed that they used some expressions that I did not recognize. "Have you changed the language?" I asked Asteriti. "People here say things differently from the way we used to speak during the war." To demonstrate what I meant, I began to speak to him in Italian. "My goodness!" he exclaimed. "Don't ever speak like that to our clients! What you are speaking is Neapolitan dialect like those black fellows in the south. It certainly would not go down well with people like the directors of Fiat."

I then remembered how our Italian tutor on the squadron had told us not to speak to the locals, because it would have a bad effect on our knowledge of Italian. We had laughed at him and told him that the only reason we were learning Italian was to enable us to talk to girls, and we saw no reason to speak better Italian than they did. He had protested, "But they don't speak good Italian. For instance, they don't conjugate their verbs!" As we pointed out to him, our main interest in girls had no connection whatsoever with their ability to conjugate their verbs. In post-war Italy, I took delight in using my Neapolitan dialect on the snobbish north Italians. I had no wish to change the way I spoke the language. After all, it had stood me in good stead with the delightful Rosa in Sorrento.

CHAPTER
THIRTEEN

Cold War Trade and HM Secret Service

Early one Monday morning, I arrived at my offices near London's Victoria railway station, and my secretary told me that a visitor was waiting to see me on a matter of some urgency. I told her to bring him up to my room, and a middle-aged man appeared, looking distinctly out of place. I must explain that our senior export executives were expected to enhance the prestige of the organization by maintaining a high standard of appearance. A range of elegant suits and ties, expensive shoes and shirts and smart haircuts were a prerequisite for my team of multi-lingual subordinates, who stayed in the best hotels all over the world and entertained influential clients in the best restaurants. In contrast, my visitor, who told me that he had come down from Scotland, looked like a country squire's gardener who had slept in his crumpled green tweed suit on the overnight train journey. He had a pocket watch on a leather strap in the top pocket of his jacket, and he wore a sinister black eyepatch. His rustic walking-stick looked eminently suitable for use in the wilds of the

Scottish highlands, but not for London. It was obvious from his appearance that he was neither a potential client nor a supplier's representative. If he had come to apply for a job as caretaker, he was wasting his time, as we already had one.

He came to the point immediately: "This is an official visit. We understand that you have recently signed a contract to supply certain machinery to China, and we know that it is to be used for manufacturing atomic bombs." I was astonished, and replied that I had negotiated numerous contracts for the supply of ordinary general-purpose metal-cutting machines, and none of them could be classed as atom-bomb-making machines. "Oh, yes," he replied, "but although the particular contract we have in mind is certainly for a number of ordinary lathes, the Chinese have ordered spherical fine-turning attachments to be delivered with them, and that leads us to the conclusion that they will be used solely for the manufacture of atomic bombs." "In that case," I told him, "the British government should place an embargo on the machines. I cannot cancel a legally binding contract without incurring a huge financial penalty, but the government could surely stop delivery, and that would let us off the hook. After all, I don't want our company to get mixed up in the manufacture of Chinese atomic bombs." He replied, "No, we don't intend to embargo the deal. You go ahead with the contract and say nothing to anybody about my visit. Some of our people will be contacting you about the matter in a few days."

I wanted to detain my strange visitor and find out something more about his mysterious background, so I asked my secretary to bring him a cup of tea and biscuits. We engaged in small talk for a further half an hour, but he did nothing to satisfy my curiosity. As he had told me that there was no official objection to the contract being fulfilled, I wondered what on earth was the purpose of his visit, and why the British government should not wish to impede the manufacture of atom bombs by the Communist Chinese at a time when our Cold War allies, the United States, maintained a total embargo on trade with China.

A couple of years previously, I had received a note from the British Board of Trade, informing me, among other things, that the government wished to encourage trade between Britain and China. The British Ambassador in Peking would be in London on leave shortly, and he was willing to meet any businessmen who might be interested. I duly made an appointment and met the Ambassador. I am fairly sure that nobody else took the opportunity. We sat alone in a small room, and I asked him, "What's the population of China?" He replied, "Nobody knows exactly, but it's certainly more than one thousand million." I did not know very much about China, but I assumed that the average Chinese family had no television, telephone, washing machine, dishwasher, refrigerator, vacuum cleaner or motorcar. I would be able to supply machinery and know-how for the mass production in China of all such items, but first I had to find out how to go about it. "What advice can you give me about the best way to penetrate the

Chinese market?" I asked. He replied, "First of all, it will be necessary for you to go to China yourself, and when you go there you should remember to take with you some toilet-paper, because they don't have any out there." He paused for thought, and then continued, "Oh yes, there is one other important thing. You will need to take a sixty-watt light bulb, because the lights in the hotel rooms are far too dim for reading by."

That was the total extent of the British Ambassador's advice. I had learned nothing of real value. I had wasted my time with him. International trade was an extremely tough business, and a man like him would not have survived in it much longer than the duration of such a worthless interview.

Some time later, when the Chinese, who had no embassy in London, opened a trade legation within walking distance of my offices, I quickly made myself known. It seemed that nobody else was showing any interest in them, and the Chinese appeared to be flattered by my attention. When numerous trade delegations began to arrive from China with very little idea of how to make contacts with manufacturers, I took them under my wing and accompanied them to engineering firms of my own choosing. The Chinese delegates were always courteous, and most of them spoke a quaint, outmoded form of English. They were not like delegates from the Soviet Union, who seemed obsessed with questions such as the number of hours it would take a British worker to earn the cost of a kilo of butter. The Chinese did not show any sign of suspicion of me, and they did not seem to be indoctrinated with anti-Western propaganda. I furnished all of them with copies of *Playboy* magazine to pass the time on long train journeys, but otherwise I treated them the same as any other important clients. Within a short time, I was able to finalize huge contracts, and was often invited to their lunches and receptions in the legation. When I learned that the Chinese typists were painstakingly typing their contracts letter by letter, I arranged to take their blank contract-forms away and get my own staff to type them out for them. The people at the legation were most grateful. Every time I returned the contracts for signature, I mentioned that I had taken the liberty of adding a clause or two to the conditions of sale. "However, if you disagree with these clauses, simply strike them out when you sign the contract." The additional clauses, which were always to my company's advantage, were never struck out. After a while, the volume of Chinese business was sufficient to justify a side-trip to China the next time I travelled to Hong Kong and Japan.

This was my pleasant and profitable relationship with the Chinese that existed when the visitor from Scotland in the crumpled suit called on me. It was not to last much longer. One morning, two men arrived at my offices unannounced, and demanded to speak to me. I told my secretary to bring them to my room and leave us undisturbed until they left the premises. I was, as usual, extremely busy, and I intended to get rid of them quickly, if they proved to be wasting my time. My secretary brought in the two men and closed the door. I guessed them to be under forty years of age, and possibly policemen in plain clothes. One of them did most of the talking while his companion looked on and spoke very little. The situation was explained to me briefly as follows: "It is known that you have excellent contacts with the Chinese, and as a bona-fide businessman you will be above suspicion, so I will tell you what you are required to do. You will write a report on each of your contacts — let us know which ones you judge to be genuine engineers — and let us have as much information as possible about all of them." I tried to broach the subject of the machines alleged to be intended for manufacturing atomic bombs, but the visitors did not want to discuss that. "Now just a minute," I interrupted, "how do I know who you people are?" One of them replied quietly, "MI5." I did not know whether I should believe them or not. I knew nothing about the Secret Service, and I was not interested in becoming involved with it. I said to the more talkative one, "How can you prove your identity?" He then produced a driving licence bearing no photograph. I laughed at him: "That merely proves that you have in your possession a driving licence with that name on it." I decided to tease him. "As a matter of fact, I think I have seen you somewhere before — aren't you employed at the Czechoslovak Embassy? I'm sure I have seen you there." He replied seriously, "No, no, MI5." I did not know if MI5 provided their people with identity documents, but I replied, "Then prove it!" He fumbled in his pocket and said, "I could show you my War Office pass." "War Office?" I queried. "But you said you were with MI5." He replied, "Well, the War

Office is just a front, of course." I decided that it was time to terminate the irritating encounter with MI5, and I told them that if they were not going to embargo the goods, they should go away and leave me to get on with my work. I explained, "I am responsible for promoting the entire export sales of twelve of the country's leading engineering factories. I control agents and branches all over the world. I travel abroad a total of twenty-four weeks each year, and control my staff of half a dozen other travelling men at the same time. In areas where we have no agents or offices, such as in the Communist countries, I do most of the selling personally, because my subordinates are reluctant to travel behind the Iron Curtain. I am far too busy to engage in any 'extra-curricular' activities. If you want someone to spy on the Chinese, why don't you get your own people to do it?" The reply was, "You are the best person because you are a genuine businessman." I replied, "I have absolutely no intention of getting involved with you people." I had not, however, realized how deeply involved I already was, and that MI5 would not be so easily shaken off.

The two MI5 men came to my offices another couple of times, and I emphasized that I was not prepared to jeopardize my company's business by any involvement with them. I told them, "Go away, leave me alone and train your own spies. I'm sure the Chinese train their own." They answered, "Oh yes, they have their own spies, but we know most of them." I wondered how on earth they could presume to know "most of them", and I concluded that they were not very bright. "Why won't you work with us?" they asked repeatedly. I was sick of telling them the same thing, so I finally answered flippantly, "The money is no good." They answered, "There isn't any." I then said, "Now listen to me. I'm a businessman. I work to earn money for the company and for myself. I am not interested in working for nothing, and I am not interested in working for you people at all. I refuse to spy on my clients. Stop coming to my offices. If my Chinese clients see you here or suspect that I am involved with you, my business with them will be ruined. I want you to stay away." Their parting words were that a certain Mr Bacon would be my MI5 contact, and they gave me his telephone number, which I had no intention of using.

A few weeks later, I was invited to the Chinese legation to discuss a further contract. Thinking that technical queries might arise, and not being fully conversant with the machinery to be discussed, I took the precaution of taking one of my technical staff with me. We were due to arrive at two o'clock. I knew the routine. I stood on the steps of the legation, ready to press the front-door bell at exactly two o'clock. As the nearby church clock struck, I rang the bell. The door opened immediately, and I knew that, as usual, the China tea would be ready to be served. We sat in comfortable armchairs at a low table. I followed the usual leisurely ritual, sipping the tea and making small talk, knowing I should not start talking business until they indicated that they were ready. We had scarcely finished the tea, when a huge Chinese man appeared beside me. His eyes blazed as he yelled at me, "You are an enemy of our country! You are trying to destroy trade between Britain and China!" I looked at him in astonishment. I was making a lot of money out of trade with China. Why on earth should I try to ruin it? I hardly knew what to say to him. I tried to explain that he was mistaken, and that I was certainly not opposed to trade with his country. He waved his arms violently and continued to bellow at me. I thought that he was less likely to strike me if I did not stand up, so I remained sitting on the low chair, and waited for his rage to subside. My English colleague sat transfixed, with a look of horror and disbelief on his face. This was his first encounter with the Chinese. He looked as though he would shit himself at any minute. It was a relief when the furious Chinese giant shouted, "Get out — get out — you are not wanted here — get out!" We grabbed our briefcases and scrambled out, fearful that he might fling us into the street if we hesitated. "What the fuckin' 'ell was all that about?" my companion asked me as we walked back to the office. "Buggered if I know," I replied.

A few days later, a written message from the Chinese legation informed my company that I was "persona non grata" — I would not receive any more invitations to their business or social functions. It was obvious to me that someone had "put the boot in". At that time, I had virtually no British competitors, as far as the Chinese trade was concerned, so I guessed that the only likely explanation was that MI5 had discredited me and ruined the business as my punishment for refusing to co-operate with them. Then I remembered an incident that had not seemed important at the time. A few weeks before, I had called at the United States Embassy to renew my visa. "Take a seat. The consul will attend to it. It will take about twenty minutes, if you care to wait," an American woman told me. Within five minutes she was back. "The consul would like a word with you. Please follow me." The consul came straight to the point. He drawled, "Waall now, I don't understand Chinese, but that sure looks mighty like a Chinese visa to me." He stabbed his finger at the open page of my passport. "D'ya mind telling me what ya do in China?" I answered, "What I do in China is the same as I do in America. I have an office in Chicago that I visit once each month, and, for instance, I sell manufacturing plant to the automotive industry in Detroit. I sell the same sort of equipment to the Chinese for making tractors." I did not tell him that I also sold equipment to Boeing for making aeroplanes — I did not think that it was any of his business. He hesitated a moment and then said heartily, "Ya know what? I'm gonna give you a visa!" As he stamped the passport, I said, "I'm glad of that, because it would not be feasible to run my Chicago operation through the mail. I've got a valid American visa in another passport, but the pages are full up with other old expired visas, so I can't use that passport." Not listening to me, he nodded wisely, "Yeah, I sure figured that was a Chinese visa. Waall, there ya go, and take it easy now!" In view of America's total embargo on trade with China, I wondered if I had now been entered in the records of their Secret Service, and I assumed that in accord with the Anglo-American "special relationship" they might be working with MI5.

When one of the company's senior employees, who was not a member of my own staff, was sacked because of stupidity and inefficiency, he made a casual reference to "your connections with the Secret Service". I felt uneasy, as I had never mentioned the matter to anybody, and I told him that I did not know what he was talking about. For some time I had felt that I was under surveillance, and I had taken to hopping on and off underground trains and doubling back on my way to my barber in Piccadilly Arcade. This had seemed like a silly game at first, but now I became alarmed, and I wondered if MI5 were intent on discrediting me among my suppliers and other members of the export business community. I also wondered if, having ruined my Chinese connections, they might start interfering with my other overseas markets.

I tried to ensure that all office waste-paper was shredded, and told my staff not to disclose my overseas destinations. "Tell people I have gone to Bosnia," I told them, knowing that in those days very few people knew the difference between Bosnia and Baltimore. The false reason I gave for this instruction was, "We don't want our competitors to find out where we are doing business, or they will try to muscle in."

Items were mysteriously disappearing from the drawers of my office desk, and I thought that my private telephone was bugged. The unpleasant incident at the Chinese legation was still on my mind. I had the distinct feeling that MI5 were still after me, and I wondered if I was becoming paranoid about the possibility of further retribution. I concluded that it was time for a final effort to shake them off.

For the past few years, I had toyed with the idea of resigning from the London company and setting up an independent company to operate solely in Eastern Europe. I recalled how one of my friends had commented, "Plenty of us would like to start up on our own, but the trouble is that we are too well paid where we are. If we were ordinary factory workers, we would take the plunge, but we are doing too well in the jobs we already have. We would need something drastic to happen before we would risk making a move." The unwelcome attentions of MI5 had now provided me with sufficient incentive to get out of my comfortable, well-paid rut.

By severing my connections with the London company, I was now taking a huge financial risk. I hoped that I might at least gain some peace of mind and be spared any further retribution from the British Secret Service, while I quietly set up a new organization for East-West trade, operating from my residence in the county of Kent.

Some of my previous clients insisted on remaining in contact with me. "We want to make sure that your new venture is a success," the investment director of a large state enterprise in Yugoslavia told me, and he immediately began to divert business to my new company. I had expended the equivalent of six years at my previous salary before the new company became profitable. My attempts to escape from the clutches of MI5 had cost me a great deal of money.

Instead of travelling all over the world, I was now operating solely with clients in the seven countries behind the Iron Curtain. My main business was with Poland, Czechoslovakia and Yugoslavia. I saw no reason why my wartime experiences should not be used to impress my clients, so I was never slow to mention, where appropriate, that I had participated in the 1944 Warsaw Uprising and in the dropping of supplies by parachute to Tito's Yugoslav partisans.

My suppliers were manufacturing firms in Britain, America, Germany and Switzerland, from which my new company bought and then resold products to our clients behind the Iron Curtain. We were able to do this because most manufacturers were not competent to deal directly in the relatively unknown markets behind the Iron Curtain.

I deliberately ignored the growing business opportunities in the Soviet Union, because my one and only trip to Moscow, years previously, had been marred by the Russians' deep suspicion of me. The officials of the Soviet state trading enterprises strongly objected when I spoke directly to their engineers in fluent Russian during contract negotiations. When I visited factories, I was irritated by attempts to stop me speaking directly to the workers by using official interpreters to censor everything I said.

Over the years, my knowledge of Russian had been supplemented by the addition of expressions in Polish, Czech and Serbo-Croatian. Most government officials in Eastern Europe were able to conduct business negotiations in German, in which I was as fluent as in English. I was now spending a third of my time behind the Iron Curtain, and making a great deal of money. I engaged extra people and trained them up so that they had good jobs with cars, foreign travel opportunities, expense accounts and higher salaries than they could have secured elsewhere.

At the instigation of one of my Yugoslav clients, I was approached by a Yugoslav commercial bank and another Yugoslav state enterprise, and requested to form a company for them in London. I got my accountants in the City of London to do the necessary donkey-work, and then, at the Yugoslav partners' invitation, I took one-third of the equity in the company and joined the board of directors. The board was to comprise equal numbers from the British side and the Yugoslav side. "Will you have any objection if we appoint an Englishman to the board?" the Yugoslavs asked. I had no reason to object to their choice of directors, but I enquired, "Who is the man? Perhaps I know him." The Yugoslavs chuckled, "He was a master spy. His name is Bickham Sweet-Escott. During the war he was the head of the Balkan and Polish sections of the Special Operations Executive." I was looking forward to meeting the retired "master spy", but in the meantime I had undertaken the task of finding a merchant banker to take the job of managing director. At a time of full employment, nobody with the right qualifications was prepared to accept a job with the unknown Anglo-Yugoslav Company, so I was obliged to

339

take over as temporary managing director myself. I was now running three companies, including an organization in Switzerland, and reluctantly spending three days per week at the offices of the new company in London.

After board meetings in the London offices, I always joined Bickham Sweet-Escott, the "master spy", for an excellent lunch of steak-and-kidney pie at the Savoy Hotel Grill. Our lunchtime conversations centred mainly on our respective wartime experiences — his as a brigadier with the SOE and mine as a lowly twenty-year-old air bomber. Knowing that our squadron's support for partisans had been co-ordinated by the SOE, I asked, "Whose bloody silly idea was it to situate dropping-zones in dangerous mountain valleys? Didn't they know we would not be able to reach the dropping-zones in the dark? It was bloody suicide! And what about the Warsaw fiasco?" Sweet-Escott's standard reply to my outbursts was, "It's no good getting on to me about that, old chap, because I was out in the Far East by that time."

Whether Sweet-Escott was already in the Far East or not, he certainly knew plenty about the background to the Warsaw Uprising. He knew about the escaped prisoner of war, John G. Ward, shot down in a Fairey Battle bomber during the early days of the war, who was on the ground in Warsaw throughout the uprising. Ward was in frequent radio contact with the British government on behalf of the Polish underground forces, whose pleas for substantial aid were largely ignored. It was clear to me that the sacrifice of so many airmen during the uprising was nothing more than a sop to some people in Britain who were urging the government to "save Britain's honour" and do something to help the starving Poles.

Contact with Ward, who had escaped from German captivity twice, might have been helpful to those of our men who survived being shot down over Warsaw and were attempting to avoid capture, but the British authorities, obsessed with secrecy, did not disclose his existence to us. The more I learned about the background to the Warsaw Uprising, the more I became convinced that the British authorities would not have been surprised if our casualty rate had been one hundred per cent instead of thirty per cent per night. We would have served our government's purpose, no matter how futile our efforts were. The Foreign Secretary was able to cite our flights from Italy to Poland as evidence that, "His Majesty's Government is doing everything possible to help the Poles." Prime Minister Churchill commented later in his war diaries that the Warsaw flights were "forlorn and inadequate". I would have liked to ask him, "Whose bloody fault was that?"

I hoped that I was now free of the attentions of the British Secret Service, since I no longer had any business dealings with China, but then I received an unexpected telephone call, instructing me to report for an interview with Mr Bacon at the old War Office building in Whitehall at 2 o'clock, on a specified date. I remembered that the MI5 men had given the name

Bacon to me previously, and as it was an unusual name I assumed that this was the same man.

I had arranged to take a young racehorse mare that I owned to Lincolnshire in my motor box, and I did not want to change my plans. I drove into London and parked my vehicle in a place near Vauxhall Bridge, changed into suitable clothes in the back, hoped that I did not smell too strongly of the horse, and took a taxi to Whitehall. In the old War Office building, I announced my arrival to a female receptionist who sat behind a large register in which I could see that my name was clearly entered among others. I was very uneasy about visiting the place, remembering that I had been told that it was a front for MI5. Now I was indignant that my name was plain for other visitors to see in the register. I had read somewhere that the people who ran the British Secret Service were "a crowd of bungling amateurs". Their lack of secrecy about their visitors seemed to confirm that description.

I was shown into the presence of Mr Bacon, who was alone in a small office. He did not tell me who he was or what he was. Without inviting me to sit down, he produced a passport-sized photograph and asked abruptly, "Do you know this man?" I answered that I knew hundreds of people, so it was possible that I had seen him somewhere. "We are aware that you certainly do know him," he told me. I replied, "Okay, if you say that I know him, you might tell me who he is. Is he one of my clients?" I pushed the photograph back across the desk. I did not see any reason to tell him that I had once seen a man like this one in Warsaw. I knew nothing about the man, but I remembered that he had sat at my breakfast table and chatted to me in Warsaw's Grand Hotel. It was not unusual, behind the Iron Curtain, for strangers to chat to me or sit at nearby tables and listen to my conversations with members of my travelling staff. On such occasions we always talked rubbish about our business activities to avoid disclosing any commercial information that might be of value to our competitors or to anyone else. We were well aware that people might be "commercially spying" on us, and if we were obliged to wait in an ante-room before starting contract negotiations with the Communist state trading corporations, for instance, we always assumed that the place was bugged, and used the opportunity to pretend to naively discuss our tactics. For example, "As all the prices have gone up by ten per cent since we made our offer, we can't give a discount without making a loss on this deal. However, if they are reasonable about the contract conditions — if we can be sure that there will be some decent business in future — if they sign the contract promptly this week, we can let them have the goods at the old prices." I always hoped the room was bugged; otherwise, we were wasting our time by trying to spread such misinformation.

"I want to ask you about Marek Piotrowski," continued Mr Bacon. I saw no reason why I should discuss Piotrowski with him, and I said, "I'm sure that you know all about my business contacts — after all you have had my phone bugged for long enough — ever since the last time your people were in contact with me." There was a look of utter astonishment on his face, and his question, "Why on earth should we bug your phone?" made me realize that this was not the same Mr Bacon as before. At that time, nobody knew much about the Secret Service, and I did not know that it comprised not just MI5, but also MI6. Apparently, I was now dealing with MI6. Why both sections had to use the pseudonym Bacon is a mystery.

Bacon continued his interrogation. "Do you think Marek Piotrowski is a spy?" I had known Marek and his delightful family for many years. He was a Polish trade delegate in London. In my business, it was essential to know important people such as he was. I answered rather sharply, "I don't know anything at all about spies. As you must surely know, Piotrowski is a commercial official of the Polish government. If he was one of my employees I would expect him to tell me everything that he thought my company should know, and I assume that his own bosses expect him to do the same for them." I wondered if my long journey to Lincolnshire with the horse was being delayed merely to ask me stupid questions, and I began to regret having foolishly agreed to come to see Mr Bacon. I had disregarded what my old Russian friend, Stipelman, had once said to me: "If it is likely to be a difficult encounter, make the other party come to you. Do not put yourself at a disadvantage by going to them." Bacon probably sensed my impatience, and he changed the subject: "We happen to know that the Polish authorities have you on a special list of trusted people." I replied, "If that is so, I am pleased to hear it. It is nice to know that I am well thought of by my clients, but how do you know anything about it?" His tone became grave as he replied, "We have people over there who keep us informed about such things. We know that the information we get from them is reliable, and we know that you are regarded by the Polish government as a person of importance to them." As he continued, I listened quietly. "You are someone who would never come under suspicion by the Poles. They trust you, and I will explain what we want you to do."

I still did not interrupt him as he imperiously issued his instructions to me. It seemed to be a foregone conclusion that I would meekly comply with his orders. I was to accept secret assignments from the Polish government and report to the British Secret Service. "When you report to us, we will tell you how we want you to proceed." I resented the note of superiority in his voice: "You would probably call it being a double agent, but if you should get caught, we would be obliged to deny all knowledge of you. Under no circumstances are you ever to tell anyone that we have been in contact with you." Now I was convinced that this man must be a different Bacon. The one associated with the Chinese affair would surely have known better than to assume that I would accept such instructions.

When he paused and seemed to be waiting for my reactions, I told Mr Bacon that my knowledge of his organization was based solely on revelations in the newspapers about traitors such as Philby, Burgess and Maclean, who were employed by the Secret Service. It seemed that Philby, a senior official, had been responsible for the deaths of a number of British agents. I had no doubt that other traitors existed within the organization, and I was determined to have nothing to do with it. "I would never trust any of them," I told him.

Mr Bacon then indignantly appealed to my sense of patriotism. "It is your duty to help us," he told me. I had willingly carried out my patriotic duty during the war. I was not pleased about the way men like me had been treated at the time, but at least the British government had not told us that it would deny all knowledge of us, if the enemy caught us. I told him, "Nobody but a bloody fool would accept such a proposition."

Mr Bacon changed his tactics: "The situation can be quite dangerous for British businessmen in the Communist countries. You could be blackmailed. There have been cases of men photographed in bed with foreign women and then hauled naked through the streets to the police headquarters. They have been told that if they don't co-operate the photographs will be used to discredit them." I grinned at him: "I can assure you, they would not be able to blackmail me." He replied, "Plenty of businessmen have been trapped and compromised by the Communist secret services. It would not do you any good if such photographs were disclosed to your company." I told him, "I own the company, so that wouldn't matter. If I ever get caught in bed with a woman, she will definitely be a very pretty one, and I won't care who sees the photographs." "But what about your wife?" he insisted. "I would simply tell my wife that I had made a stupid mistake. I would admit that I had been photographed in bed with an attractive girl. But I would never allow myself to be blackmailed. I would not expect my wife to assume that when abroad I am always hopping into bed with foreign girls. But anyway, I really don't think the people who are supposed to have me on a list of trusted people are likely to play any dirty tricks on me."

As I talked to him, it occurred to me that his own people were doubtless capable of setting me up and pretending that the other side had done it. I was becoming sick of Mr Bacon with his supercilious and domineering manner as he harped on about the potential danger of falling into the clutches of the Communist security services, while at the same time trying to persuade me to place myself in immediate danger by becoming a British agent. Double agent! I was not even a single agent! It was time for some plain speaking. "I have absolutely no intention of becoming involved with your people, because I wouldn't trust them. I am simply a businessman, and I am satisfied with that. I have never done anything wrong and I don't intend to start anything that might cause me to end up in a prison camp in Siberia." I noticed his expression harden as I repeated, "I would not trust any of them."

As I was speaking, I thought of a man named Greville Wynne who had foolishly become mixed up with the Secret Service while he was supposed to be representing some of the British manufacturers from whom I was frequently buying machinery. I had received an invitation from Wynne to attend a farewell function on the London South Bank site, before he set off on his last trip to Russia. As I did not know Wynne personally, and he had no connection with my business, I guessed that the invitation had been instigated by his Secret Service contacts. I remembered saying to my assistant, "If you are staying in London tonight and you would like some free drinks, take this invitation and tell him you are my deputy — otherwise chuck it in the bin. I don't want it." Wynne was subsequently snatched off the street by the Soviet secret police while carrying out the orders of the British Secret Service behind the Iron Curtain. As far as I could remember, the British government denied that he was a British agent. After a well-publicized trial, he was thrown into a Russian prison, where he remained in dreadful conditions until released in exchange for a Soviet spy. His business career was finished.

Mr Bacon started to repeat the rigmarole. "You should understand that it is your duty to help us. You are in the best position to help us. The Polish authorities trust you. They will never suspect you." From the start, his manner had been designed to intimidate rather than persuade me. I thought he would never have succeeded as a salesman — entirely the wrong technique! "But I won't do it," I told him.

I was sure that his talk of potential dangers behind the Iron Curtain was a veiled threat to discredit me in the eyes of the Polish authorities, but I realized that I would be in far greater danger if I became involved in espionage. I decided to change the subject. "What do you say to your friends and neighbours, when they ask you what you do for a living? You can hardly tell them the truth. Do you say you are 'something in the City'?" He glowered at me and ignored the question. I assumed he would now have to report to his superiors that he had failed to recruit me, and I wondered if the matter had already gone through various committee stages before a decision had been made to approach me. I also wondered why there was an apparent lack of co-ordination between his people and those others who had previously contacted me over the Chinese business. I assumed that the interview was at an end and I asked him brightly, "Before I go, do you think you could play that back? It was quite interesting. I would like to hear the tape." He looked startled: "Do you mean to say you think this interview has been recorded?" I replied, "Well, if it hasn't been recorded, I would say it certainly should have been."

He walked over to the door of his office and stood holding the doorknob. "So you are refusing to work with us!" As I waited for him to open the door, I said, "Well, let me put it like this. If you were to ask me to take over and run the entire British Secret Service, I would take the job, but I am certainly not willing to start at the bottom!" His face darkened: "Woe betide you, if our paths should ever cross again!" he growled as he opened the door. I went back to the woman at the reception desk on my way out of the building, and said, "I was just wondering how many people you have here called Bacon." She looked flustered and made no reply. I took a taxi back to the parking-place near Vauxhall Bridge, changed my clothes in the back of the horsebox and drove slowly through London's crowded streets onto the Great North Road. I had intended to avoid the heaviest traffic by setting out on my journey at dawn, but Mr Bacon had spoiled that plan. I ran through the interview in my mind, and smiled about my facetious remark that I would be willing to take over and run the entire British Secret Service, but that I was not prepared to start at the bottom.

What would the Secret Service do now to punish me? They had caused me to take a huge financial risk after the Chinese affair. I had now painstakingly built up a new group of profitable companies. Would they interfere with my business activities again? It would not be long before I found out. I discovered that the Secret Service was not under the control of Parliament, and there was nobody to whom I could turn for advice. Bacon had warned me, "Tell no one, not even your wife, about our approach to you." But my wife was a director of my East-West trading companies, and I told her everything. I said, "If I should fall out of a window (a common form of assassination behind the Iron Curtain), it will be because I have been pushed by the British Secret Service." I decided, for reasons of personal security, never again to travel abroad alone, but I did not risk alarming my staff by telling them the reason.

I arrived at the London offices of the Anglo-Yugoslav Company one morning to find that the place had been entered during the night. There were no signs of damage to doors or windows, so the intruders must have picked the locks — a typical Secret Service activity, as I learned later. The files in the cabinets and the documents in desk drawers had been rifled. As an apparent pretence of burglary, the office scissors had been used to force open the flimsy little tin box in which the petty cash should have been kept, but which usually contained scraps of paper on which the typist had written IOUs when she borrowed the money. Neither the secretary's expensive new typewriter nor any other office equipment had been stolen, so I did not think that real burglars had visited us. I reported the matter to the local police by telephone. They did not invite me to make a written report or to visit the police station, and nobody visited the office. When the same thing happened again, I did not bother to inform the police. I assumed that the Secret Service had told them in advance of their intention to search the premises.

Two directors came over from Yugoslavia to attend the next board meeting, and to my utter dismay they accused me of telling business people in the City of London that the Yugoslavs had been engaged in corrupt activities. I protested in vain that I had done no such thing, but I found that my fellow directors, whom I had known for some years, and regarded as my personal friends, had lost all faith in me. When the board meeting ended in an atmosphere of bitterness and recrimination, I realized that my only course of action was to resign from the board of the Anglo-Yugoslav Company and attempt to withdraw my share of the equity. I now decided to concentrate all my time on my East-West trading company, situated in Kent.

The next time I visited one of my largest clients in Yugoslavia, I found that the investment directors were aware of what had transpired at the acrimonious meeting in London. All the top people in Yugoslavia's politics and commerce knew each other. Clearly, the word had spread. They all worked for the state. They all knew, as I did, that any suspicion of corruption could result in their imprisonment. My protestation of innocence of all wrongdoing was met by mistrust and plain hostility. For many years, I had enjoyed the friendship of government ministers and other people of influence, but now I was no longer regarded as trustworthy. More than ninety per cent of my business with Yugoslavia disappeared within a couple of months, and I reluctantly decided to relinquish all my connections in that country. No longer would I be able to boast of my friendship with the Finance Minister and his family. No longer would I be able to number the President's son and the future Prime Minister among my clients. My trade with Yugoslavia, like the trade with China, was finished.

I heard nothing further from the Secret Service, but I suspected that their "dirty tricks" department was still after me. In those days, the British state-controlled GPO held the monopoly of the mail and telephone services. I began to experience irritations such as frequent telephone breakdowns and non-delivery of company mail. Then each time I picked up the phones I heard loud music. I sent for a GPO engineer and naively asked him to examine the telephones and tell me if they had bugs in them. He explained that bugs were not inserted in telephones. If telephones were bugged it was done at the telephone exchange. The music on the telephones continued, and then I began to get "wrong numbers" repeatedly. Dozens of callers asked to be connected with people who did not work for my company.

Telephone service engineers became frequent visitors to my offices, and then I started to experience harassment by the local police. My wife, who had a new MGB GT sports car, was frequently stopped within a mile of the office, on the false pretext that her car's tyre pressures were uneven. She pointed out that the car was new and the tyres were checked each time the fuel was topped up. One evening, a policeman called and suggested that I had threatened to kill a man working on a nearby building site, and another policeman telephoned to say that a woman had complained that one of my dogs had bitten her at a local horse show. I confirmed that I had taken a dog with me to the show, but it had been on a leash the whole time. The policeman insisted on the dog being produced for identification by the woman. When he arrived at my office, I questioned the woman accompanying him, and discovered that she had not been anywhere near the horse show. As I questioned her, the policeman intervened with a shout, "Don't answer any of his questions!" When I persisted in asking her to describe the dog, he became enraged and shouted, "He is trying to destroy my case!"

I pointed out that, as far as I was aware, there was no case. I reminded him that, not only had he previously told me that he wanted to bring the woman to my office simply to humour her, but also that she had spent a month on holiday in Spain since the alleged incident, and her complaint about the dog was officially regarded as frivolous. His manner then became very threatening, so I told him that microphones and loudspeakers linked the rooms of my offices and two of my staff were overhearing the encounter. Without moving from my chair, I said, "Come into my office and tell me if you heard all that!" My two witnesses appeared and confirmed that they had heard everything. I had recently read in the newspapers that a procedure had been introduced for making complaints against the police. I took the necessary action, and after investigation by a police superintendent from a different area, a letter of apology was received from the Chief Constable. The letter also informed me that, as a result of the incident, the constable concerned had now been transferred out of the district, but no disciplinary action was being taken against him. I assumed that the local constabulary had received instructions from the Secret Service to keep me under surveillance, and I thought the police had probably interpreted this as an excuse for unwarranted harassment of me.

Trouble with the telephones was continuing. Several times each day, nuisance calls were received enquiring for people who had no connection with my companies. I decided that the time had come for a change of address, so I purchased a fairly isolated farm in Sussex. The farmhouse was now used as my residence, and my two adjacent farm cottages were converted into offices and staff accommodation. I now confined my activities to trade with Poland and Czechoslovakia. My international business correspondence was conducted almost entirely by telex because I did not trust the postal service. Within a few weeks, loud music was heard every time the phones were used. I had moved my organization miles away to a different county and the telephone numbers were now different, but I still received the same sort of calls for the same unknown people as before. After numerous complaints to the GPO, a very grumpy, middle-aged "special faults engineer" made repeated visits. On each occasion, he spent a complete day prowling around in the offices and residential accommodation. I eventually gained the impression that he had merely been sent to spy on me.

The problem of wrong numbers and loud music continued, and then I received an official letter warning me of the dire penalties of using an "unauthorized radio transmitter". Needless to say, I had no such apparatus. I recalled my encounter with Mr Bacon at the old War Office in Whitehall, and his final menacing words, "Woe betide you if our paths should ever cross again." I wondered if the British Secret Service, through its cohorts, the postal and telephone services and the police, might be trying to provoke me into some course of action that I might later have reason to regret. Were my problems such as the telephone trouble and the frequent occurrences of missing mail an indication that Mr Bacon was determined that our paths would indeed cross again? Was I still being punished for rejecting his efforts to recruit me as a "double agent"? I did not know what to think, but I was determined to continue my efforts to run my business affairs in spite of the difficulties. I knew that I could seek neither advice nor redress from any quarter, because it seemed that the Secret Service was a law unto itself, answerable to no one for its actions.

At first, I had been surprised that the Secret Service had taken any particular interest in me. I had always regarded myself as an ordinary sort of chap, although perhaps a bit more adventurous than some others, and certainly more tenacious in pursuit of business deals, while thoroughly enjoying the cut and thrust of international trade. The excitement of snatching lucrative contracts from under the noses of my foreign competitors in far-off corners of the world had become an addiction. After my encounter with Mr Bacon, I began to realize that I was not quite as ordinary as I had imagined, and some of my experiences behind the Iron Curtain were indeed quite extraordinary. Although the British authorities had advised British businessmen to announce their arrival and departure to the British Embassy during visits behind the Iron Curtain, I had only done so once. Not long after the 1956 Uprising in Hungary, I had called at our Embassy in Budapest to consult with the Commercial Attaché. The Head of Chancery invited me to lunch at his residence and warned me not to say anything in front of the servants, who were obtained through a diplomatic agency and understood to be working with the Hungarian Secret Service.

After lunch, I returned with my host to the Embassy to continue our discussions, and after leaving I walked back in the direction of the nearby Duna Hotel. I stopped to look in a shop window, and was immediately approached by a very large man of sinister appearance. In harsh tones, he demanded, "Dokument!" I noted his long leather coat, slouch hat, fingers like bunches of bananas and huge boots. I briefly pretended not to understand what he wanted as he growled a few words of Hungarian at me. When I gave him my passport, I hoped he really was what he looked like — a secret policeman. I knew that I would look foolish if he turned out to be a common criminal and ran off with my passport. How would I explain why I had handed my passport to an unknown man in the street? I knew that I must have been seen leaving the Embassy. I telephoned my contact there, and he confirmed that the secret police always approached and established the identity of everyone leaving the Embassy. I said he and his colleagues would not be seeing me again, and it was twelve years before I had further contact with any British Embassy behind the Iron Curtain.

I was in Berlin when the Soviet occupation zone became divided from the Western Zones by the barbed-wire barriers that preceded the notorious Berlin Wall. One morning as I walked from my hotel in the Western Zone towards the offices of the East German central state purchasing office, I found the roadway unexpectedly blocked by barbed wire. A German youth of about eighteen, clad in an ill-fitting uniform, pointed a gun at me and gruffly demanded my identity document. I tried to adopt a nonchalant attitude as I explained to him in his own language that, as I was entering the Soviet Zone, only the Soviet occupying forces were legally authorized to demand my documents. But, although he had no right to see it, I would show him what an interesting passport I had, with numerous visas from exotic countries that he might never see. His finger relaxed from the trigger of his automatic rifle and his hostile attitude changed as he flicked through the pages of the passport. He saluted as he moved aside to allow me to pass through the barrier that would soon be replaced by the concrete wall.

Until the barrier sealed the Eastern Zone off from the rest of Berlin, valuable people, such as doctors and skilled tradesmen, were able to stroll unhindered into the Western Zones and then fly into West Germany, where they could easily obtain very well-paid jobs. Knowing that people such as the engineers with whom I had contact received excellent training by the state, I had often wondered how long such a drain on the resources of the Eastern Zone would be tolerated, and I concluded that the authorities had sound economic reasons for the erection of an impenetrable border.

All of the Communist-controlled countries of Europe were sealed off from the rest of the world by hundreds of miles of what we called the Iron Curtain, usually a high double fence with barbed wire, topped by porcelain terminals to indicate that the fence was electrified. A wide sand track between the two elements of the fence was thought to be mined. Road barriers were often made from railway-line rails mounted on concrete pillars. As the Iron Curtain border was often set back hundreds of yards from the border of the neighbouring country, any vehicle that managed to crash through the road barrier would still have a long and dangerous way to travel before it reached the safety of the West. It was said that in some places false East and West borders were erected well inside Communist-controlled countries. Anyone who managed to get through the false Iron Curtain would be met at what appeared to be the West border by fellow-countrymen disguised in fake American uniforms, and promptly arrested. It was customary for all vehicles to be thoroughly searched when passing through the Iron Curtain. Large dogs were used in the inspection of freight-carrying vehicles. Every part of every vehicle was searched. Upholstered seats were lifted. Engine compartments and luggage compartments were checked, and mirrors on long sticks were used to inspect underneath. Border formalities were often an exasperating and time-consuming hindrance, but any display of impatience would be likely to slow up the procedure. All customs and immigration officials at the Iron Curtain crossing points were armed, as were all male and female police officers. I had long since decided to be polite but never to cower when confronted by anyone in uniform carrying a gun. My frequent visits by car resulted in me being remembered by the officials at the border, especially as I passed the time while waiting for attention by distributing bars of chocolate and packets of cigarettes to all of them. The same questions were asked on each occasion. Any firearms? Any radio transmitters? Any ammunition? When it came to "Any propaganda material?" I always said yes. I had already prepared a selection of the company's advertising gifts, such as penknives, playing cards, and ball-pens, etc., bearing company logos. Propaganda material! I announced. It was never handed back to me. My car number was noted, and so long as the same people were on duty future formalities at the border were greatly facilitated.

One of my suppliers had kindly lent me a self-contained mobile workshop filled with working machinery that I wanted to introduce on the East European markets. The deal included the free loan of a driver/demonstrator and another valuable member of staff. In the spring of 1968, I organized a sales tour of East Germany, Hungary, Czechoslovakia and Poland. I already had all the necessary visas for myself, but when I applied for visas to be issued to my men, the Polish Embassy in London rejected their applications. "Don't worry," I told them, "I will fix that later." During our tour of the other Iron Curtain countries I managed to secure visas for my colleagues from one of Poland's overseas embassies, although I was told repeatedly that no visas were being issued and warned that the Polish borders were closed. Upon arriving at a deliberately chosen minor crossing-point, I found that the border was indeed closed to all traffic. Despite this difficult situation, I managed to get my party into Poland, where we found Soviet tanks massed within sight of the frontier and ready to invade. I had spent several months planning my sales tour, and I did not want closed frontiers to spoil my plans.

When it became known that I had conducted a successful sales tour despite the frontiers being closed, I was invited by the British Embassy in Warsaw to explain how I had managed it. I sat opposite an official in a room in the Embassy where loudspeakers on all four walls blared out four different torrents of sound. He put his mouth close to my ear. "This is the only safe way of talking," he told me, "as all our rooms and even our official cars are bugged." I saw no advantage in disclosing any information to him.

The Soviet troops, with aircraft and tanks, finally crossed the border into Czechoslovakia during my next visit in August. Many of the Soviet soldiers were bewildered by the hostility of the locals, as they apparently thought that they had been sent as friends to help restore order. Some soldiers seemed to think they were still in some part of the Soviet Union, especially as the locals were able to communicate with them fairly easily in both Russian and Czech. To confuse the invaders the Czechs turned round all the signposts, and even I had difficulty travelling between factories on minor roads.

During this time a correspondent from a leading British newspaper cornered me during a visit to the town of Brno, and told me that the British Embassy had advised him to contact me if he wanted any information because, "Auton is so often here he knows everything." In response to the man's leading questions, I repeatedly told him, "The situation is not the way you seem to think." He replied, "Oh well. I wrote my piece before I left London." I thought to myself, I have often heard people say, "You can't believe everything you read in the papers." No wonder people are sceptical, with such reporters working for the news media! I had several times returned from trips behind the Iron Curtain to read false accounts of incidents that I had witnessed at first hand.

Rather surprisingly, I was allowed to continue travelling freely around Czechoslovakia during the Soviet invasion. I had done so in Poland during the imposition of martial law, also when Polish shipyard strikers were being shot, and then during the rise of the outlawed Solidarity movement that eventually led to the change of regime. At the height of the Cold War, I had even dared to fly to Warsaw on one occasion to make a valuable business contact when I had no visa. "You will be arrested," a senior official of a Polish state trading corporation told me, when I met him on the plane. "It is strictly prohibited to enter my country without the necessary papers." I mentioned that none of us had visas when we visited Warsaw in 1944. "But you didn't actually land," he said. "Some of us reached the ground," I reminded him, "and some were flying at only 100ft above it." I knew that he had been in Warsaw during the Uprising, and although he knew of my involvement in it, he remained convinced that I would be arrested. Within half an hour of landing, I had secured written permission to enter the country, provided that I reported to the police within twenty-four hours and obtained a visa from them.

Nothing could have been simpler. I realized that I really must be on what Mr Bacon had referred to as a Polish list of especially trusted people, and I was glad that I had not agreed to betray that trust. No doubt, the governments of all the Warsaw Pact countries knew that I had refused to spy on them. I never felt that I was in danger from them, and they did not attempt to make me spy on my own country.

When I had first started to travel to the Communist-controlled countries, in the 1950s, most British manufacturers in my field had a huge backlog of Western clients' orders. Delivery times were long and my British suppliers really did not need any new markets for their products. Among the reasons for my early visits behind the Iron Curtain was a desire to find out what had happened to the people in countries where I had dropped bombs and supplies. I had not expected my visits to result in the promotion of East-West trade, but now, many years later, the situation had changed. British manufacturing was in the doldrums, and my suppliers were clamouring for my services as a leading exporter to Central and Eastern Europe. The British Board of Trade began vigorously to promote and subsidize exhibitions of British goods in the rapidly expanding markets behind the Iron Curtain, and British banks began to provide finance for East-West trade. Some British firms started to send sales representatives to international trade fairs in the Communist countries.

For several years, I had been exhibiting independently, but now I took advantage of the newly introduced British subsidies, and booked trade-stand space annually in the British exhibition halls in Hungary, Poland and Czechoslovakia. Within a short time, it became apparent to me that some of the new British East-West traders had fallen into the clutches of the British Secret Service. It seemed that certain firms were favoured with large and advantageously positioned trade-stands in the British pavilions. People working for those firms, although never having reasons to associate with me in England, seemed to spend an inordinate amount of time shadowing my movements and loitering on my overseas trade stands — probably at the behest of their spymasters. The common distinguishing feature of such people was a smug facial expression, as each one seemed to imagine himself to be a secret agent in the James Bond mould. It was no surprise to me when some of those naive people were arrested in England for illegal sales to hostile foreign powers of machines equipped for producing armaments.

The British Board of Trade and the British Secret Service, although having colluded in the sales, abandoned the salesmen, who were arrested, handcuffed together, locked up with common criminals in Wormwood Scrubs prison and eventually sent for trial at the Old Bailey, where they faced the prospect of long terms of imprisonment. After suffering humiliation, loss of reputation and the total collapse of their businesses, they were saved from imprisonment when the British government minister concerned had the courage to disclose, under cross-examination in court, that the British authorities had secretly connived in the illegal export of the machines for making munitions. The British Secret Service and its cohorts had betrayed their gullible stooges exactly as they would, undoubtedly, have betrayed me, if I had bowed to their pressure and been caught working as an unpaid "double agent".

CHAPTER
FOURTEEN

A Sort of Reconciliation

Over the years, I became very well known in countries of the Eastern Bloc through my work to assist in the development of sections of industry such as motor vehicle, tractor and steel production. At the same time, I did my best to give help surreptitiously to surviving victims of Nazi and Communist persecution, particularly those who, like thousands of their fellow-countrymen, had served in Britain's armed forces during the Second World War.

Thirty years after first passing the road signs to Auschwitz, I gained permission to research the archives. The former death camp is preserved in its original state as a permanent memorial to the worst of Nazi war crimes. The written details recorded by the Germans horrified me, and reminded me of my time spent shortly after the war in the company of former inmates. My research left me with feelings of great sadness and shame.

In 1989, while Poland was still a member of the Warsaw Pact, the Soviet answer to NATO, I managed to obtain official permission to spend four days at Deblin, the Polish Officers' Central Flying School. General Pilot-Cosmonaut Miroslaw Hermaszewski, the Commanding Officer, asked me how long it had taken us to fly from Italy to Warsaw and back during the 1944 Uprising. I told him our first trip took nearly twelve hours. "Not long compared with eight days in space," he joked, as he raised his vodka glass.

In 1990, as the oppressive Communist regimes finally collapsed, and the Iron Curtain disintegrated, the new Solidarity-led government of Poland hastened to award me the Gold Order of Merit. I was summoned to the London Embassy, and at the award ceremony, the newly appointed Ambassador's address included the following words:

> The turn of history during World War II has led thousands of Poles to link their destiny and hopes with Great Britain. For obvious reasons there were far fewer British people having direct relationship with Poland. It gives me particular satisfaction to meet one of them, and on behalf of Poland to thank him for his contribution.
>
> Mr Auton was first brought to my country at a time of one of the greatest trials for Poland in modern history, the Warsaw Uprising. He was one of the Allied airmen who put their lives on the line every second of the flights to help the fighting Poles. As a soldier of the Warsaw Uprising, I remember so well how much moral encouragement and material support we drew from this help

"falling from the skies". To this day Mr Auton has remained true to comradeship from those difficult times. He has maintained links with Poland as the owner of a large business, organized an association for the airmen who once flew to Warsaw and last, but not least, was the major contributor to the 1944 Warsaw Air Bridge Memorial at the Newark Cemetery commemorating the heroic past.

Mr Auton, will you please accept the token of Poland's gratitude for your time-honoured friendship, the Gold Order of Merit awarded to you by the President of Poland.

On learning how many times I had been in Poland, the consul remarked to me, "Most business people were afraid to go to our country during the Cold War." I said, "There was much more danger in 1944, but at that time we had to do exactly as we were told; we had no choice in the matter."

When the Cold War ended, I was a trusted contact, not only in Poland, but in every country emerging from Soviet domination. I was asked by the ambassadors of former Iron Curtain countries to help in their conversion to the Capitalist system of trade. The Czechoslovak Ambassador said, "You can help us because you are aware of all our problems." I certainly knew the problems, but had no quick solutions. Many people in the newly developing countries thought that, after kicking out the Communists, they would be transformed overnight into citizens of a sort of paradise, which was how they pictured the West. I tried to correct their false preconceptions. I explained that, for example, my own working environment was more like a jungle than a paradise. My advice was not to throw the baby out with the bathwater, but to retain the best aspects of the old system and evolve slowly. Unsurprisingly, much of my advice fell on the deaf ears of the impatient.

The Czechoslovak Military and Air Attaché told me that he wished to make contact with the Royal Air Force, and asked me to mediate. I knew our Chief of the Air Staff, and through him I was able to instigate visits by the RAF Red Arrows aerobatic team to Poland and Czechoslovakia.

The Czechoslovak Chief of Air Staff, whom I also knew well, gave me the use of his personal Turbo-Jet and pilot for a visit to the Pilots' Training School at Kosice. In 1990, he appointed me as an Honorary Pilot of the Czechoslovak Air Force. On handing me the relevant diploma and flying-badge, he said, "You may wear our badge on your uniform." I did not tell him that, unlike his new democratic government, ours did not provide complimentary uniforms to war veterans.

Later, I was summoned to attend the President's palace, where, in a magnificent ceremony, I received the Gold Meritorious Service Medal from former dissident Vaclav Havel, the new President. I had already been a frequent guest at previous receptions in the palace. One evening, when an attempt was made to introduce me to the President, he interjected, "We already know each other, thank you."

The Defence Minister awarded me the Military Cross of Merit. At the ceremony, he enquired if my rank was colonel or general. When I replied that I was neither colonel nor general, he asked, "Did you not receive promotion in retirement?" I was aware that, after gaining freedom from the Soviet yoke, his country had promoted all war veterans to senior retired ranks. The veterans also gained other privileges, such as free bus and train travel and free sanatorium treatment. I was embarrassed by the way our authorities treated British veterans, so I quickly changed the subject.

Incidentally, our officers received temporary wartime commissions that expired when the war ended, and they were forbidden to use their former titles. Unless they applied for regular commissions and served in the post-war forces, they reverted to civilian status, regardless of whatever rank they had achieved in wartime. For instance, my fellow company director, the wartime brigadier, reverted to Mister after the war.

I received an unexpected invitation from the Hungarian Ministry of Defence to attend a four-day meeting of reconciliation in Budapest. Only men who had been active in air combat over Hungary were invited, and these included five each from Germany, Rumania, Russia and America. I took along my old friend Peter Green, who had been with me on my squadron in Italy. We were the only men from Britain. Our hosts paid all expenses during the visit. The Hungarian Air Force took us on helicopter trips to targets that I had bombed. In the evenings, we dined with our foreign friends and compared wartime reminiscences. A very tall German fighter pilot related that because of his height he had to crouch down in the cockpit. When he was about to depart on his first combat flight in a Messerschmitt 109, the ground mechanic slammed the hood down so violently that he was concussed and could not take off. We met Junkers 88 pilots who had tried to shoot us down over the Ploesti oil refineries, and I had long conversations with jovial Russian Air Force veterans. Our programme of events included sad visits to the war graves of our own airmen and of our erstwhile enemies. In some places the foreign dead had been too numerous for individual burials. We read memorials inscribed, "Here rest 6,000 German soldiers", and we helped to repair headstones on neglected Rumanian graves that had been run over by heavy motor vehicles.

A Hungarian film crew recorded the four-day event, and one of the crew asked, "Which medal did you get for bombing us?" The Italy Star had attracted his attention, as the ribbon corresponds with the Italian national colours, which are the same as those of Hungary. I explained that I received no medals for bombing.

Many Bomber Command veterans have unsuccessfully campaigned for a medal to show their wartime combatant status. They are upset because our government continues to ignore them. I, however, cannot complain, having rejected the only medal that would have shown my own combatant status.

During my years of travelling abroad, I met many former enemy airmen and soldiers, and I never encountered any personal hostility. I always found that I had much in common with the foreign air force veterans. We had all experienced similar hazards, such as enemy opposition, official bungling, vile food and filthy weather. We had all received orders that seemed to us to be unwise, downright foolish or impossible to carry out. My greatest sympathy was for all soldiers on the Eastern Front, who suffered great hardship, and for the women and children.

My own physical scars have faded over the years, but bitter memories remain. I am often reminded of the officer who said that, if shot down, we should seek help from old people who would remember the futility of war. We thought that our war might prevent all future wars and could never be regarded as futile. But our armed forces became involved in new conflicts soon after our war had ended, and many of them now seem to have been truly futile.

It is sad to see so many lives still being wasted in futile wars. Furthermore, it is sad that our combatants are still sent into action with inadequate arms and unsuitable equipment. Our government still strives to deny pensions to disabled ex-servicemen and women.

A few things have changed since the time of our war. Media correspondents are now "embedded" with our combatants. With modern methods of communication, they can bring the plight of our fighting men and women to public attention immediately whereas our plight was never revealed. My contemporaries are reluctant to talk of the worst conditions that we had to endure. They say, "It is no use trying to tell people what it was like, because they would never understand." However, I feel that we should speak out for the sake of today's armed forces personnel, who endure much of the same hardship and neglect that we faced so many years ago. Unfortunately, I fear that nobody will listen until it is too late.